BEYOND
TALLULAH

BEYOND TALLULAH

HOW SAM WYLY BECAME AMERICA'S BOLDEST BIG-TIME ENTREPRENEUR

PREFACE BY SAM WYLY

INTRODUCTION AND NARRATIVE BY DENNIS HAMILTON

MELCHER
MEDIA

Library of Congress Cataloging-in-Publication Data

Wyly, Sam.
Beyond Tallulah : how Sam Wyly became America's boldest big-time entrepreneur /
by Sam Wyly, with text by Dennis Hamilton. – 1st ed.
      p. cm.
Includes index.
ISBN 978-1-59591-069-1
1. Wyly, Sam. 2. Businessmen–United States–Biography. 3. Entrepreneurship–
United States–Biography. 4. Billionaires–United States–Biography. I. Title.
HC102.5.W95A33 2011
338'.04092–dc23
[B]
                                                    2011031275

Produced by

MELCHER
MEDIA

124 West 13th Street
New York, NY 10011
www.melcher.com

Publisher: Charles Melcher
Associate Publisher: Bonnie Eldon
Editor in Chief: Duncan Bock
Associate Editor: Shoshana Thaler
Line Editor: Bob Roe
Production Director: Kurt Andrews
Production Coordinator: Daniel del Valle

Designed by Naomi Mizusaki, Supermarket
Additional photo research by Stephanie Heimann

Sam Wyly quotations on pages 84, 111-12, 134, 137, 143 and 294
courtesy Charles Babbage Institute, University of Minnesota, Minneapolis

First edition, 2011

10 9 8 7 6 5 4 3 2 1

Every effort has been made to contact the original copyright holders
of all materials reproduced in the book. Any errors brought to the
packager's attention will be corrected in future editions.

Printed and bound in the United States of America

Melcher Media strives to use environmentally responsible suppliers
and materials whenever possible in the production of its books. For this
book, that includes the use of SFI-certified interior paper stock.

CONTENTS

In memory of
Charles J. Wyly, Jr.

PREFACE

Tallulah was the enemy town 30 miles away. They had stomped us every Thanksgiving Day in The Big Game since time immemorial. For the entire town of Delhi —for me and my brother, Charles; for Monroe, the big Cherokee who compensated for my mistakes at nose guard; for Dupree, the 225-pound Cajun who "averaged out" my too-small 155-pound size; and for my dad, editor of the *Delhi Dispatch*—the biggest goal was to "Beat Tallulah."

Well, we finally Beat Tallulah. Then we wondered, *What's next?*

After writing my memoir, *1,000 Dollars and an Idea: Entrepreneur to Billionaire,* in 2007, I thought I had told the story of my life as an entrepreneur and I was done. But lots of letters to me said some folks wanted to know more: What were my partners and I thinking that resulted in our success or failure—in the good times and the hard times? Did I have any advice for them? A list of dos and don'ts?

I was happy that my work and writing had inspired readers to learn more about how to start a company and when to sell. But I can't write a prescription for creating a company or for getting rich. I'm not one to make up rules, but I do tell stories.

Journalist Dennis Hamilton and historian Mary Anne Davidson had interviewed more than a hundred of my colleagues, employees, family and friends to help research my first book. The Smithsonian and others interviewed me. We had lots of amazing stories still to be told about my entrepreneurial journey . . . beyond Tallulah. I built 10 different companies in nine different industries. Six of them got multibillion-dollar valuations. Three were sold for multihundred millions. Sadly, one was a $100 million disaster (economically speaking—though it helped change the world). All in the last 44 years. I hope that the book you are holding sheds more light on this journey.

I'm grateful to all who helped me with this book. For any errors or shortfalls, I take full credit. It's my hope that somewhere down the line, while trying to choose between different opportunities with uncertain outcomes, some wannabe entrepreneur will find inspiration in my story, and some other old girl or guy will smile at something that rings happy bells in her or his own memories.

— Sam Wyly
Aspen, Colorado, 2011

"If you don't know who you are, becoming an entrepreneur is an expensive way to find out."

—Sam Wyly

Rest assured that Sam Wyly knows who *he* is. Among many other things, he is the most versatile big-company entrepreneur in the history of American business. He has built wildly diverse businesses—from mainframe computers to picture frames—in every bull or bear market that has come stampeding down Wall Street over the past 45 years.

Sam Wyly has applied his unique management style to a stunning range of businesses with equally stunning success: Wyly built three hugely successful computer technology companies while competing against some of the biggest technology companies on Earth and has been a pioneer in how to make green energy, and how to make it profitable. He helped topple a behemoth and often benighted telephone monopoly as he doggedly pursued his vision of what became—thanks in large part to his sweat, brains and capital—the Internet; and the massive amounts of cash spun off by his various enterprises have made more than 3,000 of the people who worked with him millionaires. "But it's never been about the money," he says, before quickly adding, "not that I'm against making money."

It is about the money, of course, because that's the only way the important, capital-E entrepreneurs know to keep score. Jerry White, founder of the Caruth Institute for Entrepreneurship at Southern Methodist University's business school, who has been watching Wyly at close range for many years, says, "He has ten entities that grew to . . . something like a billion in revenue, a billion in market cap, public companies, any one of which would be an acceptable lifetime achievement. I don't know anybody [else] who has done ten, and I have studied entrepreneurs forever. Through the '60s, '70s, '80s, '90s and 2000s, this guy continues to remain relevant."

In 2010, Wyly sold his most recent big venture, Green Mountain Energy Company, for $450 million. At the time, his clean-air-through-clean-electricity company was the most successful energy start-up of its kind in the United States. With it, he proved that a healthy environment and a healthy economy can not only coexist, but thrive. Once again, he was looking forward, and seeing the future a few years before the curtain was drawn back for the rest of the world.

Wyly can, without hyperbole or fear of contradiction, be called a visionary. Long before that word became an empty honorific bestowed upon hairstylists and DJs, he was pouncing on opportunities other entrepreneurs were ignoring . . . or running from. His ability to spot the next trend, the next boom and, just as important, the next bust is what makes him an entrepreneur's entrepreneur. His knack for "anticipating history" is the residue of many factors—hard work, research, confidence—but it is primarily because he has a profound sense of and love for history. He turned Santayana's saw on its head—he has been able to get in front of so many trends and generate so many big ideas because he knows the past so well.

A few years ago, when asked to reveal the secret of his success, Wyly slyly said, "I read a lot." It was not a glib retort.

For him, it's that simple.

The history of great wealth, Wyly knows from all that reading he has done, is littered with the stories of miserable misers—J. Paul Getty installed pay phones in his guest rooms; Hetty Green, the world's richest woman in 1916, was called the "witch of Wall Street." (When her son Ned broke his leg, she tried to get him admitted to the hospital's charity ward, but when she was recognized, she took him home rather than pay the bill, and Ned ended up with a peg leg.)

At a glance, Wyly might seem to be one of those frugal billionaires—although never miserable. He doesn't spend lavishly, or live large, but has always been generous to partners, mentors, friends and employees. Like Wal-Mart's Sam Walton, who kept driving the same old red pickup and living in his 2,200-square-foot house long after he struck it rich, Wyly is still a child of the Depression from a small town in Louisiana who disdains the ostentatious. His closet is rigorously casual, says his cousin: "He wears his old, beat-up caps and Gap T-shirts and blue jeans, whatever he wants and wherever the hell he wants to go." When he could first afford a fine car, he bought a Buick instead of a Cadillac because back when he was growing up, folks bought Cadillacs to tell their neighbors they were rich.

His homespun values spring from beliefs he has held since he was a child studying the writings of Christian Science founder Mary Baker Eddy. "She wrote, 'Material things don't matter; spiritual things matter,'" Wyly says. "That's the background music I'm listening to when I say money doesn't matter."

"On the other hand," he laughs, "having two private jets is fun!"

Boyish in appearance and outlook despite his 11 grandchildren and two great-grandchildren, Sam Wyly is five-foot-seven and 155 pounds—his playing weight as an undersized (and wildly overachieving) nose guard on his state champion high school football team. His hair is still dark blond, still worn longish, sometimes over his collar. He speaks with a Delta drawl little changed from 50 years of living in Texas and time spent in graduate school as a Paton Scholar at the University of Michigan, and he has no airs or affectations. There is no limousine or entourage waiting for him downstairs. He remains—happily, doggedly—Bubba, the nickname bestowed upon him by his grandfather the day he was born.

Wyly is a difficult man to put in a box. "Don't label me," he says, "*whatever your label may be.*" He is a fiscal conservative, but a social liberal. He is an Adam Smith capitalist who favors a carbon tariff and a carbon tax to motivate Americans, as well as the Chinese, to "choose wisely, because it's a small planet." He embraced the free-enterprise system (and was rewarded by it extravagantly), but is an ardent tree-hugger. In his Dallas office hangs an oil painting of an ancestor, Christopher Parker, standing on the battlement of the Alamo. An equally imposing portrait of former Soviet Premier Nikita Khrushchev, banging his shoe on a desk at the United Nations, hangs between urinals in his restroom. Ask him a question about business strategy and he is as likely to quote Ralph Waldo Emerson as he is management guru Peter Drucker—and he is an ardent admirer of Mr. Drucker's work.

His proclivity for defying convention gave him the ability to see opportunity where others did not, and to take on opponents others dared not. After receiving his MBA from Michigan's School of Business, he spent five years setting sales records with IBM and Honeywell, but yearned to run his own shop, to run with his own ideas. In 1963, he made that happen, taking on Big Blue by selling a cheaper, better computing service. How he did that—and then did it again and again in a dizzying array of businesses—is a story that reveals the soul of a successful entrepreneur.

The stories in this book aren't meant to be an Entrepreneurship 101 seminar, but there are some valuable lessons to be gleaned here, about business and about life. The details of how Wyly launched his start-ups, implemented strategies for growing his companies, identified his acquisition targets, orchestrated his public offerings and takeovers, and even of how he rebounded from devastating

ALUMNI OF THE YEAR

Sam was good on the football field in high school but better in the classroom, which is why he got his picture taken after winning a history medal (1).

Six years in the Texas National Guard got Wyly a bad haircut and a worse spelling of his name (2).

No Cover Charge: Wyly was grateful to both his alma maters, Louisiana Tech (3) and University of Michigan (6), and gave generously to both institutions. When he donated $10 million to UM, he said, "My mother always told me that when someone does something for you, you say thank you. So, thank you, Michigan."

Wyly is featured on the covers of *Texas Business & Industry* (4), 1968, and *Finance* magazine (5), 1970. Always ahead of the curve, he was praised in both profiles for his instincts when it comes to his business ventures, and here, specifically, for his foresight to build a computer services company, University Computing, Co. (UCC), and its subsidiary, DATRAN.

failures reveal his unique thought processes and management style. He repeatedly started small but dreamed big, and found his stellar supporting casts by
relying on his gut instead of on some business school checklist. He set strato-
spheric goals for his people, and rewarded them richly for their attainment. And
was, himself, richly rewarded.

But this book is not titled *How to Succeed in Business by Really Trying*. There is
plenty of wisdom in these pages about how to make money, but this is about more
than a casebook on business-building or one man's trek from rags to untold riches. It
is about Sam Wyly's sprawling vision of entrepreneurship and its vital role in everything from democracy to saving the planet. And it is about his unwavering
determination to do well, while doing good. The bottom line meets the eternal.

There is an engraved inscription on a wall at the Virginia Theological Seminary,
words taught by Wyly's great-great-
great-uncle, the Reverend William
Sparrow, who helped found another
Episcopalian college, Kenyon, in Ohio,
and was a professor there back in 1841.
Chiseled into stone is this charge:

Even for high school football, Wyly was too
small to be a lineman, unless you measured his
heart and his moxie.

> Seek the truth
> Come whence it may
> Cost what it will

Throughout his professional life,
Sam Wyly tested every important decision and investment he made with a
homespun version of those words:
"What do I know for sure?"

Again, it sounds so simple. And
maybe it is.

A word to the wise: Watch for Sam Wyly's next move

IF YOU'RE ONE of the roughly 550,000 people who have moved into the Dallas-Fort Worth area since 1980, here's a business name you should know: Sam Wyly.

After keeping an uncharacteristically low profile for the past four years, the 54-year-old Wyly has re-emerged in the news during the past month.

ROBERT DEITZ

His announced plans to sell controlling positions in specialty retailer Michaels Stores and restaurant franchiser USA-Cafes will bring Wyly and his family investment group nearly $100 million in pretax cash and marketable securities, perhaps as much as half of it profit, according to calculations made from documents filed with the Securities and Exchange Commission.

The reason you should be interested in what Wyly does next is that the entrepreneurial Wyly and his brother, Charles, have a long history of making a lot of money for themselves and other people who get in early on their plays.

What the Wylys have done over the

Dallas investor Sam Wyly

past 25 years is either establish or buy small, relatively unknown companies that occupy unique market niches and possess good growth potential.

Then, once management is in place and the company off and running, the Wylys go public with their stock and raise a pile of cash for expansion. The often low initial public offering price usually rises. Then, at a time determined for reasons known only to the

Please see **DEITZ,** DI-3

LINEAGE

Sam Wyly's family story belongs to the tradition of Scots and Irish immigrants who settled the backcountry along the Blue Ridge Mountains and traveled west and south through the Cumberland Gap to build the frontier states of Tennessee, Louisiana and Texas.

BALCHES

SPARROWS

 WYLYS

c. 1657

Young Katy Cleland sails from Scotland and lands on the shores of Chesapeake Bay in the Maryland Colony. John Balch, originally from Somerset County, England, arrives soon thereafter.

1659

Katy marries John Balch, a fellow Presbyterian. They settle on Deer Creek.

1685

Katy and John's 20-year-old son, Tom briefly returns to England, where he is recruited by the Duke of Monmouth to fight in his unsuccessful rebellion against King James II.

1724

James Wyly is born in northern Ireland. As a child, he moves, with his parents and other Scots-Irish Presbyterians to western Pennsylvania. They begin the generations-long trek south and west, down through the Shenandoah Valley of Virginia and the Blue Ridge Mountains, shadowing the Great Wagon and Wilderness Roads.

1754

James Wyly and his family reside in the Highlands in western Virginia. In August, Wyly buys 2,050 acres of land from Colonel James Patten for 87 pounds currency. James's land is located on Cripple Creek, in Augusta County, which is today known as Wythe County, Virginia.

1755

The French and Indian War forces inhabitants of the settlements along the Greenbrier and New Rivers to flee. The Wylys head southward to Mecklenburg County, North Carolina, which is settled mostly by Scots-Irish and Germans. James will become a tax collector, sheriff and "gentleman"—a man of means. In his 1771 will, he reminds his wife, Martha, to "school my children."

1766

Hezekiah, Tom Balch's grandson, graduates from the College of New Jersey (later known as Princeton University).

c. 1779

For years, Hezekiah has preached in Presbyterian churches in Lancaster and York, Pennsylvania, and in the Shenandoah Valley of Virginia. He crosses over the Cumberland Gap to the newly established frontier town of Jonesboro.

1784

In disputed territory on the frontier of North Carolina, Hezekiah and his fellow "Over-mountain Men" form the State of Franklin (named for Ben Franklin) and elect John Sevier as governor. In 1796, Franklin will join the U.S. as part of the new state of Tennessee.

1794

Hezekiah founds Greeneville College, the territory's first, and serves as its president until 1810. President George Washington provides $100 of seed money to the college in 1795. (The college will merge with Tusculum in 1868.)

GAMBIER

PRINCETON

COLUMBUS

Deer Creek

Chesapeake Bay

Blue Ridge Mountains

GREAT WAGON ROAD

Cumberland Gap

JONESBORO

STATE OF FRANKLIN

GREENEVILLE

⭐ CRIPPLE CREEK

⭐ MECKLENBURG COUNTY

1817

The Sparrows sail back to the U.S., moving to Utica, New York. A year later, they have Thomas, their third son, and eventually settle near Columbus, in Huron County, Ohio.

1797

Robert Wyly, James and Martha's son, moves to Greeneville, Tennessee and marries Dorcas Balch, daughter of Hezekiah. They run a mercantile store and make buying trips to Baltimore and other cities.

1799

Living in "concealment", Sparrow marries his hometown girlfriend, Mary Roe, in Dublin before escaping to America.

1825

Educated at Columbia University, William Sparrow helps found Kenyon College in Worthington, Ohio, and the following year is ordained deacon and priest in the Episcopalian church. The college moves to Gambier in 1828, where Sparrow presides for more than two decades as a distinguished faculty member.

1798

Anglo-Irish Protestant Sam Sparrow joins the United Irish Rebels in the fight for independence from the British Crown. The rebels lose the tide-turning Battle of Vinegar Hill, near Sam's hometown of Gorey in County Wexford. He asks for clemency in a letter to the commander of the King's forces.

1801

The Sparrows' first child, William, is born in Charlestown, Massachusetts.

1805

Sam and his family return to Dublin, where a second son, Edward (Sam Wyly's great-great-grandfather), is born in 1810.

1836

A son of Robert and Dorcas Wyly, Sam Y., graduates from Princeton and returns to Greeneville to follow in his grandfather Hezekiah's footsteps as minister and teacher.

States and Territories of the United States of America
1795 to June 1, 1796

1835

Edward Sparrow moves to Natchez, Mississippi, the center of America's cotton bonanza, and meets and marries Minerva Parker, whose father owns the Mississippi Hotel—at the time, the biggest hotel in the state.

1835

Minerva Sparrow's brother, Christopher Parker, signs the Goliad Declaration of Independence and heads to the Alamo—where he and 187 other Texans perish.

1836

Sam Y. Wyly's cousin, Alfred, fights under General Sam Houston in the Battle of San Jacinto, where the Republic of Texas wins independence from Mexico.

c. 1840

Edward Sparrow becomes a lawyer, then a sheriff of Catahoula Parish, and is one of the top cotton producers in the South and a millionaire by the time the Civil War begins. Edward and Minerva own plantations named Arlington, Bellagio, Calhoun, Hopewell, Midland and The Island.

1840

Reverend William Sparrow moves to Virginia to become professor in the Protestant Episcopal Theological Seminary in Alexandria, a position he holds for the remainder of his life. During the Civil War the seminary will be used to house 1,700 wounded federal soldiers and to bury 500 of their comrades.

c. 1856

Sam Y. and Martha's son, Charles Samuel (Sam Wyly's granddad), is born in Jonesboro, Tennessee.

1861

Edward Sparrow is named chairman of military affairs for the Confederacy, after voting for secession in Baton Rouge on January 26, 1861. He is subsequently elected one of Louisiana's two senators in the new Confederate government.

1862

Yankee soldiers occupy Lake Providence and run Sparrow's wife, Minerva, and family out of Arlington. The plantation serves as headquarters for some of the North's most famous generals, including McPherson, McMillan, McArthur and, on one occasion, U. S. Grant himself, who stable their horses on the parlor floor.

1863

Sixteen-year-old Rutherford Wyly, Charles Samuel's older brother, writes home to his mother from a Confederate Army camp in Vicksburg, Mississippi, during Grant's campaign.

BAYOU MACON

LAKE PROVIDENCE

VICKSBURG

CATAHOULA PARISH

NATCHEZ

HATTIESBURG ★

BATON ROUGE

MISSISSIPPI RIVER

THE ALAMO

SAN JACINTO ★

1863

A respected lawyer and one of the foremost citizens of Columbus, Ohio, Thomas Sparrow is elected Grand Master of the state's Freemasons. He is a War Democrat and Lincoln supporter.

1865

After fighting with the Confederate Army for four years, John J. Erwin, Sam's great-grandfather on his mother's side, is wounded defending Richmond and finishes the war in a Hattiesburg, Mississippi, hospital.

c. 1865

Having survived the war, Rutherford Wyly helps manage his uncle W. G. Wyly's plantation, located along Bayou Macon about halfway between Lake Providence and Delhi, Louisiana—the towns where Sam Wyly will grow up.

c. 1870

Using a $25,000 loan on the following year's cotton crop, Edward and Minerva send two of their three daughters (including Sam Wyly's great-grandmother Anna) on a grand tour of Europe, where they are presented to Empress Eugénie in Paris.

1875

Anna Sparrow Decker gives birth to twin girls, Mary and Kate, but a month after the twins are born, she dies in Vicksburg. Edward and Minerva care for the girls, later sending them to be educated at the Athenaeum in Columbia, Tennessee.

1876

Charles Samuel Wyly graduates first in his class from the University of Tennessee in Knoxville.

c. 1880

Charles Samuel passes the English common law bar exam in Tennessee. He moves to Lake Providence, Louisiana, to learn the Napoleonic Code, which is the law in Louisiana because of the state's roots as a French colony. He works in the law practice of his uncle W. G. Wyly, now a justice of the Louisiana Supreme Court.

1882

Charles Samuel Wyly becomes the Decker twins' guardian after Edward's death.

1896

Charles Samuel and Kate Decker marry and eventually have two children, Ethyl and Charles Joseph Wyly (Sam's dad), who will grow up in Lake Providence.

c. 1900

Kate's twin sister Mary becomes a nun and a teacher in a San Antonio Catholic school.

KNOXVILLE
★

★ COLUMBIA

States and Territories of the United States of America
February 4, 1861 to February 28, 1861

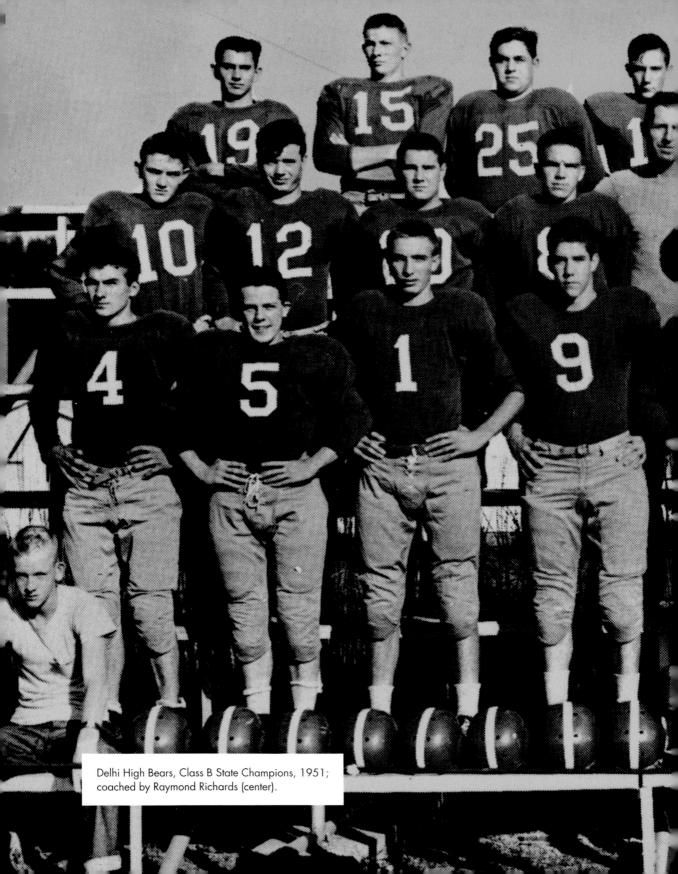

Delhi High Bears, Class B State Champions, 1951; coached by Raymond Richards (center).

THINKING BEYOND TALLULAH

Samuel Evans Wyly was born on October 4, 1934, in Lake Providence, Louisiana, a Mississippi River town of about 3,000. In *Life on the Mississippi*, Mark Twain described Lake Providence as " . . . the first distinctly Southern-looking town you come to, downward-bound; lies level and low, shade-trees hung with venerable gray beards of Spanish moss; 'restful, pensive, Sunday aspect about the place . . . '"

The region, once cotton-rich, was devastated by the Great Depression, and never truly recovered. In the 1990s, *Time* magazine called it "the poorest place in America,"[1] but Wyly disputes that assessment. "*Time* only included the bottom half of our district," he says. "If they'd included the part that runs up to the Arkansas border, we'd have at least made the middle of the bottom tenth percentile! We compete well with an Indian reservation that has no casino!"

Lake Providence is the first town in the first parish in the northeastern corner of Louisiana. Its lovely lake was formed when an earthquake buckled the ground and cut off a loop in the Mississippi. The town was originally named Providence in the early 1800s by thankful people who had managed to slip down river past a pirate named Captain Bunch, who terrorized commercial flatboats there. When the town finally got a post office, some of its incoming mail went to Providence, Rhode Island, so the town added "Lake" to Providence. It's a beautiful, clear-water lake six miles long—Abe Lincoln poled his flatboat past it on his way down from Indiana to New Orleans to sell his family's produce.

Wyly's nickname is "Bubba" because that's what his Granddaddy Evans, the local doctor, called all the white and black boys he delivered. Charles Aaron "Bubba" Smith, the Baltimore Colts' fierce defensive end in the late '60s, was the first man to give the nickname national fame. President Bill Clinton is perhaps the most recent to do so.

Sam says the first entrepreneurs he ever met were his parents, Charles and Flora, who owned a cotton farm when he was born. The Mississippi River has long

Charles Sam Wyly (1), Sam's paternal grandfather, had an office inside the East Carroll Parish courthouse in Lake Providence, Louisiana, where he served as secretary of the parish police jury.

Granddaddy Wyly, as a young man (2), set the example for his family by graduating valedictorian from the University of Tennessee in 1876, and moved to Lake Providence to work for his uncle W. G. Wyly, a justice of the Louisiana Supreme Court.

The Wyly boys did a lot of swimming in Lake Providence (3), and occasionally got pulled to church in a goat cart (4).

Charles Wyly wasn't the only celebrity at the 1950 Boy Scout Jamboree at Valley Forge (5), which featured visits from then-President Harry Truman and soon-to-be President General Dwight D. Eisenhower. That was a particularly memorable trip for Charles and Sam, because after the jamboree their parents took them farther north, to New York City, where they first saw a television, a major league baseball game, the Statue of Liberty and a Broadway show.

Above: Sam's father, Charles, in his fraternity picture from LSU in the early 1920s.

Above, right: Flora Evans, Sam's mother, grew up in Lake Providence, went to college in New Orleans and LSU, and then briefly lived in New York City, where she studied dance.

Right: When the Civil War broke out, Edward Sparrow, Sam's great-great-grandfather on his father's side, was one of the richest men in America, with cotton plantations all along the Mississippi River, including Arlington (right), that were worked and maintained by his many slaves. The plantation house was eventually seized by the Union Army, which stabled horses on its ground floor.

been a spawning ground for entrepreneurs—in the mid-1800s, Carroll Parish led Louisiana in cotton production, which made Lake Providence a favorite stop for steamboats. The town was the port of entry and departure for most everything grown, sold or bought in Carroll Parish. The river was always alive with plantation and logging barges, fishing boats and paddle wheelers, steamboats and rowboats.

Island Point was a 400-acre cotton plantation the Wylys inherited that once had been part of a sprawling 2,800-acre farm called Arlington Plantation, owned by Wyly's great-great-grandparents, Minerva and Edward Sparrow. It was one of the top 10 cotton-producing farms in the South in 1860, and the Sparrows were one of the region's wealthier families, but that prosperity ended with the Civil War, which pitted Sparrow brothers and cousins against one another—not unlike the United Irish Rebellion of 1798, which exiled the first Sparrows, Sam and Mary, to America. In 1862, Union soldiers threw the Sparrow family out of their beautiful plantation home and stabled officers' horses on its first floor.

Both of Sam's parents were college-educated and had come from prosperous and distinguished families in the area. Flora, who joined the Daughters of the American Revolution the year Sam was born, was the daughter of the Lake Providence doctor. Charles was the son of an attorney, Charles Samuel Wyly, who had been valedictorian at the University of Tennessee in 1876.

Flora, who was dark-haired, five feet tall and seemingly fearless, wanted to be a dancer when she was young. After a few semesters at Louisiana State University in Baton Rouge, she left for New York City, where she auditioned for the Rockettes and Broadway plays. (She was there for the Crash of 1929, but told Sam she didn't remember seeing any brokers jumping out windows when he asked her about that time years later.) She returned to Lake Providence in 1931 and opened a dance studio, the Flora Evans School of Dance. Charles, who loved to write, wanted to be a journalist, but Island Point was his inheritance, his legacy and his family's historical home, so he took it on. His forebearers included three centuries of scrappy survivors. "I heard stories of our folks who had helped build America," Sam recalls, "going back to a great-granddad who wintered with George Washington at Valley Forge and a grandfather who fought with Andrew Jackson at the Battle of New Orleans and Uncle Christopher who went down to Texas to help Sam Houston and died at the Alamo."

Even in good times Charles and
Flora only had enough to buy groceries
and a few books after paying down
their annual crop loan from the local
bank. They lived with their two sons in
a 1,200-foot home they proudly called
"a painted house"— white house paint
was a bit of a distinction during the
Depression, a step up from houses and
shacks with bare clapboard walls. "I
remember my mother and father reading *Gone With the Wind* to each other,"
Sam says. "It was hard times because
the price of cotton had gone to almost
nothing and a lot of people were out of
work. I remember when a dollar a day
was the going rate for men working in
the agricultural South.

The flappers of the Roaring Twenties loved to
do the Charleston, one of the many dances
Flora taught to her students when she came
back from New York to open her dance school
in Lake Providence.

"You read today about the Crash of 1929 and the Great Depression, but in the
agricultural part of the country, where we were, it started much earlier and
dragged on much longer. I remember that before I started school, we sold our
painted house in town to move into an unpainted cabin on the land, because my
parents were trying to pay down the debts to the bank to save the land."

Flora made and sold slipcovers for chairs and sofas to make some extra
money. "She sometimes traded her cloth for a supply of Mrs. Vincinci's real Italian
spaghetti and meatballs," Sam recalls, "which we picked up in an iron Dutch oven
that we returned clean."

There were other adjustments to be made. The toilet was now an outhouse,
they got their water from a pump, cooked on a wood-burning stove and heated
their home with a wood-burning fireplace. Charles ran a wire into the cabin so
they could all have better light to read by (better than the kerosene lamp or the
light from the wood fireplace that heated their home during the winter) and could
play the radio. At night, they listened to news reports on the war in Europe, and to

music by the big bands—Glenn Miller, the Dorsey Brothers. The family grappled not only with the Depression, but with the heat, the boll weevils, the famous Lake Providence mosquitoes (Twain wrote that "two of them could whip a dog and four of them could hold a man down"), the sometimes parched earth and the sometimes flooding river. A good rain could change the course of the Mississippi, and when that happened, the dirt roads became impassable, muddy pits. But that didn't mean the boys could miss their lessons—when the family car got mired in muck, Charles took his boys to school on a tractor; and when the tractor couldn't make it, he loaded them into his rowboat and rowed across the lake.

The Depression, especially in the South, made farming cotton grindingly difficult. Between 1940 and 1950, the farm population in Louisiana decreased by 286,000. In 1941, after fighting the pitiless economy for 12 long years, the family had to sell Island Point. Charles took a job with the Levee Board and Flora worked for the Welfare Department. Their luck changed when the new governor of Louisiana, Sam Houston Jones, asked their older friend and neighbor, "Mister Tib" Mitchner, to run the Louisiana State Penitentiary at Angola. The governor wanted to see if improved productivity there could help the notorious 18,000-acre prison farm pay its own way. Mitchner, who owned a 1,000-acre cotton farm, knew of Charles's business acumen and his interest in more efficient ways to farm, as well as Flora's managerial skills. Just as important, he knew they were people he could trust, so he asked them to become part of his management team.

Angola prison was far downstate, the final stop on a long desolate road through the wilderness in Louisiana's isolated interior, and its reputation for

"Captain" Flora Wyly, warden of the women's prison at Angola.

harsh conditions and brutal treatment of prisoners stretched back to the day it was opened in 1901. Charles Wolfe and Kip Lornell, authors of *The Life and Legend of Leadbelly* (who did a stretch there for attempted murder—where he was discovered by musicologist Alan Lomax), wrote that being imprisoned in Angola was "probably as close to slavery as any person could come in 1930."

The Wylys moved to Angola in 1941. Flo became the first woman in Louisiana to manage the women's prison—she was now "Captain Wyly" of Camp D, where women prisoners worked, mostly sewing uniforms for the inmates. Charles worked in the Receiving Station as administrator of pardons and paroles, where new inmates were processed—documented, examined and photographed—and records were kept of their behavior and health for parole reviews. The Receiving Station was also where they housed "Gruesome Gertie," the name inmates gave to Angola's new electric chair. (In Louisiana, condemned prisoners were executed in the parishes in which they had committed their crimes, so Gertie was moved from parish to parish: "The traveling electric chair" toured Louisiana for the next 16 years, until 1957, when it was permanently housed in the prison.)

Young Sam explored the prison extensively, and even talked to prisoners about their crimes and read their files. He also got to know the bloodhounds used to track down prisoners who tried to shorten their time in prison. "It wasn't easy to escape from Angola," he recalls, "because it was 18,000 acres surrounded on three sides by the mile-wide Mississippi River. The fourth side was a very tangled, tough place to get through. Each prison camp—like Mom's Camp D—looked like the POW camps of World War II. You had barrack-type buildings with barbed wire fences curved in at the top. The towers had guards armed with high-powered rifles and shotguns. It wasn't easy to get out of the camp, and if you did, you still had to get off the farm. One time a prisoner didn't show up for 'count' at the end of the day, so the guards knew he was gone. We could hear the dogs tracking him on the prison side of the Mississippi River. The escapee swam across the river and then heard the dogs on *that* side of the river, so he swam back to the Angola side. When he heard the barking there as well, he got back in the river and swam back over to the other side. By then he was so tired he just gave up!"

The male inmates farmed mostly sugar cane, cotton and vegetables, and some worked in the sugar refinery or the bakery. When Charles was not engaged with

Above: Abandon all hope, ye who enter here: the guardhouse at Angola State Prison, 1949.

Below: The Angola State Prison photographer took official pictures of newly arrived convicts, but found the time to snap a portrait of two new arrivals—brothers

Sam and Charles—who were only doing time in prison because their parents worked there.

Below, right: You can't (not) go home again: While he was a sophomore in college, Sam got to tour Angola as a visitor.

A prison break: From Angola, Wyly's family moved to this house in Delhi, where Sam's parents owned and put out the weekly newspaper the *Delhi Dispatch*. Sam and his brother, Charles, pitched in with the construction workers, who were paid 75 cents per hour.

the duties of the Receiving Station, he helped Mitchner introduce new seeds, planting techniques and equipment to the prison farm. They were so successful with this that by his final year at Angola, Charles had helped produce a record sugar cane harvest for the prison farm.

Even in one of the nation's scariest prisons, Wyly picked up some valuable lessons in investing. "Back then, they used convicts to guard convicts," he says. "The regular Big Stripers worked in the cane fields. Then you had Trusties and then you had Guards. Trusties wore little pinstripes and the Guards wore khaki. One Trusty was Dr. James Monroe Smith, who did typing for my dad. The reason Dr. Smith did typing rather than cutting sugar cane was that he had been the president of Louisiana State University, appointed by the former governor of Louisiana, Huey P. Long. When they were building LSU, Dr. Smith had the authority to issue bonds and use the cash to build the buildings. But he took the cash and speculated on pork bellies and soybeans. He meant to pay it back. He didn't mean to keep it. He was going to make a profit and then he was going to pay it back. But he lost. He bet wrong. This was a good lesson for me later when people were talking about betting on commodities futures. I remembered Dr. Smith and I remembered my mother saying, 'That's not investing; it's gambling.'"

Bubba's more traditional form of education came from the nearby Tunica School, where three teachers taught nine grades in a three-room schoolhouse. His third-grade teacher moved around the room, teaching a different grade in each corner. After a year of this, Charles and Flora realized that the Tunica School was not good enough for their boys and made the difficult decision to have them stay during the school year with Flora's parents, Bess and Dr. Will Evans, "Lady Bess" and "Grandaddy," who lived in Oak Grove, 180 miles upriver.

In 1945, when Sam was 11 and Charles Jr. was 12, the Wylys were ready to break out of prison, and settled in Delhi, Louisiana, a town of 3,000 that was 30 miles from Lake Providence. Charles and Flora had saved diligently from their Angola earnings, and used that money to buy the *Delhi Dispatch*, the town's Wednesday weekly. Charles became the editor and publisher, selling advertising to the local Ford and Chevy dealers, feed-and-seed stores and other local customers, while Flora wrote the social column and sent out tear sheets to advertisers with their bills.

Delhi had long been a sleepy town of cotton fields and sweet potato farmers, but in 1945, a geologist discovered a massive oil field just outside of town. It was the biggest oil discovery in Louisiana to date, and the once idyllic community was suddenly bustling with new commerce, new people, independent oil wildcatters and petroleum engineers for Sun Oil and Gulf Oil. And with all that came a lot of news to report.

Sam and his brother wrote articles, set type, cleaned presses, took subscriptions—$3 a year for 52 eight-page issues—and swept up at the end of the day. All copy had to be in by midnight Monday so that the paper could be printed and delivered on Wednesday morning.

One summer, when Sam was 16, the boys landed jobs as pipeline workers in the new Delhi oil fields, and were paid $1.35 an hour for 12-hour days, seven days a week. They got a day off only if a hard rain made it too muddy to work.

Sam had no real career goals then, and certainly wasn't thinking much about business, but he was still learning about entrepreneurship. Back when his family was still on the Island Point plantation, his father had earned a little extra money by working as a part-time insurance agent. When he took over the *Delhi Dispatch*, he added a fire and casualty insurance office as well as a Western Union desk to the office. Even then, the lesson was: diversify!

Charles did well selling insurance, but there never was any doubt about which business he preferred. When Sam was in college, he audited his father's businesses

Above: The main street in Lake Providence, Louisiana, 1940. Sam Wyly was six years old at the time.

Below: This building housed the *Delhi Dispatch,* as well as a Western Union Telegraph Agency and Wyly

Fire & Casualty Insurance Agency—all three businesses run by Charles and Flora Wyly.

Below, right: The *Delhi Dispatch* masthead, 1945.

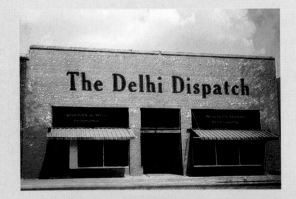

The Delhi Dispatch

Entered as Second-Class Matter at the U. S. Postoffice at Delhi, La., under Act of March 3, 1879.

CHARLES J. WYLY_____Editor-Publisher

Yearly subscription rates: In Richland and adjoining parishes, $2.00; elsewhere, $3.00.

Member:
Louisiana Press Association - National Editorial Assn.

for an accounting class exercise. The results surprised him, so he told his father, "Dad, your insurance agency makes a ton more money than the newspaper, and takes a fraction of your time. Shouldn't you spend more time selling insurance?"

"Sit down," his dad said. "There are two things you need to know: Number one, you're now a sophomore in college and that's the smartest you'll ever get. It's all downhill now, as every year you learn there will be more and more that you don't know. And number two, I like writing this newspaper." The lesson there: "Do what you know. Do what you love."

High school football has been an all-consuming passion for small towns in Louisiana since the early 1900s. Win the big game, and you were the talk of the barbershop, the diner and the pulpit for days. "For us kids who went out for Delhi football, there were three goals," Wyly says. "First, make the team; second, make the starting lineup; and third, beat Tallulah."

The Tallulah Trojans were the Darth Vader of North Louisiana prep football, and even a good season for the Delhi Bears didn't count if they lost their annual Thanksgiving Day contest against Tallulah. And no one on Sam's team could recall the last time Delhi had beaten the Trojans. Monroe Fowler can still hear some drugstore quarterbacks needling him after a loss to the Trojans. "They just outsmarted you again," Fowler's tormentors teased. "Them Tallulah boys must just be *smarter*." Fowler had no way of knowing that help was on the way, that he and his Delhi teammates were about to get a lot "smarter," and a lot better.

Raymond Richards only became the Delhi football coach because the man who had held the job before him

Wyly's Delhi Hi [sic] yearbook. He changed the spelling of his nickname at Louisiana Tech. His campaign posters for freshman class president read "Bubba Wyly for President."

was a wildly profane bully who offended local mothers with his foul mouth. The principal finally marched onto the football field one day and ordered him to "stop cussing" at his players. Instead of shutting his mouth, the coach quit. Richards, who had been the head coach's reluctant assistant for a year, was now Delhi High's head coach.

He was a lanky, six-foot-four, handsome ex-Kansan who made his points with few words—none profane—and a merciless sense of humor. "I had a turtle that had rheumatism and squeaked when he walked that could outrun Red Bailey," he once said of a slow teammate. He drilled his boys like Marines under the brutal August sun in Louisiana, found their limit, and then pushed them beyond it. "You will never tire first," he told them again and again. He demanded of his players discipline, adaptability, execution, teamwork and an unshakeable belief in themselves and their teammates.

Charles Jr. was the team's best running back. Sam was a quick five-foot-seven, 155-pound nose guard who regularly squared off against 200-pounders. Richards showed him how to get leverage on bigger opponents, and how his fleetness and tenacity could defeat their size. He wasn't fast enough to be a running back or big enough to be a tackle, but as a nose guard, he had a knack for sensing whether the opposing team was about to run or pass. "Sam was a bulldog," Richards recalled 50 years later. "He got ahold of something, you couldn't get rid of him."

From the outset of Richards's first full season with the team, 1950, the Delhi Bears were a different team, a better team, a team united around one goal: Beat Tallulah. Both teams had great seasons that year, and by the time of the Tallulah game in late November, all of northeast Louisiana was eager to see their battle. More than half a century later, Coach Richards still had vivid memories of the day: "We went over to play Tallulah for the North Louisiana championship in 1950. Thanksgiving Day, a beautiful 60-degree temperature. People were standing all around the field. The gymnasium roof was covered with people. The buildings had them hanging out windows to watch us."

Delhi walked off the field that day with a brutal 13–12 victory—the greatest win in the school's history. After the game, Sam saw his cousin Flo, a student at Tallulah, running into the stands. When he caught up to her she was sobbing, unable to believe her invincible Trojans had lost to lowly Delhi.

Charles (number 3) was the star running back for the 1951 Delhi Bears, while Sam (number 13) was an undersized, overachieving lineman (1). Their father covered every game for his paper, and kept handwritten notes (2, 3), including the team's roster. Eight of the 24 players on that team got college athletic scholarships, including Charles, but Sam's playing days were over, except for touch-football games with his college fraternity team. Sam's handwritten 1950 football schedule, when they were runners-up (4). They were state champs in 1951. Often described as Tarzan Sam, at 16 he was a small player pitted against opponents routinely taller and up to a hundred pounds heavier (5). His habit of going after the big guns would continue throughout his career.

3 DELHI ROSTER

1 - ANDREWS ☆ - QB + Passer -
2 - DEROUEN ☆ } main ball-toters, Derouen is high scorer
3 - C. WYLY ☆
4 - COLEMAN - defensive sub for Andrews
5 - DOZIER - Sub for Wyly, Derouen or Patterson
6 - G. SUMLIN
7 - BRADLEY
8 - LAPRARIE
9 - PATTERSON ☆

10 - R.G. SUMLIN
11 - ROBBINS - LE - ☆
12 - HOWINGTON -
13 - E. B. WYLY - RG ☆
14 - HICKS
15 - HARTLEY - RE ☆
16 - JONES - L.T. ☆
17 - FOWLER - RG ☆
18 - HUNTER
19 -
20 - McEACHARN
21 - WATKINS
22 - BATES - C - ☆
23 - LOFTIN
24 - DUPREE - RT ☆
25 - DUCHESNE - Regularly regls on defense

20 - KRIESCHMAN - QB
24 - L. CLEMENT - LH
21 - SCHNEIDER
23 - DEAL

4
TART	19	
ST. ALOY		
LAKE P.		
OAK GRO.	13	
MANGUM	37	0
RAYVILLE	12	12
NEWELTON	37	0
WINNSBORO	6	6
TALLULAH	18	12
RODESSA	33	12
WINTER	21	6
CLINTON	7	19

2

Delhi High School
1951 Football Schedule

SEPT.	14	.31.	START	..0..	THERE
SEPT.	21	.38.	ST. ALOYSIUS	..6..	HERE
SEPT.	28	.46.	HOLLY RIDGE	..0..	THERE
OCT.	5	.18.	LAKE PROVIDENCE	..7..	THERE
OCT.	12	.34.	OAK GROVE	..0..	THERE
OCT.	19	.33.	MANGHAM	..0..	HERE
OCT.	26	.14.	RAYVILLE	..14.	HERE
NOV.	2	.45.	NEWELLTON	..0..	THERE
NOV.	9		OPEN		
NOV.	16	.27.	WINNSBORO	..20.	HERE
NOV.	22	.14.	TALLULAH	..6..	HERE

The Delhi Bears scraped their way through the playoffs, making it to the state championship game in Clinton, the town where *The Long Hot Summer* was filmed several years later. On December 22, 1950, they lost the title game by two touchdowns. The good folks of Delhi, of course, tried to help heal their hurt. After all, they said, Delhi is a school with fewer than 200 students. You represent a town with only 3,000 people. You put Delhi on the map. *And you beat Tallulah!*

That didn't ease the pain of that loss, but Sam and his teammates learned a lesson: Don't let your goals limit your achievements. Their only true goal had been to beat Tallullah. They were now determined to be the undefeated state champions next season.

In 1951, Delhi won big, week after week, and after each lopsided victory, the town's pride grew. Sam's brother, Charles, was a fast, tough, elusive halfback, and Pat Patterson was a gifted receiver, but there were no future Heisman candidates on this team. Many years later, Sam says that Coach Richards was, in many ways, the quintessential CEO—his job was to get the best players he could find on the field, then get more from them than they believed they had. Halfway through the 1951 season, Delhi was undefeated and merciless, outscoring their first six opponents 200–13. Then, with the seventh, came near disaster—they had to scramble in the second half to tie Rayville, 14–14.

Finally, the Thanksgiving Day war with Tallulah arrived. Both teams were undefeated. At stake was the Northern District championship, and an even more valued "trophy": bragging rights for another year. The final score was 14–6, Delhi. After the game, Sam's dad got a telegram from one of his old high school teammates, Hugh King, that read, *"Le Roi est mort, vive le Roi!"* (The King is dead, long live the King!)

A few weeks later, Delhi journeyed to Logansport for the state semifinals. The game was 181 miles from Delhi, but Delhi Mayor Roy Snider declared that Friday a holiday, and urged his constituents to come out and support the team. At noon, Delhi businesses closed and doctors told patients, "You can't be sick on Friday." More than 600 of the town's 3,000 residents made the trip in a raucous caravan of chartered buses painted with victory slogans and trailing streamers.

It was one of the most brutal high school football games in Louisiana history. Delhi bent, but would not break. Final score: Delhi 32, Logansport 26.

The championship game the following week against Donaldsonville's Tigers

Christmas was very merry in Delhi when the good-news Bears won their first state championship. Charles Wyly Sr.'s *Dispatch* stories about the team were picked up by the big Louisiana newspapers.

was played at Delhi on a muddy field in a bitter winter wind, in front of every man and woman the Delhi Bears had ever known. Within minutes, the numbers on jerseys were impossible to read because they were covered by the wet, heavy muck. When it was over, the Delhi offense had amassed 227 rushing yards, while its defense had held Donaldsonville to just 31 yards rushing and a single pass completion. Final score: Delhi 26, Donaldsonville 6—and they were the undefeated state champions.

They outscored their opponents 300–53 in 10 regular season games and 82-32 in three playoff games. Ten members of the Delhi team were selected for the Associated Press All-State team. Eight of Sam's teammates got college athletic scholarships—but his own days as a football star were over, because college teams weren't clamoring for five-foot-seven, 155-pound nose guards. Sam, however, was prepared for new, bigger challenges. He had seen Coach Richards turn a bunch of also-rans into undefeated state champions. He had seen his parents realize their dreams of independence. And he had learned the vast difference between setting goals and setting audacious goals.

"You can be as big as your dreams," Richards told his team. "So how big can you dream?"

Endnotes

1   From the August 15, 1994, issue of *Time* magazine, "The Poorest Place in America" was written by Jack E. White. At that time, with the U.S. poverty level just under $15,000, three-fourths of Lake Providence's 5,500 residents had a median annual household income of $6,536.

First job: Wyly (front row, dark-framed glasses) at an IBM subsidiary, Service Bureau Corporation.

TAKING THAT HILL FOR BIG BLUE

Given the Wyly family tradition of higher education, going to college was never an "if" for Sam, it was just a "where?" LSU seemed like the obvious choice—his dad had been a Pi Kappa Alpha there, and his mom a Kappa Delta—but he decided to enroll at the much-smaller Louisiana Tech, about an hour from Delhi, after a teammate asked him, "Do you want to be a big fish in a small pond or a small fish in a big pond?"

Wyly initially intended to follow in the footsteps of his father and become a newspaperman, so he declared himself a journalism major. But he increasingly nurtured a bigger agenda—he wanted to make a difference, to lead people and to turn bold ideas into bold actions. The taste of leadership he had gotten as student body president at Delhi High had aroused the political animal in him, and he decided to run for freshman class president at Louisiana Tech, a logical step toward what became his ultimate goal—to be governor of Louisiana. His parents and grandparents had pushed him to think about local, regional and global political issues his whole life. A dinner table conversation could range from the need to keep Richland Parish dry to the Soviet Union's oppression of Hungary. In the Wyly home, politics kept the blood flowing. A high school friend of Sam's recalls that "when most of us were reading comic books, Bubba was reading *U.S. News & World Report.*"

Wyly jumped into competitive politics at Tech with his campaign to become freshman class president. His opponent in that race had a huge advantage in that he had attended a large high school with many of his fellow freshmen, but Sam made his own advantage. His model was a rousing dynamo named R. L. Ropp, the exuberant college president. "Louisiana Tech is the friendliest college campus in the South," Ropp told him. "Speak to everyone you meet." Ropp also gave Sam a bit of advice that would stay with him forever: "The sweetest sound to everyone's ear

Sam (seated, center) explored his interest in politics in the student senate at Louisiana Tech. While clerking at the state legislature in Baton Rouge at age 17, he saw that the best job in the capitol was governor of Louisiana. "I can't be governor until I'm 35, but I can lay the groundwork," Wyly remembers telling himself.

is the sound of his or her own name." Sam followed Ropp's advice, shook a lot of hands, patted a lot of backs, memorized a lot of names and made a lot of new friends. And was elected class president. Years later, he said, "Like Bill Clinton during his four years in college, I could probably greet over a thousand people by their first name. It's been all downhill for me since."

In his sophomore year Wyly took an economics class that changed his mind about business, and changed his life. "Although I liked journalism, I thought it was easy," he says. "I asked around for the hardest courses I could take. Then I checked to see who got paid well in those fields. I found out that there were two good jobs: engineers—Tech was known for its engineers—and accountants. I figured engineers built bridges and I didn't want to do that, so I decided to get a business degree." But he also studied geology because he wanted to understand the oil industry. He joined the debate team because he wanted to get elected governor of Louisiana when he was 35—the youngest one could run. He loved American history and the geopolitics taught by a military officer in his Air Force ROTC training.

The professor in his first economics class had each student do research and then pick five stocks as make-believe investments. After researching the history of International Business Machines (IBM) back to 1919—it was called Computing-Tabulating-Recording Company until 1924—Wyly picked it for his favorite "investment." He was impressed by the fact that IBM had managed to grow through the Great Depression, and had emerged even stronger under the skillful leadership of its president, Thomas Watson, Sr. Thanks to FDR's implementation of the country's vast Social Security system in 1935, which required a lot of machine accounting by both government and business—and thanks to IBM's unique and finely honed sales culture—the company dominated its market.

Wyly realized that IBM had become a world-class company in much the same way his high school football team had become state champion—through solid teamwork fostered by a powerful boss implementing solid ideas. Watson was the face, brains and heart of IBM—he had led it from the era of mechanical business machines to one of electrical equipment. And now Wyly's friends at Tech who majored in engineering were talking "electronics." That year, 1953, IBM unveiled its 701 computer, its newest product in a brand-new technology it called electronic data processing.

Taking stock: Sam's first portfolio.

Wyly also liked this company because of the lasting impression an IBM salesman had made on him. The man had driven up to his father's *Delhi Dispatch* offices in a Cadillac—only the town's bank president drove a Cadillac—and stepped out in his crisp dark blue suit, white shirt, tie and shiny black shoes. He had come to sell Wyly's parents some equipment that he said would help them automatically set and align type at the *Dispatch*. Sam recalled that the man was so polished, so well-prepared, so knowledgeable about small-town newspaper publishing and why IBM's equipment was better than the competition's— although he had the good character to know not to bad-mouth those competitors—that he came to define Sam's ideal of what it meant to be a professional.

Sam also picked Humble Oil for his "pretend portfolio." Again, he used research and personal experience to guide his choice. He remembered that Humble Oil's Baton Rouge Refinery, the world's largest, lit up the night sky. (Humble Oil is now Exxon Mobil, which earned $40 billion in profits during the crash of 2008. Its CEO, Rex Tillerson, another small-town boy—Wichita Falls, Texas— watched the 2011 Super Bowl in the suite next to the Wylys at Cowboys Stadium in Dallas.) His third pick was American Airlines (today the nation's largest air carrier); fourth was Bristol-Meyers, which sold toothbrushes and sundries on the shelves of Mr. Hopson's Drug Store in Delhi (it's now Bristol-Myers Squibb, the sixth-largest pharmaceutical company); and his fifth stock was Stone Container, which made cardboard boxes (today Smurfit-Stone Container, the nation's largest packaging corporation). These were pretty good calls, and definitely would have been great long-term investments. "If I'd had $10,000 to invest back then," Wyly jokes, "I would never have had to get a job."

Some econ classes at Louisiana Tech had adopted the "case method" pioneered at Harvard Business School, which had been borrowed and adapted from the established techniques used to teach law. Tech's econ students didn't just listen to lectures and regurgitate facts on tests, they tried to solve real-world problems. Students worked with their professors to analyze conflicting data, establish goals, persuade and inspire people with different viewpoints, make tough

Top: Charles, in his Louisiana Tech uniform, was one of eight Delhi Bears who went on to play college football.

Bottom: Sam still describes Dee, Charles's wife and his former Louisiana Tech classmate, as a real Southern belle.

decisions with vague and incomplete information and seize opportunity in the face of doubt.

Wyly instantly became fascinated with the managerial and financial anatomy of businesses. Because he was an avid student of history, he was able to put a company's performance into the context of its time. He could look at its markets and strategies, overlay the circumstances affecting it in a given era—such as the Gilded Age, the Great Depression, the war economy, or the postwar baby boom—and understand why its stocks and bonds fell or soared, why some companies survived and others collapsed.

The more he studied how companies performed over time, the more he was led to a compelling vision of business's role in the building of the nation. It spoke to his Scots-Irish soul, which embraced free-enterprise democracy. He believed that the greatness of this country was inextricably intertwined with the vibrancy of its markets, and understood why President Coolidge had said, "The business of America is business." Wyly knows that's not a totally politically correct philosophy today, but says, "Our presidents are afraid to say that, even though they believe it."

Wyly's econ classes at Tech changed his outlook on the world, on his career and on his dreams. He set new goals, and set off down a new path. He decided he did not want to wait until he was 35, the minimum age to run for governor of Louisiana, to make the world a better place. And, as always, he was high-minded but practical—he knew that starting journalists made $60 a week, while graduating

After graduating from Louisiana Tech, Sam became the first Paton Scholar at the University of Michigan Business School, where he learned the rudiments of a new tool that would change the world—the stored-program computer. Wyly got hands-on experience with an IBM 650.

engineers and CPAs were paid almost $100 a week right out of school. At the end of his sophomore year, he changed his major from journalism to business.

When Wyly graduated from Louisiana Tech in 1956, two IBM recruiters interviewed the top 10 percent of his class, then made offers to Sam, his brother, Charles, and a New Orleans boy named Jerry Germenis. "IBM had the best interviewers," Wyly recalls. "Omar Harvey was the Shreveport branch manager and another interviewer was his boss from Houston. They had this good guy/bad guy thing. The bad guy told you how tough it was to get an IBM offer and that you probably weren't good enough to work there. Then the good guy would say how great you were. They did a good job of selling you on IBM. I wanted to work for IBM and I had actually accepted the job. But then I got a chance to get an MBA at the University of Michigan. IBM said, "We will still want you after you get your MBA and do your military duty.

"Back in those days every CPA in America had a book on his desk called the *Accounting Manual*, edited by W. A. Paton, who taught at Michigan. Dr. Paton gave a speech at Tech during my senior year. My department head introduced me to him and said, 'Sam is thinking about going to Harvard or Michigan.' Dr. Paton said, 'He's got to come to Michigan. We have a new scholarship named for me and if you apply you'll probably get it.'" Wyly applied, and was accepted.

That summer, after graduating from Louisiana Tech, Sam got a job in Dallas (where both Charles and Jerry started sales training for IBM), courtesy of a friend of his father's who had a dry-cleaning shop in Delhi, and who got his son to help Sam land a junior accountant slot at a CPA firm called Brophy, Mimear and Company. On his first day on the job, Sam reported to work looking like he'd just stepped out of an IBM training manual—in a crisp white shirt, red tie and navy blue suit. To his surprise his new employers sent him out to verify inventory—counting knives and forks in a hot tin warehouse. It was summer in Dallas—100 degrees outside and stickier inside—and his white shirt and dark suit quickly became soaked with sweat. (Neither his car nor his apartment were air-conditioned, and in Texas, even scorpions seek shade in the summertime.) Counting forks seemed at first a trivial task, but Sam was soon a convert to the meticulous approach of his employer, cheerily reciting the auditor's mantra: "Trust, but verify."

That fall, he started taking his courses at the University of Michigan Business School. "The best part of going to Michigan was its good professors," Wyly says. "I took the first computer course taught there. They didn't know what to call it—the term 'computer science' hadn't been invented yet, so they called it 'statistics.' A guy came over from the engineering school to teach it.

"I really liked having an engineering guy teach us because he talked not just about the concept of the internal stored program but also about how all this equipment worked.

"We had a computer lab at Michigan. At the time, we were transitioning from vacuum tube machines to transistors. We had an IBM 650 Magnetic Drum Data Processing Machine, its first commercial computer. We programmed a payroll program in machine language to learn how it worked. But we also studied other computers. RCA had a machine. Univac had a machine. There was a joint venture between Honeywell and Raytheon on this huge Datamatic 1000 that used tape that was three inches wide. These were all the early companies that later became known in the computer business as 'IBM and the Seven Dwarfs.'"

Wyly was fascinated by the many things a computer could be programmed to do, and by its almost human ability to "think." "The engineers teaching us at Michigan were very much into, 'How does the machine work?'" Wyly recalls. "My hunger was to answer the question, 'How do you turn it into something *useful?* It's a tool, but a tool to do *what?*' It was like those farming tools back in Lake Providence—what do you do with them? A tractor did the plowing of ten mules. A mechanical cotton picker picked as much cotton as a hundred field hands. How are computers worth something?"

Wyly: "Going to Michigan was more serendipity as opposed to any great carefully planned process."

While Wyly was pondering the value of computers, IBM was busily tallying their worth in dollars and cents. The soaring sales of those 650s established IBM as the market leader in computing. In 1953, IBM projected sales of the

650 at 50 units; when production ceased in 1962, more than 2,000 had been sold. Even the great IBM had wildly underestimated the revolution it was leading—it was on the crest of a new, massive wave, and few could imagine how big it was going to become or what it was going to look like in 10 years. But some people were making good guesses: management guru Peter Drucker (whose book, *The Practice of Management*, was the bible at the Michigan Business School) had recently declared that the day of "knowledge work" and the "knowledge worker" had dawned.

Wyly got his MBA in 1957, went through Air Force boot camp in San Antonio, the first part of his six-year National Guard duty, and then took the job IBM had offered him two years earlier. He wanted a career-launching spot selling computers, but an IBM aptitude test showed that he had high technical and math skills, so Big Blue wanted him to become an Electronic Data Processing Machine engineer, designing the customer systems of software and hardware that were replacing their old tabulators. Wyly, however, didn't want to be an engineer, even an IBM engineer. "I want to be a salesman," he protested. "Sales is where I belong." He eventually wore them down, and enrolled in IBM's sales training program. (At his first training session Wyly became friendly with a guy from Texarkana, Texas, whose name was Henry Ross Perot. A Naval Academy graduate, Perot had just finished his four-year tour of Navy duty. It turned out that both of their fathers used to be in the cotton business, Perot's as a cotton buyer, Wyly's as a cotton plantation farmer. The two of them became perfect little buttoned-down IBM men, quota-busting sales reps who made the annual 100 percent clubs for achievers. And then they both struck out on their own, applied what they had learned from Big Blue's triumphs and mistakes . . . and became billionaires.)

IBM had one simple goal: crush the enemy. Wyly was trained to be just like that confident sales rep who had visited the *Delhi Dispatch* years ago. The IBM people were uniformly smart, never drank, dressed like bankers and went to bed at night with the absolute knowledge that they were part of the greatest enterprise in the world. "The basic culture of IBM was that there are those of us fortunate enough to work for IBM, and then there are all the other unfortunate people in the world," Wyly says. "Like the Marines, we *will* capture the hill. All the business belonged to IBM, and that was almost divinely intended to be. That was our story, and we believed it."

Ross Perot, who went on to start EDS, was, like Sam, a true believer at Big Blue, but soon broke off to start his own company.

That soaring confidence was drilled into new IBM sales reps until it radiated from them. It was The Aura, something they carried into every sales call. They all knew that losing was not an option—in part because IBM had a brutal but effective policy of dismissing any sales rep who lost an account, for any reason.

But all that was years down the road. In 1958, Wyly was 100 percent focused on being the best sales trainee IBM had ever seen. Six months later, the company abruptly reneged on the deal it had made with him. Bill Glavin, Wyly's manager, told him his sales program was being terminated because an oil-driven recession in Texas had dampened sales, and quotas were being missed, so staffing budgets were being cut. "We are going to make you a machine operator in Fort Worth."

"I don't *like* Fort Worth." Wyly told him. "It's a hick town. I have a nice garden apartment in Dallas, with pretty airline stewardesses out by the pool, and I don't want to move. Besides, I don't want to be a machine operator! I'm a sales rep."

"Well, there are four of you," Glavin replied. "Two are being fired and two are going to be machine operators."

"Well, in that case," Wyly said, "Fort Worth is sounding better all the time."

He moved into a one-bedroom apartment in a garage behind a Victorian-era house on White Settlement Road in Fort Worth, which he shared with an American Airlines employee, Ralph Davis.

He later saw that this accidental job was the best thing that could have happened. It gave him his first shot at running real-world jobs for customers with real-world needs, something his case method education at Tech and Michigan had whetted his appetite for. Six months later, the recession was over, and he was back in Dallas.

His job, like the one his brother, Charles, had in New Orleans, was at a newly formed IBM subsidiary called Service Bureau Corporation (SBC). It put him in the middle of the genesis of the computer services industry.

Tom Watson, Sr., had started the service bureau group in Cleveland in 1932 as

IBM leader Thomas Watson, Sr. (1), had been a business genius, which is why Sam wanted to work for his company. Wyly recalls (2): "An IBM sales convention was like an old-time revival meeting. We all wore the same uniform—white shirts, ties and dark suits. My first boss sent home a fellow young IBM-er to change clothes. His sin was to come to work in a light blue shirt rather than white. So he got sent home to change." Watson inspired his troops with maxims like, "Reach for a star. You may not get a star, but neither will you get a handful of mud!" While Wyly soon joined the ranks of IBM's prestigious Hundred Percent Club by meeting 100 percent of his sales quota for the year, he began to have misgivings. "I decided I would not be the man in the gray flannel suit," he said.

His first customers, for IBM subsidiary Service Bureau Corporation (3).

Wyly's first paycheck from IBM (4).

a minor unit of IBM. It sold tabulating services—payroll and accounting—to small customers who could not afford to lease their own tabulating equipment and hire their own staff. Customers would send accounting documents to the service bureau, then pick up the processed results later. Watson, a hardware man down to his toenails, believed that the real usefulness of this service bureau was that it helped create customers for IBM, warming them up for the day when they could afford to lease their own tabulating equipment and become "real" customers. The unit had helped IBM prosper over the years for a lot of reasons—not all of them fair, according to the Justice Department. IBM was a master at landing and locking in new business. But some of the lock-in business practices that Tom Watson, Sr., had fathered—such as leasing equipment but refusing to sell it (so there would be no "used" IBM equipment to compete with), monopolizing the punch card business and tying in free services with hardware leases (called "bundling")—had helped the company obtain near-monopoly power in the market.

Anyone who leased an IBM computer got all of the programming (software) and services needed to operate it for no extra charge. It was part of the "IBM security blanket" that covered its customers, and smothered the competition. In fact, the Justice Department eventually argued that other independent services companies—whose livelihood rested solely on selling services—could not compete with what IBM gave away along with its equipment, "the bundling." There are echoes of this in the way Microsoft bundled its software onto PCs—and got slapped by the Justice Department. Today Google has a big lobby in Washington seeking to avoid the same trouble.

Burt Grad, a historian and technology consultant, says, "IBM's view of the world was that you made your money off the hardware, and everything else you did—service, support, software—was to enable you to increase the customer's usage of the hardware." [So they would have to buy more of it.] "Let me give you an analogy. General Electric was in the business of selling electricity. It didn't own the utilities. If the utilities wanted to have more power production, they would have to buy transformers and turbines and generators from GE. So, what does GE do? GE comes up with more appliances that use electricity. 'We don't *want* to be that efficient. We don't *care* if it uses a lot of electricity. We *want* it to use electricity.' And it was the same thing with IBM."

As IBM came up with more software and services, it happily passed them along to customers for little or no charge because they generated more computer usage, which inevitably led to the purchase of more equipment. The giveaways had the additional benefit of harming competitors, who only had software and services for sale.

The Justice Department's antitrust prosecutors filed suit in 1952. In 1956, IBM agreed to begin selling, not just leasing, "electronic data processing machines." (The word "computer" was not in general usage then and does not appear in the ruling.) IBM also agreed to let others make and sell punch cards, and to spin off its service bureaus into a wholly owned subsidiary with separate books and no tie-ins to IBM's hardware sales and manufacturing organization.

At the time, Wyly wasn't too interested in all these machinations—he just wanted to work for what he thought was the best company in the world. He settled into a $130-a-month apartment he shared with a roommate, and got to know his neighbors, including the American Airlines stewardesses who lounged around the pool between flights. His next-door neighbor, a thickset 45-year-old man named Jack, ran a jazz club, and had a collection of dogs he called his children, including a treasured dachshund named Sheba that he referred to as "my wife." Jack talked to Sam about Lacy Stinson, a friend of Sam's from Louisiana who played clarinet at Jack's club. Life was good for both men.

Wyly got his own territory at SBC, which gave him the chance to go into the marketplace and see what he could do, head-to-head, against both internal and external competitors. Most important, he was solving Information Age problems. He was a knowledge worker. And his customers had a lot of questions:

"Can you solve my problem?"

"How are you going to do it?"

"How long will it take?"

"What will it cost?"

"Why should I say 'yes' to this deal?"

"Sounds complicated. Will changing cause a big disruption in our shop?"

"What's the return on our investment?"

Just as that IBM salesman had done for the *Dispatch* back in Delhi, Wyly studied the potential clients in his territory until he knew their business better than most of their employees did. He examined their structures, needs, goals and aspirations—as all good entrepreneurs must—and crafted computer services that achieved those goals. Because all this meant sitting down with clients and learning what those goals were, he got invaluable insights into a wide range of companies—how they were set up, and what had to happen for them to earn a profit. He studied the flow of information, and learned how various business units actually interacted with one another, and what kinds of information they required from one another to function. He focused on payroll and cost allocation services, but soon began to see that there was a lot of potential in a sales management system. It just needed the software to support it. The number of businesses that needed information processing began to seem limitless.

He excelled at his job, exceeded all his sales quotas and then hit a wall. He grew frustrated trying to get noticed—and have his ideas heard—as the managers above him in the corporate chain of command came and went. Each new boss seemed to Wyly not quite as smart as the previous guy. The company's policy mandated that senior people were rotated constantly (IBM, other guys at the 100 percent clubs complained, stood for "I've been moved"), so managers were cycled in and out of slots around the country, and the world.

IBM didn't make many mistakes in the '40s and '50s, but it failed to see the potential of the all-electronic ENIAC computer invented by John Mauchly, a physicist, and John Presper Eckert, an engineer who was always fiddling with his computer's 18,000 vacuum tubes.

Wyly still believed that IBM was one of the world's great companies, but maybe not great for him. If he was in a hurry to enact his ideas, to lead instead of follow, IBM was becoming a stifling, rules-driven, organizational man's bureaucratic morass. He had lots of ideas, but no one asked and no one listened. He had met and married a young lady from Dallas named Rosemary Acton. She was pregnant with their first child. They had moved into a modest home at 3736 Marquette in Dallas—Rosemary's father, Len

Acton, had made the down payment as a wedding gift. In the evenings Sam and Rosemary sat on a sofa they had plucked off someone's curb. They had no dishwasher, no washing machine and no dryer. They once had Ross and Margo Perot over for dinner and ate it beneath the clotheslines loaded with diapers strung across the room.

Wyly told himself again and again that it would be foolish to walk away from the "greatest company in the world," the leader in the most exciting new industry in decades, a pension, insurance and security, just to fulfill his personal hunger to lead an enterprise. But he felt pigeonholed. He was 26 years old, and it was time to move on.

In 1961, he wrote letters to IBM's badly overmatched competitors in the computing world— the so-called Seven Dwarfs—looking for a job. A few days later, he hadn't received any firm offers, but he felt uncomfortable staying when his heart was no longer in the job, so he told his boss he was leaving IBM, and went home. A couple of hours after he got home, a call came from Honeywell asking him to come up to Boston for an interview. "Back then I thought that I would work for IBM forever," Wyly says. "Maybe be president of IBM—that was my thought early on. But three years later they hadn't even made me a branch manager. Then Honeywell came along."

Seeing IBM's huge success in computing, Honeywell had joined the fray in the 1950s, but it had problems. Its first computer, the Datamatic 1000 (1957), a vacuum-tube machine that weighed 25 tons (with 26-pound, three-inch-wide tape reels), took up 6,000 square feet, and cost $6 million in today's dollars. With just seven units sold, it never threatened IBM. But it was the company's second generation of solid-state computers, set to roll out in late 1960, that Honeywell had in mind for Wyly. Honeywell wanted to poach some of IBM's best and brightest, so they offered him an 80 percent increase in base pay. Honeywell was preparing to deliver its first solid-state computer, the Honeywell 800, and Wyly was to assemble a team of sales reps and technicians that he would manage, and they would sell the 800 in Texas, Oklahoma and Arkansas.

Wyly was intrigued. "My IBM territory was just one little piece of Dallas, and Honeywell said, 'We'll give you two and a half states; we'll make you the area manager and you will get to hire the first salespeople, hire the first programmers and be in charge.'"

He was stunned—and thrilled—to learn that he would be on his own in the field. During one of his interviews with Honeywell, he realized that his new boss,

John Cheely, would be 1,000 miles away, in Chicago. "Cheely told me, 'Now, Sam, if you have a problem—*don't call me!*' He said, 'Just sit down and see if you can't figure it out by yourself. Or maybe call another regional manager somewhere to see what *he* would do.'

"They didn't have everything planned out," Wyly recalls. "An amazing level of anarchy existed in this brand-new division. I loved it. Honeywell sent me to Wellesley, Massachusetts, for training; I'd never spent time in Boston. I'd never been around houses that were 200 years old. I had never ridden on a train before. I was in the city and taking the train out to the suburban office in Wellesley Hills. I had a per diem and they paid for my hotel, which was kind of neat!"

Wyly wasn't just another rube blinded by the big city lights. He knew what he was doing, and he knew what he had to do to be successful. Once again, he had stumbled into a perfect training ground for an entrepreneur. He had been expecting to join the polished, well-directed marketing machine of an 80-year-old corporate giant. Instead, he was being asked to create that machine. When he started with Honeywell, his territory market share was zero. But he had some advantages: Thanks to his education at Michigan and his experience with IBM, he was now Honeywell's de facto computer industry expert in Texas.

Wyly was ecstatic. It was his first real shot at testing himself and his ideas about what computers could do and about the many new markets that were still untapped. All he had to do to be successful was outsell the other six Dwarfs and a sophisticated, entrenched IBM, which had 70 percent of the market and just a few months earlier Wyly believed was invincible. He went after his initial customers himself, while recruiting his team. "I'm Sam Wyly and I'm from Honeywell and we sell computers," he would tell prospects, who would laugh and reply, "Nah, Honeywell sells thermostats. *IBM* sells computers."

"I was young and naïve," he recalls. "I didn't understand the difficulty in going up against a company with a 70 percent monopoly with a new product. It was not easy, but I loved it." He kept knocking on doors, making calls, helping prospects analyze competitive systems versus what Honeywell offered, and pushing his product. It began to pay off. He learned that for all its market power, IBM had chinks in its armor. Its equipment was reliable and its cradle-to-grave service was unbeatable, but upgrade deliveries were always done on IBM's schedule, not the customer's. And with so many huge and growing markets, IBM had ignored a few niches.

And Honeywell had its own edge, a potentially sharp one: performance.

Wyly visited Honeywell's headquarters in Wellesley, got a look at the new 400 and 800 series computers, and was delighted to hear that they were faster and had more capacity than IBM's new machines. But they wouldn't be ready for 18 months, so he had no deliverable product. Wyly handpicked a five-man team and set about showing them what he had learned about beating IBM. It would not be easy, because IBM had cultivated relationships with thousands of companies for decades, and knew how to use that 70 percent market share like a sledgehammer. Wyly, who had once swung that hammer, now found a way to turn the bully's tactics against it. He got an audience with Republic Insurance Company in Dallas, a longtime IBM customer, and made his pitch to six vice presidents on the committee charged with determining Republic's future in IT. They voted for IBM, 4–2. But Wyly wasn't deterred—"The selling starts when the customer says no"—and he went to Russell Perry, Republic's CEO. Wyly knew Perry had clashed with IBM after he had swapped delivery dates with another IBM customer, shortening his delivery time from 18 months to 60 days. IBM had slapped him down for that move, and Perry was still stinging from their arrogant, high-handed treatment. "IBM had this thought-control structure where *they* manage the account, *they* tell customers what the rules are," Wyly recalls.

Wyly told Perry about the superior performance of Honeywell's machines—and of Honeywell's determination to keep clients happy—and Perry said, "I'm overriding the committee." Wyly got the contract. Republic converted to Honeywell, and their IBM representative—whom Wyly had known since their Sunday school days—was fired (per company policy) for losing the account. (Weeks earlier, Wyly had warned his old friend to get off the account, but this IBM man bled blue, and didn't believe IBM could ever lose. He was wrong—and looking for a new job.)

Wyly's small sales team beat the sales numbers for some cities with 30-man Honeywell teams. In two years he nearly doubled his income again, to $30,000. Then came a pivotal day. He urged his bosses to invest in Dallas with a large-scale computing center dedicated to serving the oil industry and other customers. He could see that some of IBM's competitors had great hardware and software systems, and would be moving into that market. IBM had commissioned a study that investigated the potential market in North Texas. The conclusion was that the new $3 million computer would make a profit, but not *enough* profit. Wyly felt the assessment was wrong. He saw an opportunity to make money. "This study triggered a thought for a similar but different business that might work," he says. "I didn't have $3 million, but I had $1,000 and an idea. I knew there were a whole lot of people out there who wanted the power and productivity that a big computer system offered, but who couldn't afford a multimillion-dollar mainframe. How could I create a company to fill that gap?"

He chewed on that idea for a while, and slowly put the pieces of the puzzle together in his mind.

And now he had a tough decision to make. If he wanted to follow directives for the rest of his career, move anywhere on short notice and get a nice paycheck, he should stick with Honeywell. But he could see that there was no way he would be able to stay in Texas, and get to the top at Honeywell.

So there he was, feeling dead-ended again. "It became clear to me that if I really wanted to be independent and control my own destiny, I couldn't be with any big organization, whether it was Honeywell or IBM," Wyly says. "I really needed to have my own business, just like a good cotton farmer does or a good newspaper publisher does."

But striking out on his own now meant exposing his family to even more risk than what he'd faced when he'd left IBM. He was 28 years old. His first son, Evan, had arrived. He had two cars. His family was now living in a two-story house on a tree-lined street in a great school district. There was, however, another factor to consider: his newfound confidence, based on his experiences since getting out of school. Establishing Honeywell—then an unknown name in computing—in Texas convinced him he could do the same thing for his own company. And beating IBM proved to him that he could compete against the best. And he was eager to meet that challenge, to prove himself. He was ready to become an entrepreneur. "When people ask me if I started my own company to get rich, I tell them I didn't. I had a vague notion that you could acquire wealth, but that was not really my purpose. I was already making far more money than I had ever thought possible when I was in college. In fact, I had figured out that the most I would need to make was $10,000 a year and I was already making $30,000. So it wasn't about money. My purpose was freedom; my purpose was independence."

The Toastmasters Club was a mutual self-improvement society, or you might call it media training in the Dark Ages—members were called on randomly to provide a two-minute response to any question or topic tossed to them by the chair. About every fourth session, each member had to give a six-minute talk on his own topic.

CHAPTER THREE

THERE'S A PONY IN THERE SOMEWHERE

State-of-the-art, fully transistorized, circa 1960: the IBM 7090, which sold for nearly $3 million. "It could do great scientific calculations as well as business data processing," Wyly says. NASA's Saturn moon rocket ran thousands of virtual test flights on the 7090 before the rocket's actual launch.

On a hot summer day in July of '63, Sam Wyly was strolling through his Dallas neighborhood with his small son, Evan, when they came across a man mowing his lawn. They had met Eldon Vaughan casually at the Third Church of Christ Science, so Wyly knew he was a lawyer with his own practice. He and Evan walked over and sat down to chat under a lovely mimosa tree, its feathery hot pink flowers bobbing in the meager breeze.

"I need a charter for a corporation," he told Vaughan.

"Sure, what's on your mind?"

"I'm starting a company."

"What kind of company?"

"Computer services."

Vaughan looked at him curiously. "Now what exactly is a computer?"

Wyly smiled, then gave him the basic hot-day-under-a-tree crash course in software services, and how computer technology was going to change the world. When he was done, Vaughan said, "I'm not bright enough to assess the potential of your company, but I do know how to incorporate one."

On July 23, 1963, while still working for Honeywell, Wyly took $1,000 out of the bank and had Vaughan file the papers of incorporation for a new company. Just like that, the easy part of becoming an entrepreneur was done. Then he hit a few minor obstacles. For one, the computer industry in the early '60s was a frantic jumble. While there was the superficial appearance of a defined industry, beneath the surface there was a stew of new markets, new players, new applications and new needs. And the parameters changed often, and quickly. Where others saw only chaos, Wyly saw opportunity.

Following IBM's lead, the major computer-makers simply wanted to move as many machines as they could. That's where the big money was—so much money, in fact, that they were ignoring niche markets. "In focusing on multimillion-dollar

Left: When Sam faced the decision about whether to leave his lucrative territory and budding career with Honeywell to start his own business, he had a new factor to consider: his first child, Evan Acton Wyly (left, in 1962, with his grandparents Flora and Charles Wyly).

Below, left: Sam with his eldest son, Evan.

Below: Driven to succeed: Sam's first wife, Rosemary, with his twin daughters, Laurie (left) and Lisa and Evan in a modern-day version of the Model A Ford, which had a fiberglass body and a brand-new engine.

computers back then, IBM was separating the trivial many from the vital few," Wyly says. "And no one did big computers for big businesses better than IBM."

But Wyly had learned at Service Bureau Corporation that only the wealthiest companies could afford the in-house computer operation IBM was peddling. Thousands of smaller companies desperately needed the speed, accuracy and flexibility of computing in order to lower their costs and improve their decision-making. The business Wyly had in mind went back to the market analysis IBM had done that said a $3 million computer center in North Texas wouldn't be profitable. He saw that that cost-analysis was based on using an expensive, new IBM computer. *How about a used computer?* he asked himself. *I can buy a used car for less than a new one. Dad couldn't afford a new printing press for the* Delhi Dispatch, *but he found a secondhand one that did all he needed done.* Wyly was sure he had a good plan, but asked himself, *What do I know for sure?*

What he knew for sure was that this industry was in its infancy, wildly unsettled and growing fast, much like the steel industry when Andrew Carnegie jumped into it in the 1860s. And he knew from his time as an IBM salesmen that there were plenty of customers to compete for, and there were going to be many more. He knew that despite their vast wherewithal, IBM and the Seven Dwarfs were lumbering giants that could not react quickly to all the market opportunities. He knew that he, on the other hand, could totally focus on this niche, and have lower operating expenses, focused customer service and lower overhead. And the macroeconomic backdrop was promising. The economy was gaining strength, and growth meant more discretionary corporate spending for things such as computer services. It might make banks more willing to loan to new ventures.

Wyly's market analysis had identified his niche—scientific and petroleum engineering applications in North Texas—a relatively small number of companies. He knew he could create a lean business plan for companies such as Sun Oil and for some engineering consultants. He needed a mainframe computer system that was fast, had lots of storage, had a good Fortran compiler and a place to house it, because his target customers were engineers who had written their programs in the Fortran language. Then he had to get some customers to believe that his start-up was a better, more secure alternative to what they could get from IBM or the other big guys. And then he had to deliver. That was a daunting mountain of challenges, but the optimist in him said, *Start digging—there's a pony in there somewhere.*

Finding a low-cost, used computer wasn't his only problem. He needed low over-head. He needed some kind of substitute for equity capital. How could he create equity? First, he needed to do some old-fashioned bartering. Wyly remembered a former Texas Instruments engineer at Southern Methodist University, in the heart of Dallas, J. B. Harville, who was heading up the university's computer lab. Wyly knew Harville was a man with a problem: He and his data processing students were still using a massive, antiquated UNIVAC 1103 vacuum-tube computer—the Model T of information processing—that bore little resemblance to current machines. That meant Harville's students were entering the job marketplace poorly trained, which hurt their chances of landing jobs and tarnished SMU's reputation.

Wyly dropped in on Harville one day and told him about his venture. "I'd like to install my computer operations on the SMU premises," he said. "In exchange for the space, the electricity and half the maintenance bill, and if you pay for the raised floor to put the cables under, you and your students can have access to the computer on evenings and weekends."

"We will do it," said Harville. "If you can put your deal together, our trustees do not want to spend cash for a new computer system, but our alumni keep giving us lots of money for buildings."

And so University Computing Company was born.

Wyly now had a name, a plan, a customer and boundless optimism—none of which paid the bills. The next two items on his to-do list: find a used computer, and the money to pay for it.

Finding the right secondhand computer was a thorny challenge. It had to be old enough to be reasonably priced but new enough to have the current technol-ogy. It had to be powerful enough to handle the needs of whatever customers he landed and reliable enough to serve them without fail. It had to be advanced enough to justify replacing the SMU UNIVAC computer and simple enough that he could program and maintain it without hiring a hundred computer scientists.

Wyly knew that there was no viable secondhand market for the IBM machines.

In 1951, Remington Rand's UNIVAC I—to the abject horror of Tom Watson, Sr.—had been selected to handle the U.S. Census Bureau's calculations. IBM's tabulating machines had monopolized the hugely prestigious contract for seven decades. Perhaps the most bitterly lost commercial customer in the history of enterprise, the switch had one world-changing outcome: it focused Watson Jr. on electronic calculators at IBM. Sam got introduced to the Information Age firsthand on an IBM 650 Magnetic Drum Data Processing Machine (1) at the University of Michigan. "A radical difference was the stored program," Wyly says of this era, when the term "computer" was still unknown. In 1953, IBM projected sales of the so-called calculator at 50 units; when production ceased in 1952, more than 2,000 had been sold, making it the first of its kind on which IBM banked a sizable profit. Even Big Blue had wildly underestimated the revolution it was leading. Wyly learned machine language and Symbolic Optimal Assembly Program (SOAP) on the 650, authoring and debugging programs to calculate payrolls and to sort labor costs.

By the time Sam looked to set up his first company, the UNIVAC 1103 vacuum-tube mainframe—a descendant of the UNIVAC II (2)—installed at Southern Methodist University was an antiquated, heat-producing clunker, much like Honeywell's first big bet, the motel-sized Datamatic 1000 (3), jointly produced with Raytheon. Eager to challenge IBM's 70-percent-and-rising market share, Honeywell had, in 1958, announced the 400 series (4), a true second-generation, transistorized computer that would go toe-to-toe with IBM's 1401 (5), targeting small and medium-sized businesses. Smaller, faster, less expensive and more reliable as a source of computing power, one transistor could replace 40 vacuum tubes. Of the 1401, Wyly says, "It was a low-priced computer, basically a bookkeeping edition."

New business computer models faced the need to turn a profit, quickly. "The military didn't need any promise of payback," Wyly says of the R&D process that gave birth to the first supercomputers. "Can you blow away the Germans or Russians quicker? That's the question."

Whenever the lease on an IBM ran out, it installed new equipment, then picked up and disassembled the old computer. That meant IBM controlled the supply and maintained very high gross profits. Since there was no secondhand market, if a company wanted an IBM computer, it had no alternative but to lease IBM's latest equipment. Although that 1956 Consent Decree with the Justice Department had compelled the company to begin selling its computers, IBM priced them so high relative to the rental price that used IBM machines were scarce and expensive in 1963.

Wyly scoured the trade journals and poked through every dark corner of the industry for weeks. It felt like a needle-in-a-field-of-haystacks search, but he finally found what he was looking for. While in Washington, D.C., for a software association conference, he met Bob Holland, president of the Corporation for Economic and Industrial Research (CEIR), which had grown too fast, gotten in over its head and was running big losses. Holland had been brought in from RCA's computer business to fix things after CEIR defaulted on a $4 million bank loan. In trying to pay down some debt, Holland was ready to sell some of the company's older computers.

One of them was a Control Data Corporation 1604. They had two, but only needed one, and Control Data would not buy it back. They'd paid $1.5 million for it, but their asking price now was $650,000. This was exactly the machine Wyly needed, but he was about $640,000 short—he only had $10,000 saved. He told Holland about his vision for University Computing and that he really wanted his 1604, really *needed* his 1604, and wanted to pay for it with a five-year note.

"We can't," Holland said, "Our bankers require that we get cash for any asset we sell and pay down our debt."

That meant Wyly needed a big loan. He started at the largest bank in Dallas, Republic National Bank. After all, his personal account was there. A young loan officer had once loaned him $2,000 to invest in stocks when he was a "Saturday morning and 10 shares" investor, and he had diligently repaid that. *This can be done.*

He wore his best IBM outfit: conservative dark blue suit, white shirt, understated tie and polished shoes. He detailed his business plan, recounted his real-world experience at IBM and Honeywell, and told the bankers about the untapped niche of petroleum and other engineering services. He made it clear that his intention was to build a computer center in which these scientists and engineers, hungry for computer access, could run their specialized programs and would pay only for their time on the computer.

The mainframe that got Sam into the game, the Control Data Corporation's 1604A, he was able to buy at a fire-sale price. Designed by legendary supercomputer architect Seymour Cray, at age 35, the all-transistor 1604 put Minnesota-based CDC on the map, helping to establish the company's reputation for building the fastest and most powerful mainframes of the 1960s. Writes tech columnist John Dvorak: "This machine could do just about everything from real-time data processing to weapons control." It retailed for $1.5 million.

"The bottom line?" the bankers asked.

"Gentlemen," he said, "I need to borrow six hundred and forty thousand dollars."

The bankers laughed. "And I mean a real belly laugh," Wyly recalls ruefully. But he was not dissuaded. The old college debater in him knew he had to add meat to his presentation, as well as substance to his deal. That meant forecasting expenses, revenue and income with more specificity, and providing a potential customer list. He had to demonstrate that the solitary missing ingredient to this can't-miss venture was the loan. And what if he could line up some customers who promised to *use* University Computing Company when it went live? To do that, Wyly realized, he needed a company that needed him.

From his work with Honeywell, he knew that petroleum engineers at Sun Oil Company up in Richardson, Texas (north of Dallas), had to drive 27 miles to Grand Prairie every time they wanted to use the IBM 7090 computers at Ling-Temco-Vaught Aerospace, where they rented excess time. But LTV wasn't a computer service business and had no guaranteed access or reserved usage times. Sun Oil engineers sometimes made the long drive only to find that someone at LTV had bumped them at the last minute because they always had priority.

Wyly approached John Rice, an engineer at Sun. "How would you like a shorter drive?" he said. "And how would you like to save money? And your guys will have priority scheduling."

Wyly told him about his plan for University Computing, about the Control Data 1604 he had lined up, and explained that he needed Sun Oil to come on board

The Sun Oil Production Research & Development Lab, outside Dallas, provided the first customers for Sam's new computer services company. In those days, you had to be close to your customers, because all the data had to be delivered by hand.

before he could get the bank loan. The quid pro quo: the contract he'd give Sun Oil would be a super bargain—$500,000 over five years—that would cut their costs by two-thirds, but $250,000 of that had to be paid in cash in advance. "Otherwise, I can't sell a bank on making a loan."

Rice liked the scheme, and agreed to become a customer if Wyly could put the other parts of his deal together. Cutting costs and making Sun Oil's engineers more productive and happy were his motivations. It was 20 miles closer to their shop, and they would be helping SMU professors and students move up to a second-generation (transistorized), large-scale computer system. They liked that.

Though Wyly had nothing on paper, he took his new pitch to the second biggest bank in Dallas, First National Bank. The loan officer didn't laugh this time. But he did turn him down. Again, it came down to collateral for the loan.

Wyly knew there had to be a solution. Coach Richards had said, "You will not tire first."

At 11 a.m. on November 22, 1963, a beautiful Friday morning, he went to meet with loan officers at the third-largest bank in Dallas, Mercantile Bank. He had asked for an 11 a.m. meeting because President and Mrs. Kennedy were driving through town at noon, and he wanted to watch their motorcade. This Texas trip was the launch of President Kennedy's reelection campaign for 1964. It would pass down Main Street, where the bank was, and he figured he would have time after the meeting to get to a good viewing spot.

The meeting with the loan committee went pretty much like the first two meetings. Disappointed but neither surprised nor deterred, he left the bank shortly after noon. He crossed the street to Neiman Marcus and scampered up to its third-floor windows. At 12:25 p.m., he watched the motorcade pass below, heading toward Houston Street and Dealey Plaza. President Kennedy, sitting in the back of a big convertible with the top down, was waving, smiling. Jackie, dressed in pink, was radiant. The parade crowd was exultant. As he headed for his car, it felt like a good day, despite his bad news from the bank. He was looking forward to a meeting with J. B. Harville and an attorney that afternoon at Southern Methodist University. As he was paying for his parking the cashier, listening to her radio, looked up at him and said, "The president has been shot!" It was 12:30.

Stomach churning, Wyly drove to his one 1 p.m. meeting at SMU, but everyone there was in shock. Kennedy was officially pronounced dead at 1, and CBS News anchor Walter Cronkite famously announced it on television 38 minutes later. No one in that meeting had his mind on business, so they all went home. Like most of the world, Wyly watched television for the next four days, caught up in the horrific drama.

On Sunday, November 24, he was still in front of his TV, watching the man arrested for the shooting, Lee Harvey Oswald, as he was transferred from the city jail to the county facility. Oswald was in handcuffs, being led to a vehicle, when a man burst from the crowd of journalists and photographers and fired one shot into Oswald's belly. Moments later the gunman was identified as Jack Ruby, a downtown nightclub owner.

"That's my old neighbor!" Wyly said, jumping from his chair. His former neighbor with the dachshund for "a wife" had just killed Lee Harvey Oswald—live on national TV. When police found Ruby's car parked down the street, Sheba, his cherished dachshund, was inside.

It was hard to imagine normalcy ever returning to the nation after the assassination of President Kennedy, but over the next few weeks Wyly saw that the stock market, which dislikes a crisis, was not going in the tank. The market dropped three percent the day Kennedy was shot before it was closed down. But it was in the middle of what Wyly had concluded was a multiyear expansion (six months after the assassination, the Dow was up 12 percent). The Federal Reserve Bank was supplying lots of liquidity to the U.S. banking system. He continued to see opportunity, though he wondered if conservative bankers could see what he saw. He knew from his dad's friend who ran the

Howdy, neighbor! In Dallas, Sam briefly lived in the same apartment complex as Jack Ruby, seen here with his cat and beloved dog, Sheba. He hadn't seen Ruby for a few years— and then saw him on TV, gunning down Lee Harvey Oswald.

bank in Delhi that the bankers' mantra called for the "three Cs" before making any loan: character, credit and collateral. He felt he could win on character, and he did have a brief credit history. But he was short on collateral—big-time.

When he finally returned to thinking about business, he knew he was running out of time. How long before CEIR sold off its computer to someone with a fistful of cash? How long before SMU found some other way to replace its old UNIVAC? How long before Sun Oil solved its reservoir simulation needs without University Computing?

Then one day, his answer walked in the door.

An insurance agent, having heard that University Computing was installing a $1.5 million computer at SMU (he didn't know about the fire-sale discount Wyly had gotten), came to sell Wyly some property insurance. After hearing the man's pitch, Wyly said, "I love your policy, but I have to get in business first." He explained his collateral dilemma.

"I can solve your problem," the agent said cheerily. "What you need is a performance bond that guarantees, in this case, that the insurance company would repay Sun Oil pro rata if you failed to deliver the computer services any time in the five years of the contract."

Wyly happily (and quickly) agreed to buy the bond (and the insurance), and went back to Sun Oil, who immediately agreed to a five-year contract, with $250,000 cash up front.

Now Wyly went to the fourth-largest bank in Dallas, Texas Bank. Jack Garrett was the vice chairman; Sam had met him at church. Garrett introduced Sam to a loan officer, who currently had a much safer bundle to look at than the one Wyly had pitched to the first three banks, and the officer recommended making the loan, provided Sam could get one more guarantee. Garrett recommended a company Texas Bank had worked with called Diversa, which Wyly liked, because he also had a connection there. His father-in-law, Len Acton, was a dealmaker in the Texas financial world, and knew the top Diversa people well. He introduced Sam to his partner, a lawyer named Guy Mann. The two of them had helped buy and sell companies for "Big Rich" Texas oilman Clint Murchison. Guy Mann's brother, Jerry, ran Diversa, which had been bought from Murchison by John D. McArthur's insurance company. Jerry had a diverse resume: He had been known as "the little red arrow" as a football hero at SMU, which made him an enduring local hero. He had studied at Harvard Law School, where he'd been a part-time preacher in small towns outside Boston, then had come home to Texas, where he served as the state's attorney general. In 1941, he ran for the U.S. Senate as a Franklin Roosevelt Democrat against Lyndon Johnson, then a congressman from Austin and the Texas hill country. But they both lost to the governor, W. Lee "Pass the Biscuits, Pappy" O'Daniel. The nickname came from the catchphrase for his radio show, which was sponsored by a flour company. O'Daniel was a charismatic man who regularly toured the state with his Hillbilly Band and won over audiences with a song he'd written called "Beautiful Texas." Johnson and Mann couldn't compete with all the radio exposure O'Daniel got with his country band.

After Wyly talked to Jerry Mann, Diversa agreed to guarantee Wyly's note to Texas Bank in exchange for equity in University Computing. Wyly was desperate to wrap the deal up, so he made them an offer he knew they couldn't refuse: 49 percent of the company. Jerry Mann agreed—verbally.

But when they sat down to sign the deal, a lawyer sitting next to Jerry Mann casually told Wyly that Diversa really had to have a 51 percent share. Wyly was stunned. "That's *not* the deal we made," he said. "If I give you fifty-one percent, I sabotage the very reason I quit IBM and quit Honeywell and started this business. I *have* to control this company. You do not have a clue about this business. I don't want to have to clear every move with you and your accountants and lawyers. I don't have time for that. You bring nothing to the table. No cash; no intellectual contribution; no energy. Your guarantee is fifth in line in financial importance."

Diversa wouldn't yield, and Wyly saw his deal slipping away. He had to do something, fast, so he asked everyone in the room to step outside so that he could talk to Jerry Mann privately. When the two men were alone, Wyly did not complain that Mann was reneging on their verbal deal; instead, he said, "I'll accept this agreement if you give me your personal word that I can buy you out at a market price later."

Mann agreed. They shook on it, and the deal was signed. Diversa got 51 percent, and Sam Wyly got his first company.

UNIVERSITY COMPUTING C

Wyly: "Early on, with the creation of University Computing, probably the first and best decision I made was to ask my brother, Charles (right), to join me as a partner. He brought knowledge and experience. I needed somebody I could trust and who could trust me; that was my brother."

NEVER LET YOUR WALLET TELL YOU WHAT YOU CAN DO

At the opening of the company's Tulsa office, UCC employee number three, Ross Rumore (far left), and first investor, Ben Voth (second from right), stand by while Sam greets local dignitaries, including the governor of Oklahoma, Henry Bellmon (center).

Sam Wyly's idea had finally become a real business, with $650,000 of capital, boundless ambitions and one employee: Sam Wyly. Whatever happened next was up to him, not a committee, and he felt tentative about absolutely nothing. He didn't worry about repaying that big loan—instead, he was busily dreaming up new ways to grow the company. *What's the next city? The next state? The next technology? How do I make the puzzle pieces fit?* He couldn't turn his brain off, and didn't want to. While most start-up computer services companies in the '60s were thinking about how many customers they could land in their hometown, Wyly was thinking: *How do we become the biggest player on earth?*

His first priority was to find the right people to help him, and his choices were sometimes odd to everyone but him. He hired a 65-year-old retired insurance executive who knew almost nothing about computers as chairman of the board. He brought in a high school dropout who would go on to lead several companies for Wyly. *You mine gold where you find gold*, he thought.

He wanted to build his corporate team by following the same principles Coach Richards had used to build the Delhi Bears football team: "Assemble the best players. Put them where they excel. Train them beyond old boundaries. Learn the opposition better than they know themselves. Execute your assignments quickly, exactly and with inevitability. Innovate when you need to. Believe in yourself, and what you're doing. Tenacity matters more than size. Be the last to tire. Play like you belong among the best."

He first needed to compile a strong sales team because "nothing happens until someone sells something." He needed help recruiting those people, as well as help getting more customers and running the business. That meant getting his brother,

Charles, involved. Shortly after Sam got his deal nailed down in late 1963 he called his brother, who was settled in Houston—married, a father and a very successful salesman for IBM. But Charles quit IBM, packed up his family and moved to Dallas as if he had been just waiting for Sam to call. Their parents, Flora and Charles, who had sold the *Delhi Dispatch* and moved to Houston when IBM had transferred Charles there, now moved to Dallas, too. "Early on, probably the first and best decision I made was to ask my brother, Charles, to join me as a partner," Sam says. "He brought knowledge and experience. I needed somebody I could trust and who could trust me. Those principles went through almost everything we did after that. It was a difficult process, but I had to learn to delegate to others."

Sam and Charles scoured all of Dallas, then all of North Texas, looking for customers. They refined their presentation as they learned from each call. They focused on the petroleum engineering market because they understood oil company guys—Delhi, Dallas and Houston were all oil towns. Their main pitch to prospects was that UCC was convenient ("We're nearby"), they wouldn't have to invest multi-millions in a computer ("Use our CDC 1604 by the hour") and they'd get great personal service ("Got a problem? Here's my home phone number"). The business concept for UCC was simple: "We buy computer power by the acre and sell it by the square foot, just like real estate." The scientists and engineers would come to the University Computing Company center at Southern Methodist, run their programs for as long as they needed to complete the jobs and pay only for the time they used.

UCC ended 1963—with just two months of live operations—with $67,000 in revenue and a $5,000 loss, but interest was mounting. Wyly could see that he would have to expand sometime, and *right away* struck him as as good a time as any. Why should he confine this useful service to North Texas when there were so many opportunities in other cities, in other oil-producing states? Tulsa still called itself "The Oil Capital of the World," but in truth, that title belonged to Houston. And nearby Texas A&M had a freshman class of 3,000 petroleum engineers. Soon, Wyly knew, there would be limitless opportunities for his company beyond the petroleum industry.

In his endless thinking about expanding, one idea dogged Sam: *What if we could make our computers accessible via a telephone line?* He knew American Airlines used

Young UCC President

A close look at the success story of University Computing Company, 1300 Frito-Lay Tower, and its young founder and president, Sam Wyly, should convince anyone of the opportunity-filled world in which we live. However, it does take a man like Sam Wyly to take advantage of these opportunities.

At age 28, when most other young men are anxiously awaiting a junior-executive title, Wyly quit his job with Honeywell and formed his own company. To make things even more exciting, Wyly chose to make his way in the country's newest industry — one where some of the country's largest corporations have lost millions endeavoring to establish a market position.

sales. In 1966
4½ million
profit should
000."

In predicti
his dynamic
said, "There
itations on
computer's
there are som
tations which
for a while.
any home in
will be able
ford the use
plan budgets,
Maybe some
while to com
limit these us

Wyly is no
In his past h
of Business
from the Uni

Top: Wyly quit Honeywell at 28 to start UCC: "After being at Honeywell for a while I realized that it was really going to be like IBM for me, and I was not likely to be made president of Honeywell. I was more likely to be fired for insubordination."

Above: UCC's new Dallas computer plant, early '70s.

Above: Sam's brother, Charles, taking a tour of the Dallas plant at its opening. Charles had a promising future at IBM, which he gave up to help Sam start UCC. Note the images of COPE-45 components on the wall behind him.

Teletype machines to make reservations that were stored in an IBM 7090 computer system. Could he improve on that model, using a telephone line and a high-speed printer or interactive keyboard? Instead of bringing raw data into the computer center and then carting off the processed results, what if customers could just make a phone call—send their work to be processed from a terminal linked to a telephone line and receive the results the same way? It was a brilliant idea, the fastest possible track to becoming a global company, and thinking about it electrified him. He wanted to connect the world to Dallas through phone lines, but the technology— especially AT&T's slow analog phone lines—wasn't ready yet. AT&T's telephone lines handled voice-based analog signals very well, but not the computer's digital data. The analog lines were both too slow and too expensive for Wyly and his customers to use.

Until the technology caught up to Wyly's vision, growth meant replicating his Dallas model—a computer center located close to his clients—and he was ready to do that in every city in the country. He first wanted to expand north, to Tulsa, but didn't have the capital to start another service center. No matter—he lived by one of Len Acton's favorite sayings, "Never let your wallet tell you what you can do." He hustled up a big contract with a Tulsa firm, Sunray DX Oil Company, and it, much like Sun Oil in Dallas, would be the base for his second center. Sam knew that the closer this new center was to Sunray DX, the better, so he went looking for office

Tulsa was prime territory for Sam and UCC because of the confluence of computers, oil money and engineers desperate to crunch a lot of data. (This photograph dates to 1945.)

space. An office building across the street from Sunray that had once been its head-quarters had space to rent, so he walked over to investigate. There he met the owner, Ben Voth, a 65-year-old retired insurance company president. Sam explained the concept behind University Computing, and Voth liked the idea. He also liked it when Wyly agreed to lease space in his building.

Wyly soon learned that Voth knew Sunray DX and many of the other large Oklahoma companies intimately—they had been some of his largest insurance customers, and Voth had golden relationships with many of the company officers and directors. He was an old-school businessman from an era in which the hand-shake was more binding than a 100-page legal document.

"My half-century of experience has convinced me that there is one basic principle which every successful, lasting business enterprise must follow," Voth wrote in his autobiography, *A Piece of Computer Pie.* "It may sound corny, but it's the age-old principle of the Golden Rule. There is a notion in some quarters that most fortunes are made through avarice and greed, such as despoiling our natural resources or exploiting the poor. Quite to the contrary, the way to make a fortune in this country today is to follow the Golden Rule, giving the other fellow the kind of deal you would like to get from him."

Voth told Wyly that early in his career he had been helped by many people, and he never forgot it. He thought it was his duty to help others as others had helped him, so he introduced Sam to prospects and decision-makers in Tulsa, and helped UCC's branch office get off to a good start.

It soon became clear to Wyly that despite being retired—and with several million dollars in the bank—Voth was bored. He had his office space to manage and some investments to monitor, but he clearly ached to reengage in something real, something challenging. And although he knew almost nothing about computing, the tantalizing promise of this information age technology had rekindled his competitive fire for commerce.

Sam invited Ben to visit Dallas, where he got a tour of the operation at Southern Methodist University. They then had dinner at Wyly's home, where Sam introduced him to his family. During this visit, Voth told Wyly he wanted to buy into the company, so Sam offered him five percent for $50,000. "I'll give you a hundred thousand dollars for ten percent," Voth said.

Wyly was thrilled. "That will give us the capital to build on."

"I believe you're going to make this work," Voth said.

Wyly decided to take it one step further. "What would you think about becoming chairman of the board of University Computing Company?"

Without hesitation, Voth accepted. He was officially unretired.

Wyly knew people would question the call: why bring in someone who doesn't know the industry? This is just like the opening song in *The Music Man,* "But he doesn't know the territory!" But Wyly knew better, and told friends, "Despite our conservative suits, white shirts and ties, most of us in the company look like runny-nosed kids to these mature VPs we are trying to make deals with. It'll be good to have some 'grey hair' around here." (Even though, Wyly recalls, Voth was bald.)

So Ben Voth became the first outside shareholder of UCC, and this small business with big ideas that almost never had a board meeting now had a chairman of the board.

By the end of 1964, the company's first full year, revenue was $692,954, with a net profit of $136,000. But it wasn't easy. "It was always a competitive marketplace with whatever you offered," Wyly says. "I remember picking up the Chicago yellow pages and noticing that of the people who were classified under service bureaus or computer services, 33 percent of the names dropped out every year. The list was getting longer but a third were dropping out, so it was clearly survival of the fittest."

And UCC was clearly one of the survivors. The two data centers were profitable from Day One and Wyly was wondering which major city they should go to next. But his most persistent dream still had a dial tone. "When I imagined the future, I saw a computer with a phone line on it." He called that intersection of two existing technologies "the sweet spot," and was certain that a merger would take both to another, extraordinary level. He imagined a company that anyone— business, school or individual—could connect to with just a phone call, paying only for the time they were on the line. Computing services would be "on tap" for users, like water and electricity. Just as people didn't have to be an electrician to turn on a light, they would not have to be a technician to use a computer.

The main obstacle was an ancient, immovable monopoly called American Telephone & Telegraph. AT&T, content with its state-guarded profits and monopoly,

Right: A full-sized model of the Tel-star experimental communications satellite at AT&T's Bell Laboratories.

Below: The race was on in the '60s to find a better, faster way to deliver data to computers, and to link up customers to those oversized mainframes. The communicative oscilloscope device at the Bell labs, was one innovation in data storage and retrieval.

had little incentive to invest quickly in new technology, even though the brilliant researchers in Bell Labs had invented a lot of it, including the transistor, the basic component of second-generation computers, which Bell licensed out to Texas Instruments and others.

Wyly continued developing his big idea despite seemingly insurmountable hurdles. It would mean diversifying outside of the scientific and engineering services University Computing had provided for the oil clients. He envisioned a string of computing centers, each specializing in applications for different industries, such as manufacturing, banking or accounting. Ultimately, all of those services would be accessible from anywhere. He knew there had to be better ways to move information around, and he knew that the future of University Computing Company—in fact, the future of computing—hinged on being able to solve that problem.

As UCC began to take off, he hired Gene Smith, a top-tier software technician at General Electric, to lead its software development. Smith pulled together young technicians who had been involved in designing airline reservation systems. The development effort they launched was for the COPE-45, short for Communications Oriented Processing Equipment. It was a remote job entry terminal, and would let users anywhere—down the hall or across an ocean—send data over telephone lines to a mainframe computer for processing. "Leroy Towel was the architect of the COPE 45," Wyly says. "We derived the name from the Colt 45—the fastest gun in the West."

University Computing's first proprietary product for data communications was about the size of a desk with an oversized typewriter on top, and it marked the tangible beginning of Wyly's chase for the Holy Grail in computing. Once people and computers could efficiently communicate over long distances, there would be no geographical limitation on his business growth. And that, he thought, would just be the first of a thousand changes in the technology. Instead of having to put a computer center near a client, he could sell a COPE-45 to anyone with a telephone. Customers could run their jobs from their own offices, and get the processed results printed out right there faster than ever before.

While the COPE-45 was faster than most other communications terminals at the time, Wyly didn't kid himself that it was the future. The system ran five to

Above: Sam and Charles with UCC's COPE-45 (Communications Oriented Processing Equipment) that sent data over phone lines. It was clunky, but revolutionary in its day.

Above, right: (From left) Smiles Click, Jeanette Gibson, and Ray Hannon, UCC's first PR guy, who dealt with the press and Wall Street analysts, are all watching a demonstration of the COPE-45.

Right: UCC's red, white and blue all-American computer, 1970s.

Opposite: When it was all about the hardware, UCC's line of products for data transmission and retrieval in the early '70s. The COPE-45 was named after the Colt 45 Texas Ranger pistol, the "fastest gun in the West." Says Wyly: "We engineered the product to push data through the lines faster . . . We were working on the cost of the line and the cost of the terminals. We were using whatever digital equipment anyone came up with to provide a better answer than what we had. We were more innovators than inventors, because we weren't starting from scratch. We had to take what was there and figure out how to use it smarter and quicker and better at low cost." The COPE ran up to seven times the speed of most earlier competitors. Dick Fagan, who managed University Computing's overseas operations, says, "The COPE put us on the map."

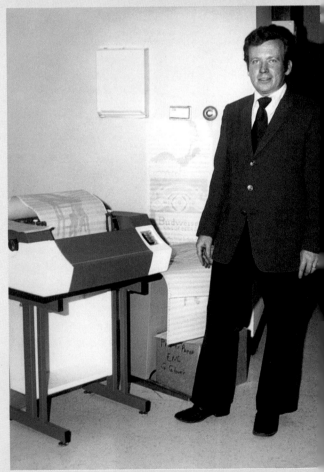

seven times the speed of most devices of the day, and would cut customers' average return time from two hours to just 20 minutes. But with exponentially growing processing demands, the world was going to need even faster communications—thousands of times faster. Still, its design enabled many users to process their jobs simultaneously, virtually eliminating the need to schedule sequential time on the computer. It was an evolutionary product, not revolutionary, because it had to use AT&T's molasses-slow analog lines—but it was a tantalizing peek under the curtain at what was to come. If he could kill the batch cart, University Computing would have a supreme competitive edge.

Wyly prepped his team and then turned them loose.

Even while he was aggressively growing his computer services business, Wyly began to imagine other business opportunities. He soon found one on a New York City sidewalk. He had gone to New York City in 1966 for a trans-Atlantic cruise and was staying at the Waldorf-Astoria for a couple of days before embarking. Walking down Park Avenue one beautiful afternoon a few hours before he was due to board the *Queen Mary,* he looked up to see Bob Holland, the president of CEIR, the man who had sold him University Computing's first computer three years ago.

"Bob Holland!" Wyly said. "I've been thinking about you."

The two men grabbed a booth in a nearby coffee shop, and Wyly told Holland he wanted to hire some of the impressive CEIR people he had met and worked with. In turn, Holland told Wyly he was almost done at CEIR. Wyly said that was very good news, because he was interested in hiring

PR chief Ray Hannon framed the note, in which Sam says "Meet me at office at 6:00," and pictures for Wyly. "It could be either six a.m. or six p.m. Well, likely for me, p.m."

Holland; a public relations man named Ray Hannon; an executive named Warren Burton; and a fellow who worked for Burton named Tommy Lyons (who at 28 had two PhDs). "I am interested in bringing you and the others into the University Computing family, and perhaps heading up a new company that would lease computers."

Links to the past: UCC was a big success in the computer world but never had the same impact in the fashion world.

Holland wanted more details, but Wyly's ship was boarding in 90 minutes. "We can't resolve this today," Wyly told him. "I'm out of time. I've got to be on that ship at two o'clock."

"Well, I'm on my way to a board meeting at CEIR," Holland said. "I can give them my resignation, but I don't want to do that unless we're clear on what you want to do."

Wyly hated to miss this opportunity, so he wrote a check for $250,000 to Holland's private business. "This will bind us until I get back."

When he returned to the States six weeks later, Wyly laid out for Holland his idea for a new business, one that leased computers to big companies, a bit different from University Computing's founding business of buying by the acre and selling by the square foot.

Holland was interested, in part because of a new law he had recently heard about in D.C. that affected computers. It was one sentence in a bill that allowed banks to loan money for the lease of computers and not have to carry the full asset and liability on their balance sheets. If a bank had, for example, made a loan for $100 million dollars of computers that were going to be leased, they would have $20 million declared as a liability, and $80 million, which would normally be a liability, was suddenly not a liability. That created more "money in the bank," so they could lend not $80 million but $800 million, 10 to 1.

"That's ridiculous," Wyly told Holland.

"I agree," Holland said. "It's ridiculous, and I don't know how long it will last. But to change it, regulators have got to go back through the congressional process. It can't be changed by administrative fiat, and it has a lot of friends. The banks love it."

In other words, this was the perfect time to speculate on computer leasing.

Wyly moved quickly, formed the Computer Leasing Company, and the business took off. The First National Bank in Dallas, the biggest bank in Texas, and Citibank in New York were eager to compete for the loans. The mood at the banks was similar to the recent frenzy of mortgage-lending that bankers engaged in at the start of this century, which led to the boom, bubble and bust that ended with the Great Crash of 2008. "And this was going to end the same way," Wyly says, "but we didn't know it at the time, and we were exuberant. The easy-money era of the 1960s was like the alcohol in the punch bowl—it fueled the party."

Wyly knew that many opportunities were transient, so it was important to be ready to move on them. While UCC was showing strong growth and nice profits, bold ventures would take more cash than he had. A lot more. That meant he needed to defy conventional timetables for an IPO and take UCC public after just two years. But would there be any takers?

The timing for this IPO was both good and bad. After decades of focusing on steadiness and dividends, a sea change was occurring on Wall Street. The big word now was "growth." Traders and long-term investors knew computing was a growth industry, maybe *the* growth industry, and they wanted in.

What Wyly knew for sure was that running a publicly held company would be a new game. He would have to deal with shareholders, and write quarterly and annual reports. He would have more people on his board of directors to deal with. He would have to interact with Wall Street analysts. There would be a hundred extra phone calls a day. And he would have to spend more with lawyers and accountants and Wall Street people who had nothing to do with the vital functions of creating customers and competitive products.

What Wyly didn't know was that those weren't the worst frustrations of an IPO. He soon learned that none of the conventional underwriters wanted anything to do with him or his company. While University Computing had become known in Texas and Oklahoma, the suits in New York City didn't have a clue about UCC. Texas? Oklahoma? "That's *oil* country," they said. They acted as though his computers sat on bales of straw and he had a hitching post outside his office.

Pulling off this IPO would require one of his best sales jobs, and big assists from a few smart people. He reached out to his father-in-law, Len Acton, whose Dallas

UCC's first board of directors, 1963 (from left): Len Acton, Guy Mann, Sam, Ben Voth and Charles. In 1963, Acton and Mann helped Sam secure the bank loan he needed to get his start-up up and running. Voth invested the first $100,000 of equity and got 10 percent ownership that, at its speculative peak four years later, was priced at $20 million.

broker, Til Petrocchi, was with the St. Louis–headquartered firm of A. G. Edwards. Petrocchi was great at spotting good companies in growth industries, and as he watched Wyly build University Computing, he became a believer. Petrocchi was a second-generation Italian who grew up in Boston. At 17, he had joined the Marine Corps. He was headed to the South Pacific for an assault on Saipan when the atomic bomb was dropped on Hiroshima, ending the war and, he says, "saving my life." He went to college on the G.I. Bill, studying political science and business at Boston College and Harvard.

After he got fired from a meat-cutting job (for boning three chucks an hour when the union standard was two), he chose jobs where initiative wasn't punished. On weekends he filleted fishes and sold cookies, starting with a dozen of them, and was shipping them by freight car three years later. He never stopped learning about business.

Some lessons were more painful than others. At 18, when most guys were thinking about prom dates, Petrocchi figured out a way to undersell the market for lobsters in Massachusetts by importing just the lobster meat from Maine, where it was cheaper. Business was great, but six months later, after the lobster lobby howled, the state passed legislation banning imported lobster in meat form. But he had made enough to buy his wife a diamond ring, which she is still wearing 50 years later.

Petrocchi hustled his way into a job as a stockbroker in Fort Worth. It was commission-only and he was starting at the bottom. His first month in Texas he made $58, and filleting fishes back in Boston suddenly didn't look so bad. In his second month he sold an investor 10,000 shares of an underwriting his firm was doing. The commission was $3,000. He put away the filleting knife. He later partnered in a start-up called Parker Ford and helped grow it to 12 offices, at which point it was bought out by A. G. Edwards.

When Petrocchi met Sam on that June day in 1965, University Computing was a year and a half old. Len Acton and Sam told him that University Computing wanted to seek capital in the public markets, knew they didn't have the requisite five-year track record, but still wanted to find a way to make it happen. Petrocchi had an idea. He explained that A. G. Edwards had never done an underwriting, but that Benjamin Franklin Edwards III, the new president of A. G. Edwards and the great-grandson of the founder, was just out of Princeton and eager to get into that business. So Wyly and Petrocchi went to St. Louis to pitch their plan to Edwards.

It did not go as they had hoped. Wyly explained the concept, history and success of University Computing, and outlined the immediate growth plans for Edwards. "We'd like to raise a million dollars worth of public equity at five dollars." Edwards was doubtful, but Petrocchi's passionate arguments finally wore him down. He agreed to put together an alliance of brokerages that would sell the stock if Wyly promised to hit the road and persuade investors that University Computing was the real thing. Sam knew Edwards thought he couldn't do it. But no one believed in UCC as fervently as Sam Wyly did, and no one could sell it better.

After three months and a score of dog-and-pony shows, Wyly had lined up and converted plenty of believers. He also learned that he loved talking up the company, answering investors' questions. The give-and-take was instructive, telling him what was important to investors and how they measured investments.

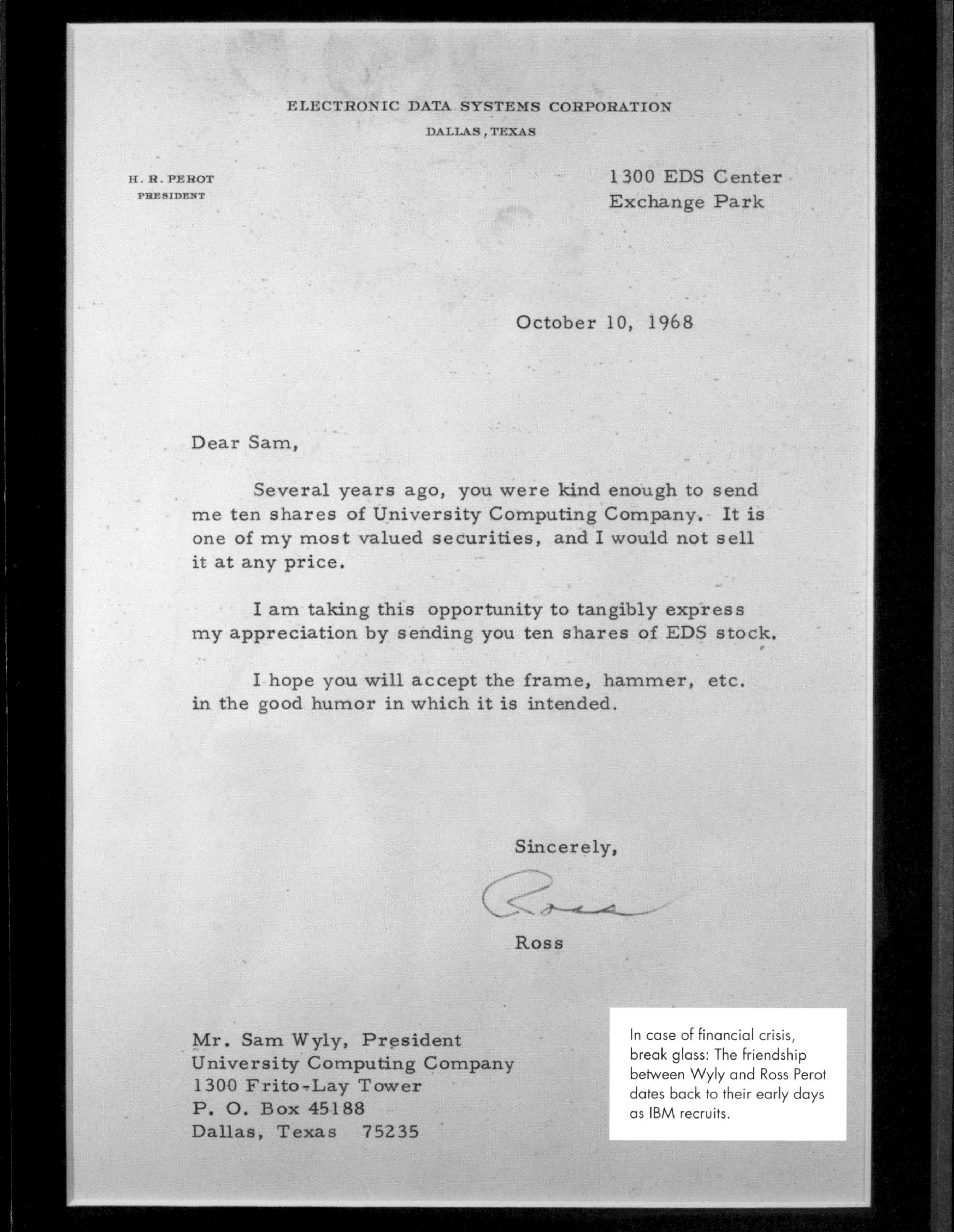

ELECTRONIC DATA SYSTEMS CORPORATION

DALLAS, TEXAS

H. R. PEROT
PRESIDENT

1300 EDS Center
Exchange Park

October 10, 1968

Dear Sam,

Several years ago, you were kind enough to send
me ten shares of University Computing Company. It is
one of my most valued securities, and I would not sell
it at any price.

I am taking this opportunity to tangibly express
my appreciation by sending you ten shares of EDS stock.

I hope you will accept the frame, hammer, etc.
in the good humor in which it is intended.

Sincerely,

Ross

Mr. Sam Wyly, President
University Computing Company
1300 Frito-Lay Tower
P. O. Box 45188
Dallas, Texas 75235

In case of financial crisis,
break glass: The friendship
between Wyly and Ross Perot
dates back to their early days
as IBM recruits.

Petrocchi took the deal back to Edwards and said, "Okay, we're going to sell five hundred thousand shares." Edwards knew they had gotten a positive response from their road shows, but not *that* positive. "To *whom*?" he demanded. Edwards, who had never done an IPO, was torn between the possible rewards in commissions and warrants and his fear that a flop IPO would tarnish the firm built by his grandfather and father, and of which he was now the manager and part owner.

Just one week prior to the IPO, Edwards was still saying it couldn't get done. But Petrocchi, Acton and Sam had already found buyers for almost half the offering, and Ben Edwards finally signed on. The company was capitalized in the public markets on September 22, 1965, 13 days before Sam's twin daughters, Laurie and Lisa, were born.

When it came time to divvy up all that new wealth, the Wall Streeters—the people who had shouted "smoke and mirrors" three months earlier, the people

A quick start-up: UCC doubled its revenue every year for the first five years, and the stock appreciated 100 to 1.

who had doubted the viability of the deal until a week before the offering—now claimed to have done all of the work and insisted that they deserved all of the pot. Edwards told Petrocchi he would be dealt out.

"I want my part," Petrocchi told Edwards.

"What part?" Ben replied. "We did it. You didn't do anything."

Petrocchi went to Wyly, who told Edwards, "You're giving Til Petrocchi twenty thousand A. G. Edwards warrants. Or you ain't going to see me anymore."

Petrocchi got 20,000 shares, and the deal was still a boon for A. G. Edwards. The firm that had balked all the way to the altar ended up with 50,000 shares as its fee. Founded in 1887, the company had grown to be worth about $9 million when Sam walked in the door. As a result of Wyly's underwriting, its valuation doubled to $18 million in four years.

With cash in hand, Wyly moved on to his next order of business: he bought out Diversa with a secondary stock sale. Jerry Mann honored their handshake agreement.

Wyly also gave away UCC stock in 100-share lots to 50 people who had been in some way instrumental in helping him get to where he was. This ranged from blood kin back in Lake Providence to high school and college instructors to friends, including Ross Perot, who later responded in kind, sending Wyly a framed certificate for 10 shares of his own Electronic Data Systems (EDS) stock. It hangs on a wall in Wyly's house in Dallas. The frame has a small metal hammer attached, and bears the inscription, "In case of emergency, break glass."

University Computing Company's stock rose and split three times in the next four years before peaking at $187.25 a share in 1968. Sales that year hit $57 million, with a net income of about $5 million. A $9,000 investment in the 1965 IPO with the 100-to-1 increase in only five years, was worth $1 million by 1968. Ben Voth's $100,000 investment had grown to $20 million. The company was by then worth $1 billion dollars, and based on market prices on the New York Stock Exchange, it was the fifth most valuable company in Texas.

Some would call that the success of a lifetime. Wyly called it a good start.

E. W. "Mac" McCain (left) could have been the president of Univac (the original computer company), but signed on with UCC as executive VP instead.

TALENT GOES WHERE THE ACTION IS

In those early days, UCC was run the way most start-ups have always been run: a few guys in the field scrambling after customers, part-timers keeping the books and getting out the bills. Wyly had one-fourth of a secretary, whom he shared with his brother, Charles, Len Acton, and Guy Mann.

But less than a year after his IPO, even while operating with a skeleton staff, Wyly saw that he needed to ease himself out of sales and focus full-time on growth. He wanted to organize the company in a way that let him seize opportunities as quickly as he found them. He had to come up with a management process that would support his opportunistic idea machine.

He already had a clear vision of what his management style was, and would always be: Communicate his goals, strategies and ideas to his managers, then turn them loose and pay them on performance. He felt he had done a pretty good job picking his managers, but he knew he needed to do better in order to get better, so he resolved to hone his management skills and learn to lead more effectively.

"Pretty quickly I realized I didn't know how to run a company, so I wondered who could teach me to be a president," Wyly says. "You really don't learn that in school. The American Management Association had a management course for presidents in upstate New York, so I went there to learn how to be a company president. I was surprised to find that my neighbor and ex-IBM co-worker Ross Perot was there at a big round-table. I was also surprised to learn that August Bushell, president of Gulf Insurance Company, who had just made a big investment in my company, was there. August had been running his company for twenty years and yet he was there to try to learn how to run the insurance company better."

Wyly also joined the Young Presidents' Organization and read a mountain of business books. (A mountain he is still climbing—he reads voraciously, especially history, biographies and historical fiction. He loves to read the stories of great entrepreneurs such as Andrew Carnegie, Mary Baker Eddy, Sam Walton, Mary Kay Ash, Steve Jobs and Mark Zuckerman.) He was thinking more about what it takes to be a great entrepreneur. "We were doing new things and we were doing creative things," Wyly says. "I particularly enjoyed the creative part. Being an entrepreneur is a creative process. There were huge opportunities to innovate and you could do new things in all areas. You could do it in the technical part and you could do it in the business part. I always had a sense of doing something that was worthwhile—

Ross Perot and Sam Wyly
Management Course For Presidents
Upstate New York
July, 1965

Sam Wyly and H. Ross Perot, two young entrepreneurs trying to learn how to run their companies better, both attended the Management Course for Presidents in New York in July 1965. "We were both trying to learn how to manage our companies," Wyly says. "After four years in Annapolis, and then four years as a Navy officer, Ross was actually deeply in love with white shirts. When Ross started his own company, he out-IBM-ed IBM with that and other military-type disciplines brought into the world of business. Initially, Ross hired only ex-IBMers and ex-military officers. It worked. They built a great company, and as time went by, the company culture loosened up. My target market for UCC was engineers and scientists who were more shirt-sleeve guys than the controllers and corporate VPs at the core of Ross's market. So we were a bit more casual in dress from the beginning, but our sales reps who called on the business market looked pretty much the same as Ross's team."

creating a good tool would help people be more productive. It was like seeing the way McCormick's reaper, Ford's tractor and hybrid corn seeds each help agriculture and help the world."

Wyly also wanted his business to be one of the best in its field, to pioneer international markets. He foresaw the AT&T telephone monopoly converging with IBM's near monopoly in computers—that sweet spot—but predicted neither would be able to keep out a gold rush–like stampede of new competitors because the technology was changing so fast. He wanted UCC to develop data communications capabilities and a transparent internal financial reporting system that would work for multiple companies. And he wanted to minimize the interdependence among the companies he owned so that he could add or subtract businesses without disrupting the others.

University Computing grew in three distinct directions: scientific and engineering services, commercial and business processing services, and computer leasing. Its revenue had more than tripled, to $2.1 million in 1965, and was on track to more than double again in 1966, to $4.5 million, with profits rising from 12 percent to 19 percent. It was a good start, but Wyly wanted more. A lot more.

Driven to have every unit become "best in class," he needed an organizational structure that would get the most out of each. He decided to establish divisions of specialists within the company—groups of *intrapreneurs*—rather than keep all under one generic management group. In creating separate entities, Wyly concentrated specific expertise at the top of each unit. He could add or subtract units in a modular way. If one unit (or product) ceased to be a good fit, he could sell it. If a unit was a breakaway success, he could put more resources behind it or even spin it off.

He also laid out plans to expand into Houston, Oklahoma City, Chicago and Los Angeles. His immediate goal was to become a national computer services supplier; his long-term goal was to go global, which meant launching his remote processing services. The L.A. installation was the first to deliver the remote processing capabilities over analog phone lines. His vision of a "computing utility" was under way, though slow and expensive, and error-prone phone lines made it far from ideal. Barely three years after the doors opened at UCC, he had customers in 23 states. The company had to evolve to accommodate them.

The Computer Utilities Division was the original business of large-scale computer centers for scientific and engineering applications. The Data-Link Division marked the company's expansion into commercial and business-oriented processing services in major cities. The Computer Leasing Company leased computers independent of the computing business and raised capital with public equity and debt. To expand his pool of skilled knowledge workers, Wyly added another division, the Academy of Computer Technology, which taught the use of large-scale computer systems, improved applications, specialized computer languages and advanced programming. The premise was that if his people were able to educate customers (and themselves) in all the ways businesses could use the new processing services and technologies, it would be good for America and *very* good for University Computing.

Finally, to drive the development of the hardware and software needed to stay ahead of the curve, he created a Technical Services Division. A lot of these people had already developed important software for the big hardware-makers. The pitch Wyly used to land them was that their achievements had been heralded inside the software subculture, but ignored by their bosses, the "glassy-eyed hardware zombies who loved to push iron." Join us, Wyly said, and we'll not only acknowledge you, we'll build a company around you. Like his friend Ross Perot, Wyly believed, "Eagles don't flock—you have to find them one at a time."

But he also believed that talent goes where the action is, and with his aggressive growth strategy, one of great attractions of working at University Computing was that it was always changing, always moving forward. One recruit named Tom Lyons said that working at UCC was "like riding the nose cone of a rocket!"

When picking his managers, Wyly lived (and hired) by Peter Drucker's proclamation: "The only difference between any two companies in the same business is the quality of management at all levels." Wyly quickly figured out another central truth, which he shared with all his managers: "You succeed when you put your best people to work on your best opportunities, not your problems."

Wyly was already thinking ahead like a big-time entrepreneur, not just a computer guy, so he wanted to create a management structure that would support a range of businesses and thrive under his style of leadership. If that style had a name, it would probably be "macromanaging"—the art of leading decision-makers.

Straight-arrow Sam became an honorary
Arapahoe in the late '60s, after he built a Datel
computer-terminal plant on the Wind River
Reservation in Wyoming.

It would have elements of both centralized management (strategic planning and financial reporting) and decentralized management (autonomous the rest of the time). He did not want to micromanage anyone; he saw that as a waste of everybody's time, and knew that the smart people he was hiring would resent it. But while his executives would have great freedom to think and act like entrepreneurs, everyone had to speak a precise and common language. This would be rooted in financial reporting. He went back to the revelations he had gleaned in college about reading businesses by the numbers. He wanted a team that 1) understood numbers as well as he did—that is, how those numbers revealed the company and represented its goals; and 2) could manage those numbers with great autonomy—but great accountability.

Strategic decision-making—new opportunities, mergers and acquisitions, emerging technology, national and global expansion, etc.—would be done in meticulous detail at annual meetings, with progress monitored in quarterly reviews and monthly updates on progress. At those quarterly meetings, Wyly also wanted to hear entrepreneurial ideas, big ideas. He wanted his managers to look hard at their fields and ask: What's next? What's the next breakthrough? What's the next step they have to take to spur it? What's the next acquisition? Where's the next opportunity? Wyly believed in challenging ideas, and in having *his* ideas challenged, and he showed his top executives how to do it. He told them a good plan would survive an attack by a round-table discussion. Software managers say these quarterly and annual grillings by Wyly were the toughest part of working for him, but they forced the managers to think through the answers to everything.

Each manager would run a division of the company, and would convey to his team leaders and employees the goals and plans that had been agreed upon in the annual reviews, along with the manager's *own* goals and tactics. Wyly likes to quote Harold Geneen, former CEO of International Telephone & Telegraph, who took that company from $760 million in sales to $17 billion in 13 years. He used the same three words in the same three sentences and provided three different lessons. He said, "MANAGERS must manage. Managers MUST manage. Managers must MANAGE."

But he also knew that no one is perfect, and problems will come up. He used two methods to spot those problems: "red flags" and regular audits. A manager would raise a red flag for anything that could cause his division to fail to achieve its plan. Managers had the autonomy and the duty to fix things, but also the charge to report them immediately if they couldn't.

The red flags were to alert managers; the audits were to alert Wyly. He wanted transparent financial reporting, plus audits. The CFO—along with an audit committee of the board—would have the job of maintaining that transparency. The CFO had to feel confident about the numbers he was presenting from each of the divisions, and be able to justify his data. Auditing did that. Again, the whole process went back to that sweltering warehouse in Dallas where Wyly counted forks: "Trust, but verify."

When Wyly found an ideal candidate, he could motivate that individual with a good paycheck and, more important, stock grants. Early in 1967 he also instituted an employee stock plan for all employees. He believed that this was more than a reward; he knew it engendered a mind-set of ownership and pride. No one fights for a child like a parent, he thought, and the results bore him out. Over the years, he created more than 3,000 millionaires via their holdings in his companies.

To lead his technical projects, Wyly went after the software managers who had done the best job developing software for IBM and the other big companies. He had been convinced by his time with Honeywell that some of the best work being done at General Electric was by Eugene Debs Smith, so he hired him away. (Smith's parents had named him for their hero, the late Eugene V. Debs, the perennial Socialist Party candidate for president of the United States in the early 20th century.) Smith immediately became Wyly's chief of defections—he helped raid the best and the brightest software people from GE.

With his talent on board and the new organization structure in place, Wyly focused on that "sweet spot." Over the next couple of years, University Computing's computer terminal manufacturing needs increased so rapidly that Wyly created a subsidiary to turn them out. Again, he sought out a star to run it. Seymour "Sy" Joffe was a big-game Univac salesman who had sold more than $100 million of computers to NASA, and had worked on the first space computers in the Gemini program. Those machines not only had to be fail-safe in space, but

Above: Arty Smith had a day job as UCC's CPA, but he loved to fly and encouraged Wyly to purchase the company's private jet, a Falcon. Smith (left) and copilot Clay Hancock share a laugh about UCC's high-flying style during its late-'60s ascent. The Datel Time Sharing Terminal was a UCC product for professionals who used computers every day and whose processing workload challenged older technologies' capacity to handle it. Its sales success confirmed that remote processing demands were growing almost insatiably—and that UCC had, once again, bet well in buying Datel for stock.

also had to communicate back to Earth. This was exactly the guy Wyly wanted to head up his communications enterprise.

Joffe was a 12-year Univac veteran with all the attendant income and perquisites, so he was reluctant to take the leap until his wife gave him some advice: "Sy, sometimes you've got to move on in life . . . and ask for stock."

Hoping to close the deal, Wyly asked Joffe to join him and some friends for lunch. In the room with him were some good ole Texas headliners: Ross Perot, who was now running his own very successful company, Electronic Data Systems; the billionaire Hunt Brothers—Bunker, Herbert and Lamar (who would discover oil in Libya, start the American Football League and then go bankrupt trying to corner the silver market)—and Jimmy Ling, chairman of Ling-Temco-Vought, who had just been on the cover of *Time* as chief poster boy for Wall Street's current mania for "conglomerates."

Wyly said to them: "Here is the guy I was tellin' y'all about!"

Joffe was dazzled. And he got his stock.

Under Joffe's guidance, UCC not only made the COPE increasingly faster, but introduced two more specialty terminals. The FASBAC keyboard software was the first technology that could be used by just about anyone. Another product, the Datel Time Sharing Terminal, was a fast device for professionals who used computers every day and whose processing workload was increasing beyond the existing technology's capacity to handle it. The robust sales of this product proved that the demand for remote processing was almost insatiable.

Wyly now knew that the future of moving data over phone lines—online processing—was going to be nearly boundless, but also that the competition was going to get nasty. AT&T, using FCC challenges and threats of lawsuits, was already reminding everybody that it had a long-standing monopoly on any devices that could be electrically connected to its phone lines. Those devices were all manufactured by AT&T, of course. But the key word was "electrically." This opened the door for acoustic couplers—users just stuck their telephones into a molded hard-rubber transmitter and made a mechanical connection instead of an electrical one.

But Wyly saw things that promised change—maybe revolutionary change—within the communications monopoly. A Texas oil field services innovator named

Tom P. Carter had been marketing a connecting device called the Carterphone, which patched radio calls into the telephone network, since 1959, and had been fighting AT&T's monopolists almost as long. By 1966, his company had sold 3,500 Carterphones to dealers around the world.

One inspiration for Datran was the Carterphone, which patched radio calls in the telephone network. "We have Nokia and Apple's iPhones because of Tom Carter," Wyly says.

Often companies face the question of whether to buy or to build the products and services they sell. The answer, Wyly realized, depended on the situation. He wanted to grow aggressively and used two divergent tactics to do it. He thought the development process—at least on the fundamental business and scientific services he sold—was a lot like reinventing the wheel. R&D was expensive, slow and usually fruitless. "You have to kiss a lot of frogs to find one prince," he said.

Wyly believed his customers wanted something simpler: computers and computer services that handled their work dependably; reliable companies that charged them a fair price, provided convenient access and would be there for them when they had a problem. Selling something "unique" was far down the list of qualities they were seeking.

This made acquisition a valid strategy for growth. The research and development he wanted to do was mainly in data communications; that's where he might change the world, and that's where his two goals dovetailed. His "breakthrough technology" would be the delivery vehicle for the array of other services. The technology didn't yet exist in any viable form, so he had to devise it. Increasingly, he now had the means to make the acquisitions he wanted. He found that a well-researched acquisition usually got him a good company, good employees, good products with a good reputation, and his momentum wasn't disrupted. That was key. As long as he could get what he needed for a good price (and not carry too much debt), he could claim revenue and income instantly. He could also build on an existing customer base instead of doing a lot of cold-calling.

Wyly saw that he could buy a company, break it up and sell off some of the parts at a profit. But he also recognized that this was not an entrepreneurial strategy, but a capital one, and he was looking to build businesses. His goal with acquisitions was to buy a good company and make it better. He would keep most of the acquired company's key personnel—technical support staff, sales staff and certain executives (including the president/founder, when that was possible and appropriate)—to assure continuity and quality. This would cut into the short-term profit, but provide a foundation that would lead to even greater profits long-term. He could sell parts that did not relate to his objectives to reduce debt from the purchase. From there, he would build the company name through quality control, customer service and improvements in the product line.

Wyly knew how to deliver computing performance, but he knew that wasn't enough to win a market, especially a foreign one. He knew customers prefer to deal with people who know them, who are familiar with their companies, who speak their language, who understand their issues. That meant keeping the core personnel when he bought in.

It followed, then, that he had no interest in hostile takeovers. For one thing, there were plenty of companies willing to sell, so the expense of a proxy fight seemed wasteful. And people commonly assumed that hostile acquisitions of software companies would cause the best tech people to leave, maybe even go into business against you. So his general rule was to avoid hostile takeovers.

It was a rule he would break only once.

In 1966, Wyly acquired D. R. McCord and Associates, Inc., a Dallas-based, internationally known petroleum engineering and consulting company that had pioneered the use of large-scale computers to simulate petroleum reservoirs, and did geological evaluations and reservoir predictions for oil fields in North Africa, Australia, the Middle East and North America. It provided instant international heft to University Computing. Wyly put McCord's executive vice president, Dick Fagin, in charge of his overseas operations. In May of 1967, University Computing acquired the largest independent computer services firm in the United Kingdom. With those two assets in hand, Wyly was now itching to give the world a taste of the processing revolution he envisioned.

He called a meeting with Fagin; his communications guru, Joffe; and some other staffers. "Now we've got to do something *great*," he told them.

The idea they hatched was a satellite link between London and Dallas. They demonstrated the feasibility of a worldwide network of computer centers and telephone lines by "hosting" an exchange of greetings between the mayor of Dallas and the lord mayor of London. Using UCC computers, they transmitted via ground lines in each country and then by satellite across the Atlantic. Wyly bought a full-page ad in *The Wall Street Journal* showing pictures of each mayor beside a COPE-45 terminal. Data messages like this had never been sent before by civilians. The military, of course, was more advanced, but for the civilian world, this new method of transmitting data was exciting, and tantalizing.

Toward the end of 1967, Wyly made another international investment: Automation Centre, A.G., based in Zurich, Switzerland, which already had massive processing operations in 10 European countries. The man who'd built this company was Walter Haefner, a debonair 57-year-old millionaire entrepreneur and

London calling! Wyly and Dallas mayor Erik Jonsson (a founder of Texas Instruments) connect to the lord mayor of London on the first digital transatlantic link, part of UCC's push to become a global player.

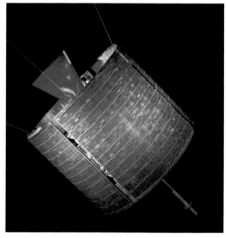

When the Early Bird satellite was launched in April 1965, it became the world's first commercial communications satellite. It could relay 240 telephone calls or the signal for one television channel.

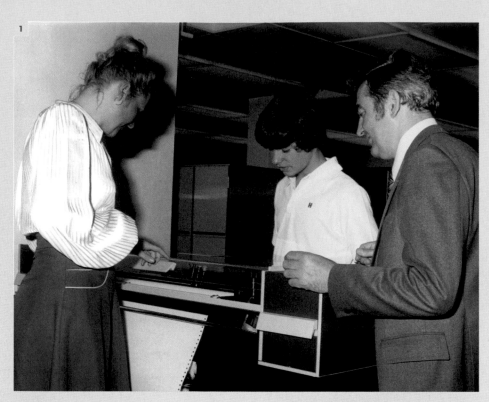

Evan Wyly (center), visiting UCC's London office with University Computing's Doreen Halford and Jim Harvey. After graduating from Harvard Business School, Evan went into the family business—rather, businesses (1).

Wyly and his ace engineer, Ed Berg (far right) at a dinner hosted by Nippon Electric Company (NEC), which built digital radios for UCC subsidiary Datran (2).

In Zurich, both the Swiss and American flags were on the wall (3).

The hair was big, and so were the mainframes in the 1970s. The era of the personal computer was just around the corner (4, 5).

Wyly: "I saw the computer as a tool, just like the plow is a tool and the tractor is a tool. A tool that would help people, a tool that could liberate them, educate them and make the world more democratic, more transparent and more productive."

Thoroughbred owner who still lived in the home on a Zurich mountainside he had bought for $25,000 back in 1948. After college, he worked for Esso selling oil products to service stations, and when World War II came and cut off oil imports he shifted to selling charcoal engines for cars because there was almost no gasoline available for civilians. After the war, he got Zurich dealerships for Chryslers and British MGs, then negotiated exclusive dealership rights for Volkswagen in Switzerland. Riding the postwar boom, he acquired 22 dealerships. In 1957, Haefner was among the first European businessmen to install a business computer to manage his payroll and inventory processing, and when other dealerships began asking if Haefner would use his computers to do the payroll for their dealerships, he saw a vast market and founded Automation Centre.

Wyly liked and admired Haefner, and Haefner became a significant investor in University Computing and joined its board of directors, and later became a big investor in Wyly's monopoly-busting strategy—Datran.

Looking back nearly 40 years later, Wyly still has a clear memory of what he envisioned, and what made him one of the great pioneers in computer technology. "I saw the computer as a tool, just like the plow is a tool and the tractor is a tool," he explains. "A tool that would help people, a tool that could liberate them, educate them and make the world more democratic, more transparent and more productive. When I started school there were thirteen and a half million agricultural jobs in the old South; today there are less than half a million. That's because of a tool— the mechanical cotton picker did the work of a hundred people. It was a better tool. And I saw the same thing happening with the stored-program computer and all of the digital possibilities that it opened up. I sensed that at some fundamental level the computer was like all of those earlier tools—from the plow to the steam engine—that made manual labor faster and easier. Here was something that helped man do his mental labor—it was a tool for thinkers. And work was becoming less and less manual labor and more and more knowledge work.

"My technical contribution was virtually zero, at best that of a blunt-pencil architect and visionary. But I had a feel for taking complexity and simplifying it, and a gut instinct for where things had to end up. Sort of like what Wayne Gretsky said when asked what made him such a great hockey player: 'Don't skate to where the puck is, skate to where the puck is going to be.' That's what I was trying to do.

My role was conceptual—to see that we could create that 'sweet spot' where the telephone met the computer, and make a great leap forward in providing productivity tools for knowledge workers. My job was to bring in people who had the technical and marketing skills and to get out of their way."

In just three years, Wyly had taken University Computing from a single-focus Dallas start-up to a multidimensional global corporation. Its stock tripled in the first half of 1966. Then Wyly got his first inkling of how fickle the market could be. That summer, money abruptly became tight and the stock dropped 50 percent. "We had been growing, we had been profitable, we had a lot of cash and little debt, and as far as we knew, we hadn't made a misstep," he says. The drop hurt his wallet, and his ability to take care of his people, since an important part of his reward system for key executives was based on that stock price. And shareholders obviously weren't looking for the stock price to go down.

    Then in the latter half of the year, money eased and the stock doubled before Christmas. *So that's the way it is going to be*, Wyly thought. By the end of 1968, the stock hit a split-adjusted $187.25 per share (on $57 million in revenue), and had a billion-dollar market valuation (20 times revenue). The markets were then capitalizing fast-growing young companies with an irrational exuberance not to be seen again until the euphoria of the dot-com boom of the late 1990s, and the latter-day booms of Google and Facebook, Twitter and Groupon. It was a good time to be a visionary, and a very good time to be an entrepreneur.

Wyly created the term "computer utility" to describe the marriage of the telephone and the computer, the happy union that would change the world. His red 1966 Mustang is parked outside.

Even while building his business empire, Wyly kept his family close to mind.

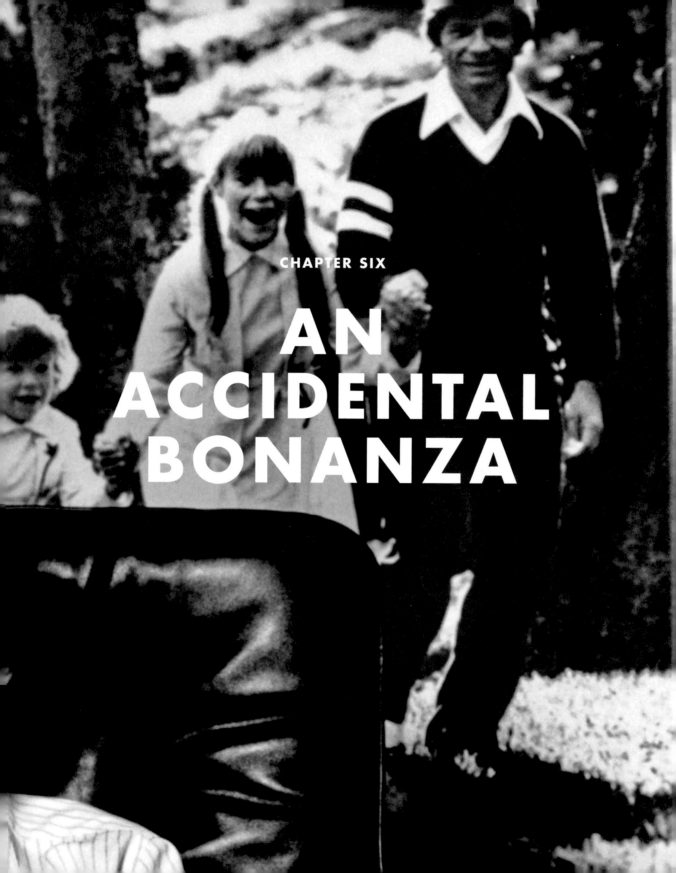

CHAPTER SIX

AN
ACCIDENTAL
BONANZA

Sam Wyly's friends, family and colleagues all say that humility has always been one of his most endearing qualities, but his quick and soaring success with UCC, his new friends in high places (the White House and beyond) and his many entrepreneurial ventures called to mind the adage: "When you know you're being humble, you're no longer humble."

He was just 35 years old, and when somebody told him how smart he was, he didn't argue quite as hard as he once might have. And because of his many con-quests in commerce, he was now being flattered a lot in the press, and fielding scores of inquiries from people with "opportunities." He passed on most of them, but one day he got a call from Guy Mann, who told him that his brother, Jerry, needed help rescuing one of the businesses Diversa had bought.

The big conglomerate was struggling across the board, Mann told him. (They had missed out on the 100–1 four-year run-up in University Computing stock because they had sold outright, back to Sam, after the IPO.) Diversa had been living up to its name: it had bought into diverse enterprises ranging from oil rigs to real estate to dog food, but was squeezed for cash—the bank was demanding payment of a $1 million note collateralized by a 12-restaurant chain called Bonanza. Mann asked Wyly for a favor. "We have all these debts and we have Bonanza hocked and the bankers are calling the note," he said. "But with a little time, we are sure we can sell that company to PepsiCo, which is looking for restau-rant companies. They just bought Pizza Hut. We need you to guarantee our note or we'll lose the opportunity to do something better than just defaulting it to the bank. I just need six months. And if we don't sell it, you'll own it."

"I don't want to own restaurants," Wyly told him. "I don't know anything about the restaurant business. I've already got a computing business and I'm still trying to learn how to run *that*." But he thought about it overnight, and the next day he told Mann, "I owe you. You helped me get UCC started, so I'll help you." He signed the note.

By then, Wyly had moved University Computing's headquarters to the 13th floor of the Frito-Lay Building in Dallas (13 was his lucky number). As corporate neighbors, Wyly had gotten to know Herman Lay, the chairman of PepsiCo, who told him his company was indeed looking at restaurants. That told Wyly it was a safe bet that the Bonanza sale would go through.

But it didn't, and suddenly the software genius owned a dozen not-very-well-done steakhouses. What Wyly knew from Dun & Bradstreet was that 19 out of every 20 new restaurants failed, and restaurants were the worst entrepreneurial bets of any kind of start-up, even if the entrepreneur was a chef. Plus, the $1 million he'd paid the bank was only the first of many desperate calls for Bonanza cash. Everything about this deal screamed, "Get out NOW!" But Wyly loved challenges.

"Okay, what do we have here?" he asked himself. The word "disaster" came to mind, but so did others. Here's what else Wyly knew about his newest acquisition: Bonanza (named after the very popular TV Western featuring Pa Cartwright and his three sons, Hoss, Adam and Little Joe) focused on budget dinners and lunches—diners in these cowboy-style eateries could get a steak-and-potatoes dinner for less than two bucks, well below the cost of most steak dinners. The menus and pricing were designed to attract families as well as couples, which made it a solid option for budget-conscious families eating out. It filled the gap between McDonald's and the higher-end "white tablecloth" restaurants. Wyly also knew that more and more women were going to work, including young women in the emerging two-income families, as well as the many "Rosie the Riveter" workers who had filled the factories in the 1940s when 16 million men were shipped off to fight Hitler and Tojo, and had found that they enjoyed their jobs and their paychecks. Wyly figured that many of them would want to dine out at the end of a long day instead of putting on an apron and cooking dinner.

But he had serious questions about Bonanza that started at the top of the management team. The chairman knew nothing about restaurants (he was just a chum of Jerry Mann's), nor did the president. But Wyly saw that bit of bad news as good news and wondered: what if we had a manager who could manage, who knew what he was doing?

Next on the Bonanza ladder was a vice president, Charles "Chuck" Green, who didn't have much more experience in restaurants than the top guys, but Wyly sensed that he was an instinctive businessman, and he did have some working knowledge of the Bonanza concept. He also was candid enough to break bad news to his new boss. "I hate to tell you this as the new owner," Green told him, "but we're going to have to file for bankruptcy next month if you don't put more cash into this place right now."

Bonanza was looking more and more like a loser. Wyly knew the easy solution was: forget the steak and eat the loss. But there was that nagging challenge—could he fix a business he knew nothing about? He decided to find out, so he fired the two top guys and put Chuck Green in charge.

Wyly then set out to learn everything he could about the industry—the winners and the losers, the viability of the Bonanza concept, and how to grow good store managers and make franchisees competitive. Because it was a franchise concept, Wyly realized he had to make Bonanza into a good corporate partner for local entrepreneurs in towns ranging from Tupelo, Mississippi, to Dayton, Ohio. The core market was the folks in small farm towns and blue-collar boys working in the city or suburbia. He had a hunch that the next recession (which he predicted was coming soon) might depress big-ticket items like houses, cars and TVs, but that strapped middle-class Americans might reward their families with steak dinners that didn't bust their budgets. He concluded that if Bonanza was run right, it could expand all over America's heartland, maybe even go coast to coast.

The board of Bonanza had 14 members in 1970, including Lorne Greene (third from left), the star of the immensely popular *Bonanza* TV series. This was before Wyly decided that less is more for company boards.

"The family steakhouse has no true national franchise name," he told Green and his store managers. "We want Bonanza to be that name." It was a familiar refrain from Wyly, who was never content to be just a player—he wanted this company not only to survive, but to thrive.

To fund Bonanza's growth in 1969, a few months before the market crashed and a tough recession rolled in, Wyly raised equity capital on it and opened more new stores. His architects came up with a design that looked like a barn. They dubbed it the "B3" and built more than 300 of them over the next few years.

By early 1970, though, bank lending became Scrooge-tight and Bonanza began feeling the pinch. The aggressive expansion, which had focused on opening company-owned stores instead of franchises, took a lot of capital. By 1974, Bonanza had grown from 12 restaurants to 350 (250 of them company-owned), and had $20 million in equity and $30 million in debt as all the money markets seized up. Wyly had built the largest steakhouse chain in America, but it was only breaking even and stores were being shut down.

"The '70s were painful all over," Wyly recalls. "It didn't make any difference whether you were in restaurants or in computers or in whatever. Even though we were having lots of success with the steakhouses, it was a blue-collar market, which was the first sector to get hit with layoffs and unemployment. We were suffering from the worst inflation since the Civil War, which made all costs go up.

Ultimately, Wyly decided that three or five members was best for a private company, and seven members, for a public company.

The stock dropped to near nothing, and debt went to high interest rates. You need a lot of capital to own restaurants and their real estate."

But capital was disappearing; losses were rising, and his University Computing stock crashed from $99 to $13—Ross Perot's EDS dropped from $160 to $16 by 1974.

"You will never tire first," Coach Richards had told his team. Some days those words sounded to Wyly like a curse. Still, he felt that the 350-unit chain they had built was substantial and he didn't want to give it up. Chuck Green had helped him build a solid foundation, but Wyly felt they now needed help. In the fall of 1974, he called in his turnaround wizard, Don Thomson, who lived for the quick turnaround: take on a troubled enterprise; thoroughly study its books, operations and managers; and remake it into a profitable business. In fact, Don seemed to have a three-year internal clock—work somewhere for three years and then move on. His restlessness was probably residual from his time in the Army. Thomson had been preparing to leave Korea in 1950 after his two-year hitch, but his company commander persuaded him to skip his boat ride home the next day and pitch one more baseball game for the division's team. The colonel promised him a trip home on a fast plane instead of a slow ship, so Thomson agreed. But when the North Koreans invaded South Korea around the bottom of the third inning, Thomson's hitch in Korea was extended by the start of the Korean War. After that, he never hung around anywhere a day longer than it took to fix things. Day-to-day operations bored him, and he would leave after a crisis was resolved, looking for the next forest fire.

Thomson was a high school dropout, a second-generation Irishman who grew up in the Bronx, where his family thought him mentally handicapped until an Army intelligence test in 1948 determined that he was dyslexic. He went on to astonish Harvard Business School professors at an advanced management seminar, and learned how to operate IBM equipment in the Army in Japan. Harold Geneen, the legendary chief of International Telephone & Telegraph, spotted Thomson's potential and gave him a subsidiary of ITT—called General Controls—to run in the 1960s. He dazzled even the notoriously tough Geneen. Thomson saw that 90 percent of General Control's sales came from 300 of its 7,000 products, so he promptly dumped the majority of them. *Reducing* sales took the division from a $3 million loss to a $6 million profit, so Geneen gave Thomson another company,

ITT WorldCom (the Telex subsidiary that competed with AT&T and Western Union in markets outside the U.S.), to run, which he took from a $3 million net to $20 million. After leaving ITT, Thomson managed a printing and lumber company called Arcata up from zero profits to $25 million in two years.

He smoked like a coal locomotive, loved his Irish whiskey, enjoyed the horse track, closed down many a disco at 3 a.m. and seemed like a mismatch for the reserved, teetotaling Wyly. But over almost a quarter-century of working together, Wyly never had a bad moment with him. And even though Thomson's experience with steaks at that time was confined to grilling them in the backyard, Wyly knew he had picked the right man for this job, and named him Bonanza's new CEO.

Thomson continued to expand, hitting 600 stores by the end of 1977. The company moved from a $4.2 million loss in 1974 to break even in 1975 and finally into the black (with a $2 million profit) in 1976. Meanwhile, Thomson and Wyly upgraded the steaks and paid down the $30 million bank debt to $16 million. In three years, sales increased from $210 million to $310 million.

How they did it is a lesson in knowing how to read numbers. One of the key changes came from Thomson's analysis of company-managed stores versus franchised restaurants. Thomson and Wyly found that other restaurant chains were making their best margins from franchises. "McDonald's earned over ninety percent of its profit from the licensees, not from the company-owned stores," recalls Wyly, "and some of its best marketing ideas came out of the licensees. Ronald

Don Thomson, whom Wyly appointed as CEO of Bonanza, was a turn-around wizard. A dyslexic student in high school, his facility with numbers and instincts about what made businesses tick gave him the ability to build winners quickly. Sam refers to him as "the greatest manager I ever met."

McDonald was *invented* by a licensee." A McDonald's licensee in a Catholic district saw his sales of hamburgers dip on Fridays, and invented the Filet-O-Fish sandwich, which was a hit and is still on the menu today.

"We had one manager in a company-owned store who was doing $35,000 in sales a month," Thomson recalled. "He bought the store, and a month and a half later was doing $44,000. I asked him, 'Why the hell didn't you do that for us?' and he said, 'Don, I've got a cot here now. I sleep in the store.'"

All this made perfect sense to Wyly, who tried to make lots of people owners in his various endeavors, which in turn generated the enthusiastic involvement, shared experience and "what's next?" thinking that he knew bred successful companies.

Thomson wasn't done. He next launched an aggressive plan to convert company stores into franchise operations. When that conversion was completed, he and Wyly had reduced the number of company employees from 5,000 to 50, and had helped turn a lot of them into owner-managers and millionaires.

Thomson's scrutiny of the books told him that renovated restaurants enjoyed sales increases of up to 30 percent, so he designed three overhaul packages for franchisees—with price tags of $25,000, $50,000 and $100,000. He introduced new menu items, including the steak-and-shrimp and steak-and-chicken meals that became staples. One of his biggest contributions to Bonanza was the salad bar. They were already being featured in a few high-end restaurants at the time, but Thomson introduced them to the budget-restaurant world, where they were an instant hit.

After a long slog, and with a good operations model in place—1978 sales hit $346 million—Thomson said his clock had run out and Bonanza was ready to operate without him. In April 1979, he stepped down as CEO, but stayed on the board as Wyly's assistant, while Sam became chairman. Wyly then promoted Kenneth Horstmyer, the chief operating officer and a former

Salad bars were just becoming popular in fancy restaurants, and Thomson pounced on the concept for the Bonanza chain, with great success.

Wyly wasn't interested in owning a restaurant chain, and his research told him that the margins were low and the failure rate high in that business. But when Bonanza fell into his lap, he couldn't resist the challenge, and gradually built it into a huge national chain.

Center, left: Sam and son-in-law Jason Elliott at the Bonanza Restaurant in Tupelo, Mississippi, Elvis Presley's hometown.

BONANZA

1973 Annual Report to Shareholders
BONANZA FAMILY RESTAURANTS

In 1980, the chain introduced a new marketing theme: "Bonanza—the family restaurant that respects you." The lead spokesman was Rodney Dangerfield, the comedic master, as the forlorn, eternal underdog. The pitch: Dangerfield "never gets any respect"—except when he goes to Bonanza.

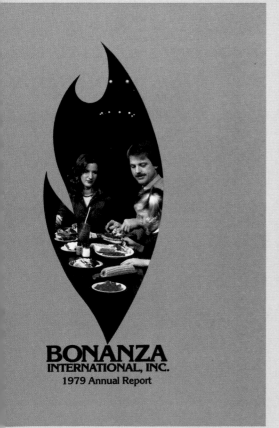

BONANZA
INTERNATIONAL, INC.
1979 Annual Report

Bonanza International, Inc.   1975 Annual Report to Shareholders

executive of Burger King, to CEO. But Horstmyer had his own ideas about building the company, and it took him only six months to get crossways with the numbers-hawking Thomson.

On May 2, 1979, Thomson sent Horstmyer a letter after Horstmyer canceled a direct-mail campaign Thomson had scheduled. Thomson told him: "As you know, we have some fundamental disagreements on how to run the company. The first-quarter loss of company stores is approximately $1 million. Of that amount, almost $850,000 was due in part to inaction on your part as related to sales and operations for the months of January and February . . . In my opinion, [canceling the direct mail campaign] will make it extremely difficult to franchise the stores if you are wrong." Horstmyer was wrong, and in 1979, Bonanza lost money ($215,000) for the first time in three years. By June, he was out.

Wyly persuaded Thomson to return, and the company regained its footing quickly; by the end of 1980, it had $395 million in sales, and soon had more than 650 restaurants in more than 30 states. "There's room for six hundred on the West Coast alone," Thomson predicted.

In 1983, Thomson was ready to move on—again—and Jeff Rogers, who had come up through the marketing ranks, was named CEO. Thomson—again—stayed on as Wyly's muse.

Wyly, by now a veteran acquirer of software companies, was convinced that the best way to further expand Bonanza was by acquiring its competitor, the Ponderosa chain, which also had around 600 restaurants, and in 1984 he decided to make his move. Thomson and Wyly figured they could change the Ponderosas to Bonanzas and get more bang for their advertising buck. Like Bonanza, Ponderosa had gone through stark ups and downs, but unlike the Bonanza chain, 60 percent of Ponderosa restaurants were company-owned, so converting them to Bonanzas would be easy. Wyly saw a lot of potential if the chains were merged and the best managers from each were running things on the ground.

He pounced when he saw Ponderosa's stock price drop to around $10. "This is a good time to merge the two companies into one identifiable brand. Let's go after them," he said to his executives. "It's time to 'holler Drexel'!" In other words, time to get his leveraged-buyout partners, Drexel Burnham Lambert, on the phone. (On his bookshelf, Wyly still has a brass bullhorn given to him by his friend Peter

Ackerman, the number two guy at Drexel, at one of the annual Drexel sessions, which the press had dubbed "The Predators' Ball.") This was during the frenzied leveraged buyout (LBO) and hostile takeover days fueled by Drexel's Mike Milken, whose great innovation, the junk bond, enabled "little guys" like Wyly and T. Boone Pickens to go after the corporate giants who were always defended by "white shoe" bankers like Goldman Sachs and Morgan Stanley.

Wyly set a $20 bid for Ponderosa, and was wary about leaks driving up the share price. He had recently read in *The Wall Street Journal* about a Wall Street bank whose employees had bought stock in a client's takeover target, leaked acquisition information and made money on the bounce. "I don't want any of that going on," he told Drexel and his own people as he waved the *Journal* article two inches from their noses. "If there is one share sold or bought by insiders, I'm firing you immediately."

Drexel approached Ponderosa, explained Bonanza's bid and the strategy behind merging the chains. Ponderosa said it was not for sale, but, nonetheless, word got out that the company was in play. Traders began buzzing, and the shares went over $20. Wyly stopped buying and pulled back.

Takeover artist Asher Edelman then made a bid for Ponderosa and bought the company for $29.95 a share in 1986. "We made a nice profit on the shares that we bought," Wyly recalls, "and Edelman paid too much and now had to try to pay off his debt."

Only a year later, Edelman admitted that he could not pay the debt, and sold the chain to John Kluge of Metromedia Company for nothing but the assumption

Thomson spun off a slightly more upscale chain, the Peoples restaurants, in 1981.

of the debt. That same year, Bonanza enjoyed its best year ever, with a net income of $8.6 million on sales of almost $500 million. Wyly called the profits his family's "grocery money" because the Bonanza dividends were now so reliable. Coincidentally, just a short while before, he had realized that his CEO had a gambling addiction, and had been thinking through how to deal with that problem.

Just then, he got a call from Ackerman, who told him, "There is a guy here who wants to buy Bonanza—he's already bought the Ponderosa and Steak & Ale chains."

It was John Kluge, and *he* wanted to execute Wyly's merger plan. Wyly was ready to sell, but he could not resist pressing Kluge about his interest in steakhouses. When Kluge came to Dallas, Wyly asked him, "John, *Fortune* says your cell phone licenses are worth $5 billion, which makes you now the richest man in the world. You made your money in broadcasting, and your son is six years old. Why do you want to own steakhouses?"

"I used to drive a Frito-Lay truck and sell to these guys," Kluge explained. "I understand the business. I was a vendor. Besides, I think the intellectuals are wrong about people not eating red meat."

Kluge then asked Wyly why he wanted to sell Bonanza. "Well, I've had it for twenty-one years and I have been through three recessions selling steaks to a blue-collar market," Wyly told him. "When times are tough, folks cut back on steaks and eat hamburgers, and I would rather not go through a fourth recession with this business."

Kluge told him, "I don't worry about recessions."

The deal closed in 1989 for $83 million, and Bonanza became part of Kluge's Metromedia conglomerate. Wyly's CEO was immediately ousted by Kluge's people. Roger Lipton, a restaurant market analyst with Ladenburg Thalman, told *Nation's Restaurant News* that Ponderosa "had been mismanaged for years," while Bonanza had "a good management team in addition to profitable stores." But that was no longer Wyly's decision to make. He no longer had a stake in that game. The question for him now was the same one that had driven him for decades: what's next?

By 1987, there were more than 600 Bonanza steakhouses in the U.S.

Wyly, investor Walter Haefner (center) and
Datran CEO Glenn Penisten.

CHAPTER SEVEN

IF YOU CAN'T JOIN 'EM, LICK 'EM

Datran was the most ambitious, wrenching, exhilarating and costly venture in Sam Wyly's career. His promise to change the way the world did its computing was far more than pep-rally bravado for shareholders—thanks to the astounding success of University Computing's first five years, his long-held (and -pursued) dream of launching a communications revolution that would change the world was at hand. He had the vision, he had the team, he had the "throw weight" and he had the money.

The May 15, 1969, issue of *Forbes* magazine listed UCC as 155th of its 500 highest market value companies in the USA and fifth in Texas, with a market cap of $899 million. (The first four companies were Tenneco, Texas Utilities, Texas Instruments and Pennzoil. Exxon had not yet moved its headquarters to Dallas from New York City, nor had AT&T and other giants. By 2011, Texas had more Fortune 500 companies than California or New York, and the lead was growing.)

Wyly had been stockpiling talent for years for this project, and University Computing's first stab at a communications solution, the COPE-45, had been a success. "The COPE is what put us on the map," said Dick Fagin, who headed up University Computing's overseas operations. "The machine acted as if your computer was in your office. It just tore up the business that we had."

Still, Wyly knew he needed to come up with a new communications model for computing. He sensed that AT&T's vast monopoly was fraying, and on June 26, 1968, the FCC handed down its decision—against which AT&T had battled for 10 years—and enabled Carterphone to attach electric devices to telephone receivers that patched radio calls into AT&T lines. The FCC also decided to permit a start-up company called MCI to sell long-distance voice services via microwave links along the highway between Chicago and St. Louis. *The rules of the game are a-changin'*, Sam thought.

Sy Joffe, whom Wyly had brought in from Univac, told him that the smartest telecommunications engineer at his old company was an ex-Navy man named Ed Berg, who had floated around on a rubber raft for two days during the Battle of Midway after Japanese dive-bombers and torpedo planes sank his aircraft carrier. Berg was the brains behind the UNIVAC machines that married computing and telecommunications, so Wyly hired him as soon as he was able. "He was a brilliant engineer," Wyly recalls, "and he told me computers were destined to shift from being giant calculators to a means of communication, and that he could engineer it all like a beautiful digital symphony. I liked the sound of that. Ed became our architect-in-chief for America's first nationwide digital network, what we envisioned as a 'highway' for computers.

"Ed said we would need to transmit data at the speed of 25,000 words per second. That doesn't sound fast today, when we talk about nanoseconds and terabits per second, but it was lightning-fast compared to AT&T's analog phone system. We believed that if we could send data that fast, our project might develop into a low-cost system for 'electronic mail'—people could send written messages back and forth over distances more quickly and more clearly than they could with the U.S. Mail. We were going to be faster and better, just as the telegraph had beat out the Pony Express riders on horseback. The problem was that we couldn't efficiently do what we needed to do using analog phone lines. We studied satellites and fiber optics, but they were too far into the dim and

Two Univac recruits helped Wyly get Datran off the ground: the brilliant marketer Sy Joffe (above, second from right) and engineering wizard Ed Berg (right). These guys fell just short of creating a commercial computer network two decades before most people had heard of the Internet.

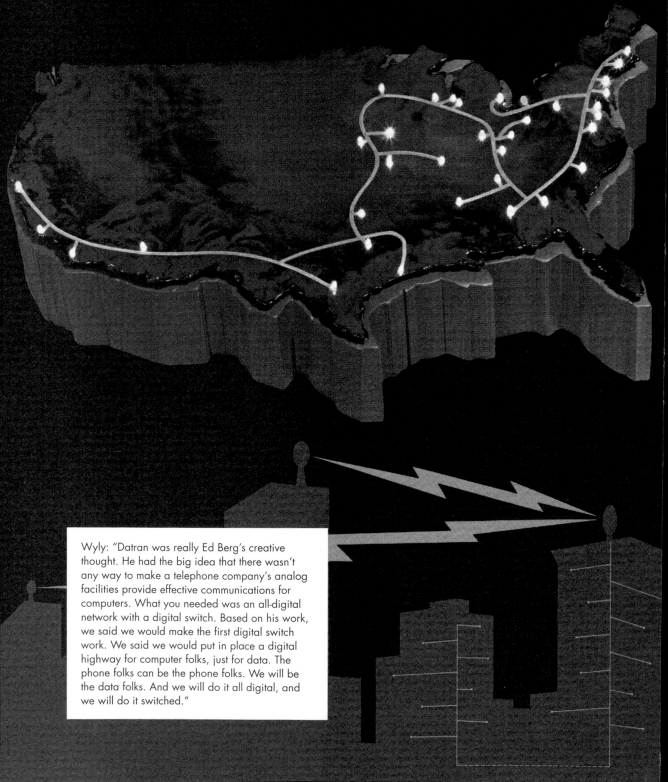

Wyly: "Datran was really Ed Berg's creative thought. He had the big idea that there wasn't any way to make a telephone company's analog facilities provide effective communications for computers. What you needed was an all-digital network with a digital switch. Based on his work, we said we would make the first digital switch work. We said we would put in place a digital highway for computer folks, just for data. The phone folks can be the phone folks. We will be the data folks. And we will do it all digital, and we will do it switched."

distant future. So we decided that the
best available technology was digital
microwave."

Joffe and Berg proposed building a
high-speed digital data-only network,
using microwave as the basic technology.
It would entail erecting transmission
relay towers 20 to 30 miles apart all
over the country, but when it was done,
their digital network would have a 10–1
cost and speed advantage for computer-
to-computer data, and would be able to
transmit 25,000 words a second.

This page from a Datran catalog shows one of
the proto-modems that enabled the network to
dramatically improve the quality of digital
phone calls and reduce costs tenfold. Wyly bet
his corporate net worth on Datran, and lost the
bet when money dried up in the mid-'70s and
the Ma Bell monopoly slashed prices to drive
Datran out of business.

Wyly loved the idea but knew the
time and expense of establishing
rights-of-way and building relay towers
would be daunting. That's when he came up with the idea of buying Western
Union. He had concluded that even though AT&T controlled most local phone
companies and all the long-distance business, there was one way around its
monopoly: the old telegraph rights-of-way that followed the railroad lines. After
reviewing both telegraph and telephone law, Wyly declared that "Western Union
is sitting on a mother lode of long-distance rights-of-way and a mother lode of
local copper wire connections. We can quickly convert them into a 'telephone
company for computers.'"

In April of 1968, University Computing ($42 million in assets) made a tender
offer for Western Union ($741 million in assets). Western Union's managers and
board were shocked. Wyly had approached them about a friendly merger, but they
just stared at him in disbelief. (*Forbes* magazine, writing about this bid, said: "Sam
Wyly's motto is 'If you can't join 'em, lick 'em.'") No one in the computer industry,
on Wall Street or in the executive offices of Western Union could believe the nerve
of the little Texan. Acquire a historic national treasure that had linked East and
West, North and South, at the same time that the railroads were built? *Unh-uh.*
Western Union thwarted Wyly's takeover bid by hiding behind an obscure 1905

New York State law that said no one could own more than 10 percent of a "tele-graph company" in New York without the approval of the legislature in Albany. (This wasn't the first time Western Union paid dearly for its shortsightedness. In the late 19th century, it declined to buy the rights to Alexander Graham Bell's tele-phone for just $100,000, believing no one would want to talk over a line when they could send a telegram.) "Those laws passed to protect a monopoly by law-makers in Albany, New York, were the stopper," Wyly says. "That plus the stolid bureaucracy that Western Union had become."

In August of 1968, Wyly thought of another way to "lick 'em": he formed Data Transmission Company—Datran for short. His plan was to take the company public and finance its development with the equity proceeds, much as he had done to grow University Computing. In November 1968, Datran filed a minutely detailed petition (the stack of documents was almost seven feet tall) with the FCC to become a digital data carrier. The plan called for a string of microwave towers to be built 20 to 30 miles apart and, using digital switching computers, transmit data at high speeds for business customers, so there would be no incursion into AT&T's residential voice business. The cost was estimated to be $375 million.

He began hiring elite communications engineers, software wizards, lawyers, economists and rate specialists, and making connections with the relevant power brokers. Without the FCC's express approval in hand—but certain it was com-ing—he ramped up Datran's system design and development, entered negotiations with equipment suppliers, took options on tower sites and worked on obtaining frequency clearances over the proposed routes. He got his University Computing investment bankers, Kidder, Peabody and Solomon Brothers, signed up to raise private equity.

He also assembled a prestigious board of directors, including Sol Lenowitz, chairman of Xerox; Bob Strauss, chairman of the Democratic National Committee (a balance to his Republican friends in the White House); Erwin Canham, editor of the *Christian Science Monitor* and president of the American Chamber of Com-merce; Dr. Glen T. Seaborg, a Nobel Prize winner for nuclear chemistry (who discovered plutonium, the key element in the atomic bomb) and chairman of the Atomic Energy Commission under Presidents Kennedy, Johnson and Nixon. Wyly

The DATRAN System

OCTOBER 1975
20 CITIES

Boston · San Francisco · Detroit · Chicago · Hartford · Cleveland · New York · Pittsburgh · Philadelphia · Columbus · Baltimore · St. Louis · Kansas City · Washington · Tulsa · Oklahoma City · Los Angeles · Atlanta · Dallas · Houston

Above: Less than a year before the company declared bankruptcy in 1975, Datran had 59 microwave towers transmitting digital data to cities between Dallas and Chicago.

Right: Datran chief marketing officer Ray Cotten (left), Penisten and Wyly at an industry convention.

Wyly: "After we were stopped from merging with Western Union, we decided to try to get a franchise from the Federal Communications Commission . . . We made our own filing. It was a huge thing. We had a lot of receptivity from the people in the FCC's Common Carrier Bureau, who had been wrestling with what to do with the phone monopoly for a long time. We started in 1967 and we didn't get permission until 1972. It was FCC Docket 18920. What we got was the authority to build a data-only network with no phone calls, a data-only, all-digital, switched network, which was really what the world needed.

Bottom: Bernard Strassburg (left), the FCC executive in charge of telecommunications matters, saw that there needed to be a competitive alternative to AT&T's telephone monopoly and was a staunch supporter of attempts by Datran, MCI and Carterphone to level the playing field. Wyly refers to him as "my favorite civil servant."

hired Glenn Penisten, a sharp 17-year Texas Instruments vice president, to be Datran's CEO.

In his 1976 book, *The Innovation Millionaires, Fortune* magazine senior editor Gene Bylinsky wrote that Wyly had attracted the best engineering minds in the country to build his "digital highway for computers," and that "Sam Wyly [was] one of the most, if not the most, successful post–World War II entrepreneur in the United States."

Little did Bylinsky know that the best was yet to come for Wyly.

And so was the worst.

Datran set up headquarters in Virginia just across the Potomac River from Washington, D.C., so that it was within counterpunching distance of regulators, politicians, lobbyists and AT&T. He knew Datran would need buckets of cash for several years—the tab by the end of 1970 was $6.6 million.

But then, a little serendipity came his way. Back in 1967, on a visit to California, he had been walking down the hallway of a competitor's offices and noticed a sign on one of the doors that read: Software Products Division. He was puzzled. "Software isn't a product," he said to himself. "It's a *service*. It's a bunch of instructions you write to get the machine to provide a service function." But soon the words went from riddle to revelation. "Why *couldn't* those instructions be packaged and sold as a product?"

Wyly hadn't thought much about software as a product. For one thing, there were IBM's anticompetitive practices—he knew of a company that had sold a program for IBM 7040 computers that was better than what IBM had, but went out of business when IBM developed a new, similar program and gave it to customers free as part of a software "bundle."

But he also knew that the game had changed when the Justice Department antitrust agreement consented to by IBM on June 23, 1969, forced Big Blue to separate its software from its hardware, and to price it fairly. The decree launched a tsunami of competition, and Wyly snatched his chance to get into software products when Jimmy Ling's company, LTV, floundered. LTV was a Dallas company that had originally built fighter planes for the U.S. Navy, but had evolved into a conglomerate that brokers called "Meat Ball, Golf Ball and Goof Ball," because it owned a meat-packer, a manufacturer of golf clubs and a drug company. Ling had also bought one of the big U.S. steel companies, Jones & Laughlin, but his bankers, Lehman Brothers and

Goldman Sachs, had to renege on their promise to refund the bank debt with long-term bonds. So Ling and other leaders of the conglomerate boom had their crash—a bit sooner than the crash computer stocks would face in 1970.

Within a year LTV's stock had plummeted from $167 a share to $11, and the company was frantically divesting businesses. One of the ones they were dumping was Computer Technology, which had huge aerospace contracts. CT also had begun to develop software products, but like many companies rocked by the recession, it had big problems. In the easy-money, go-go '60s it had wildly overspent on office accessories—including leopard-skin rugs and hand-carved boxes for executive phones—and on luring over a battalion of IBMers, who'd signed expensive five-year contracts.

Wyly snapped up CT, and had E. W. "Mac" McCain, a Wharton honors graduate who had run Univac's computer business, handle the brutal restructuring. In short order, the baubles were sold off and the overpriced ex-IBMers were pushed out. Wyly had discovered that IBM managers needed to leave Big Blue and get their noses bloodied elsewhere before they could become good managers for him.

As University Computing began to add products to its software line Wyly saw a number of things happening. One was that the computer services revenue that made up his company's principal business was dropping because more and more companies were buying their own computers. But that wasn't all bad news, because this proliferation of new computers meant there were many more customers with software *product* needs. Wyly also saw that the profits from software products, particularly the systems software that directed a computer's internal operations, could be staggering—even with a huge commitment to a sales force and customer service, University Computing made up to 40 percent margins on systems software. But those profits for the few products the company was selling could not compensate for the hits it was taking elsewhere.

Over the next few years, University Computing's software team kept rolling out or acquiring software products. It earned a small profit of $2.3 million on $109 million in revenue in 1971, but a year later had a staggering $82 million loss on $101 million in revenue, mainly because of the ever-growing investment in Datran and the success of Digital Equipment Corps' new $100,000 minicomputer that was an affordable option for some computer services customers.

Right: Breaking ground on Datran's nationwide digital computer communications network: Datran was a noble failure, but it led to the breakup of AT&T, which knocked down the walls and opened the way for the digital revolution that is still spreading today.

Below: Wyly, Haefner (center) and Penisten pose in front of the microwave tower on Cedar Hill, near Dallas, on December 31, 1972, the day the first leg of the Datran network—Dallas to Houston—went live. With an anticipated $375 million capital outlay to build the nationwide microwave tower network, Wyly found his biggest investor in Haefner, who committed $40 million and remained a loyal supporter until the project was halted.

Wyly decided to reorganize his company: UCC Communications Systems, Inc., was sold for $20 million in cash, and UCC's corporate office became a small parent company for University Computing, Datran and Computer Leasing. He changed the parent name to Wyly Corporation.

He continued pouring cash into Datran, his determination steeled by the FCC's 1971 ruling that approved its petition to build a nationwide digital microwave network. In April of 1972, the FCC formally issued permission for Datran to begin building its microwave towers and other infrastructure throughout 27 American cities. As the first telephone company for computers, UCC's stock rallied from its single-digit lows in the 1970 Crash up into the 30s. But money for Datran was increasingly hard to come by, in part because the AT&T monopoly was fighting Wyly with every tactic in its arsenal, even preannouncing its digital service *years* before it would be ready in an attempt to dissuade equity investors and commercial bankers from putting money into Datran. But Wyly somehow continued to find more cash to expand the UCC Software Division. He knew something important was going on there, but with Datran taking so much of his time, he needed someone new to manage it. Someone special.

On November 3, 1971, Wyly asked Sterling Williams, UCC's top sales rep, to manage the software products unit. Wyly also began selling software products in Europe, and in year two, the international business had record profits. They looked even bigger because the dollar was dropping versus the mark, the Swiss and French franc, and the pound. In 1972, University Computing further beefed up its software operation when it acquired a three-year-old Dallas banking software company called Results that had been founded by Ed Lott, a 43-year-old father of nine who had helped pioneer the automation of bank credit cards in Indianapolis and Chicago.

Wyly asked Lott to stay on as president because he cherished his technical skills, his managerial talent and his good name in bank data centers. Results was morphed into the UCC Banking Software Division.

The moves with Lott and Williams paid quick dividends. By the end of 1974, three systems software products had $2 million in sales each. Two of Lott's banking software products had $5 million in sales each. UCC's software products were now providing most of the revenue for the company—and sales were soaring despite the dismal economy.

In 1972, Wyly offered Don Thomson the job of CEO at Datran, but Thomson turned him down. "AT&T's monopoly is unbelievably tough," he told Wyly. "You may ultimately bust up their monopoly—God knows it ought to happen—but how long is it going to take? Why don't you offer me the job of running the computing business? I know I can do that."

So Wyly brought in his 42-year-old fire-jumper to be president of University Computing. The move didn't impress everyone. The headline of the *Forbes* story about Wyly was "Man With His Back to the Wall."

Thomson quickly redirected the company's marketing and business thrusts and pared some nominal businesses, and showed a $3.2 million profit that first year. His great gift, as always, was to look at a company's books, find the cancer and cut it out. He centralized the big computer systems in Dallas and London, and focused the U.S. operations on specialized services for banking, hospitals, insurance companies, and energy, consulting and engineering industries. In 1974, University Computing posted profits of $6.8 million, a 200 percent increase.

Most of those profits from software products were going into Datran.

On December 31, 1973, after five years of research, planning, engineering, construction and testing, Datran went live on the Houston-to-Dallas leg of the nationwide network that would link up 27 major cities. It worked flawlessly. Wyly and CEO Glenn Penisten got their picture taken beside the microwave tower on Cedar Hill, the highest point in greater Dallas from which to send and receive radio signals. "Datran, our major new business strategy of the past five years, is now serving customers," Wyly proudly announced to shareholders. Then he added: "It will need more money in the next two years. We expect to get it." By this time he had invested $55 million in the project. And he was going to need a lot more. AT&T was fighting Datran at every turn. It now complained to the FCC that Datran was disrupting its phone service, driving up local and long-distance prices, and was "unneeded and ultimately unfeasible."

Wyly's rebuttal: "If the USA and the 50 states are going to continue with a monopoly forever, then AT&T is right; but that's changing and that change will continue until there is a truly competitive market for the transmission of data."

But AT&T's guerrilla warfare was starting to pile up some casualties. In July of 1974, a bank that had agreed to put together a much-needed $50 million line of credit

Datran brochures from the early 1970s: Wyly faced the familiar entrepreneurial challenge of finding the right words to describe innovations that the world might not be ready to understand. "I've always been intrigued with the words people use and what they call things. I noticed that my doctor grandfather had his own jargon. The engineer who taught computers had his own jargon. Later, programmers developed their own jargon. So you have all these words. And then you have some people who are trying to understand the whole business, and they create their own category. Long before we started Datran, there was the problem of how people in the digital world . . . adapt to using telephone capability for computers. The computer 'language' was totally alien to what was in place for people to talk to other people. The quality of the analog system was not bad; it was good quality for phones, but it was bad quality for computers . . . It was a different way of thinking."

for Datran told Wyly it could only arrange $20 million. The bank called again a short time later to say that none of the credit would be coming. "Sorry," the bank said. "You just got squeezed in the credit crunch."

More like a credit crush. The despair in the 1970s capital markets was still choking the money supply: venture capital investments dropped 95 percent; Wall Street firms went bust; brokers and bankers got jobs as teachers and truck drivers. The public equity and debt markets almost shut down. It was the worst economy since the Great Depression, as oil prices went from $3 a barrel to $12 a barrel, triggered by the Israeli War and the Arab oil embargo. Adjusted for inflation, the stock market crash was worse than the Crash of 1929.

Despite the bad times, Wyly was determined to fight on. "We need to bet on Datran because its future is so vast," he said with unflagging optimism. A major engineering hurdle had been eliminated when they made that first digital switch work. When the system went live from Houston to Chicago—with 59 microwave towers connecting them—it worked perfectly. It was fast, error-free and less expensive than AT&T. The new digital network had a 10–1 cost advantage over carrying a data call over the analog network for voice calls. The people who said it couldn't be done had scattered in the wind.

Then AT&T finally rolled out its digital service, which it priced 30 percent below Datran, and it subsidized that with higher rates for its monopoly of local and long-distance telephone calls. They then began lobbying Congress to pass an astonishing piece of legislation that would have prohibited further competition against AT&T. The so-called Consumer Communications Reform Act (widely referred to as "the Monopoly Protection Act of 1976") sought to eliminate "wasteful or unnecessary duplication of communications lines." Wyly was stunned that a third of Congress would endorse a bill that would outlaw competition, but there it was, and Datran was in D.C.'s crosshairs.

Bad news kept coming. One of Wyly's A-list board directors, watching the mounting losses, suggested to him that "maybe it's time to stop chasing your dream." But he pressed on, although 1975 was the worst financial year in the company's history. "It was obvious that we were going to need more capital," says Penisten. "Sam and I made a deal with Kidder, Peabody to raise fifty million dollars of private money. It was all set to go, and the day it was supposed to close, I got a

A helicopter delivers a microwave receiver atop Heritage House in St. Louis, Missouri.

Fortune magazine writer Gene Bylinsky said Wyly was building a "highway for computers" that would allow data to pass quickly from computer to computer.

call from Peabody that we were going to have to stop. Calls had been made, they said, and they couldn't go any further with it."

Calls had been made. Penisten had heard that before. When he asked about the substance of those calls, the Kidder people answered carefully; but to Wyly and Penisten, AT&T's fingerprints were clear. The Wall Streeters could not afford to lose their lucrative positions in syndicates for Bell's bonds and stocks, the biggest and easiest transactions that generated fees. Lots of fees.

"After that, we were getting desperate," Penisten recalls. "I made another deal with United Telecom to acquire a piece of the company. Again, we had it all worked out, then we got a call at the last minute from the president of United Telecom. He said, 'We are not going to be able to do this. We have to live with AT&T. We use them for delivering our long-distance calls all over the USA and around the world. We can't be in business without them. They tell us what our share of long-distance calling revenue amounts to. They have made it clear that we can't partner with Wyly in a competitive business for computer-to-computer calls.'"

It was over, and even Wyly could see it, says Penisten: "That's when Sam decided to close it down and try to get his money back by suing AT&T."

Wyly told him, "We're going to have to start winding it down, and I think it is best that before I do that, you leave and find something else to do. I will give you a year's salary. I'll see that each employee gets six months' pay." It was as graceful an exit as Wyly could orchestrate for the people he had invited to join his revolution.

Two weeks before filing bankruptcy for Datran, Wyly filed a lawsuit against AT&T charging that it had impeded fair efforts to launch the company through "abuse of its government-granted and government-protected monopoly power." Then, after 15 years of dreaming, eight years of struggling, and an investment of more than $100 million—more than $400 million in today's dollars—Sam Wyly closed down his big dream in August 1976.

He worked out a plan for recapitalizing University Computing—a plan that would save the rest of the company from bankruptcy, but reduce his ownership of it to only 2 percent, with most of the equity going to pay the debt. Despite the losses from Datran, part of the company had continued to generate profits and grow fast: software products. That made recapitalization possible.

Recapitalization called for the exchange of $105 million face amount of bonds for a combination of stock and cash. Commercial banks would advance the cash and have a senior lien on the assets of a healthy company. This enabled the computing business to survive the fall of Datran, but more important, Wyly's decision to expand software products—even as he was generating cash for Datran—enabled the company to prosper over the next decade, and a $9 share got in exchange for debt in 1978 was worth $45 by 1987, thanks to these same software products he had developed continuing to grow at a 25 percent annual rate.

Datran's demise and the bear market and charitable gifts had by 1975 cost Sam Wyly 80 percent of the net worth he'd had when that May 15, 1969, *Forbes* story declared that University Computing was the fifth most valuable company headquartered in Texas.

In 1980, four years after filing that lawsuit against AT&T, Wyly won a $50 million settlement, half of the lost $100 million. That, with similar wins in court by Tom Carter of Carterphone and Bill McGowan of MCI, resulted in the 1982 Justice Department Consent Decree that broke AT&T into eight telephone companies, all competing with one another, and led to today's competitive telecommunications market, to today's Internet, and, eventually, to the hundreds of thousands of thriving software and hardware companies such as Facebook and Google and Apple. Some of the folks who do legal work for Wyly today remember that when they were junior lawyers for AT&T, Sam Wyly was the most feared name at headquarters.

Wyly likes being an important footnote in history, but also recalls an Abe Lincoln story: Abe, when told he was going to be tarred and feathered, said, "If it weren't for the honor of the occasion, I'd just as soon stay at home."

But Wyly wasn't the stay-home type—he was already looking ahead. Not long after the dust from the Datran war had settled, he sat down with his yellow legal pad and began to scrawl ideas for building the world's greatest software products company. Again.

Man with His Back to the Wall

With his once-proud empire crumbling around him, UCC's Sam Wyly is still hanging on.

WHAT DO YOU DO when your company has just lost $81 million of its $143 million in equity capital and you know that during the current year debt repayments will exceed cash flow? Your company's current debt-to-equity ratio of 2½-to-1 already violates the covenants of an outstanding loan and the company's revolving credit agreement. Add to that the fact that Wall Street will not touch you; your stock is around $5 a share compared with $187 a share just five years ago.

Do you slip ignominiously into retirement and let the bankers take over? Not if your name is Sam Wyly and your company is University Computing Co. of Dallas. A devout Christian Scientist, Wyly sincerely believes that will power can conquer all, even overwhelming financial odds.

But it was will power that got Wyly into trouble in the first place. Supremely confident, he tried to do too much with too little. As considerable as UCC's accomplishments were, Wyly's commitments were soon out of all proportion to his financial means.

At any rate, money is what Sam Wyly needs now, lots of it. This year alone he needs $40 million; next year he will need $44 million and by 1975 he will need perhaps another $28 million. His debt is already $150 million.

Where is all the money going? More than $100 million will be needed by Data Transmission Co. (Datran), UCC's Virginia-based subsidiary, which Wyly believes is the company's most promising operation.

In April Datran began construction of a nationwide system of microwave towers that will transmit data—much of it from computers—among 27 American cities in direct competition with American Telephone & Telegraph. At stake is an estimated $5 billion worth of business by 1980. To get even a small slice of that business, Wyly believes Datran must be operational before AT&T's system is set up and working, currently slated for sometime next year.

Ask Sam Wyly where he is going to get that kind of money and he leads you right into the office of Dean Thornton, UCC's treasurer for the past

Problem. *Sam Wyly made money in computers. Now he needs much more.*

three years and the former treasurer at the Boeing Co. Thornton unfortunately doesn't have any firm answers either. "This is a critical year for us," he says, "I can get us through 1973, but then we fall off a cliff. We must find a way to accommodate Datran."

Even getting through 1973 will require a bit of fancy financial footwork. If Thornton's figures are correct, UCC this year will generate a cash flow of $20 million. But it needs $20 million to service debt, plus $22 million for Datran and another $18 million to pay off the Western-American Bank of London on a note whose terms the company has violated because of UCC's high debt/equity ratio. Net of cash flow, UCC needs $40 million. Wyly claims Datran will be able to get the money it needs this year. But how about the other $18 million?

Earlier this year Wyly and Thornton planned to raise $10 million by spinning off UCC's insurance subsidiary, the Gulf Group. But when the Equity Funding insurance scandal became public knowledge, souring Wall Street on all insurance issues, underwriter Bear, Stearns & Co. and Wyly decided to forget about the offering. In March Thornton did manage to renegotiate the terms of both the $18-million note and the company's revolving credit agreement of $25 million. This does not eliminate the inevitable, only postpones it. According to Thornton, the banks have given

UCC several months to find new sources of money.

Now Thornton is attempting to do what seems impossible: obtain more long-term debt. There are two package deals involved. His plan is to use Gulf's stock to secure a $35-million loan and increase the loan secured by UCC's computer leasing portfolio by $10 million.

UCC was established in 1963 on the premise that it could do businessmen's computer work for them more efficiently and cheaply than they could do it for themselves. It was a good idea and revenues soared: $700,000 in 1964; $7 million in 1966; $60 million in 1968; $128 million in 1971. But Sam Wyly got overambitious and began investing in other businesses, some of which turned out losers. He spent millions trying to build a computer terminal that was better than IBM's. Last year he sold the operation to Harris-Intertype, writing off $32 million in the process. He also tried to establish a computer programming school. Losses on that gamble in 1970 and 1971 totaled $9.2 million. With these losses, much of the profits made in the computer operation went back down the drain. Then last year the computer operation soured, and with heavy write-offs UCC lost $83 million.

Smart and charming Sam Wyly, 38, has one last card to play—but it is slightly soiled: Copying from his friend James J. Ling, the Dallas conglom-

Wyly with his mother, Flora, his wife, Rosemary, and Louisiana Tech president Jay Taylor in 1968.

LEARN, BABY, LEARN!

"Success is never achieved alone" is a line that might be entwined with Sam Wyly's DNA. It's what his great-great-grandparents used to preach and what every subsequent generation of the Wyly family was taught. As was "Share with others what is shared with you." Sam always says he could not have succeeded without the guidance of his parents, the wisdom of good mentors and the diligent labor and tireless devotion of the professionals with whom he surrounded himself. That is why he has always felt obligated to pass on the lessons he has learned. His mentoring has taken many forms, but never a more significant one than in the calamitous year of 1968, when America seemed on the verge of being torn asunder.

On April 4 of that year came the shocking news that civil rights leader Dr. Martin Luther King, Jr., had been shot in Memphis. The immediate, visceral response of many young men in black communities was violence. Riots were rampant, and vast areas of Washington, D.C., Baltimore, Detroit and other cities were burned. Hundreds of neighborhoods and tens of thousands of businesses were razed. Wyly understood the sorrow and the rage, but not the impulse to destroy one's own neighborhood. *Why*, he wondered, *did young men burn homes and businesses, the sources of refuge and sustenance?*

The answer, it seemed to him, was that they didn't own anything, so they were punishing those who did. The solution, he concluded, was to invite black Americans to the economic party.

But how? The lack of black ownership was pervasive—from homes to property to businesses—long after the big migration from the cotton fields of the south to the "promised land" of California and the big cities of Detroit, Los Angeles, New York City and other northern centers. A century after abolition, there were still crippling holdovers from the days of slavery—too many black Americans did not have jobs, property or a proper education.

Wyly knew a successful black entrepreneur named Joe Kirven, whose story laid out the obstacles to, and potential for, minority entrepreneurship. Kirven had taken a small idea—an office-cleaning service—and built it into the largest black-owned business in Dallas. Like Wyly, Kirven had built his company with a lot of sweat and shoe leather. "I made a sales call at a place called Associates, which was pretty close to where I grew up, and the president, G. E. Litton gave me an opportunity," Kirven said. "That was my first sale." The entrepreneur was off and running.

It wasn't a fluke sale. Like Wyly, Kirven had a talent for salesmanship. Tall, dedicated, college-educated (a soccer and football player at the small, all-black Wiley College in Marshall, Texas, made famous by the movie *The Great Debaters*, starring Denzel Washington) and eloquent, he was a persuasive presence. But whereas Sam Wyly's big obstacle when starting UCC had been wrenching business from established big companies such as IBM, Kirven had to lure his clients away from entrenched local white competitors. And that meant he had to work harder just to stay even.

"I'm not bragging," Kirven said, "but I was a pretty good salesman. I tried to make a good appearance because I knew from the beginning that I was competing against the Caucasians. But I knew if I called on enough accounts each day, I would eventually get my quota. I had to do three times as many. If they called on four or five accounts, I had to call on fifteen."

Wyly drew two conclusions: First, if aspiring black entrepreneurs were to have a prayer, they needed access to bank loans and venture capital. Even limited capital, applied to good ideas, could get them started. He had started University Computing with only $1,000 and an idea, so he knew how much could be done with not much. Second, he knew an understanding of business was the key for people of any ethnic heritage. He needed to get successful entrepreneurs willing to share their knowledge, their frustrations and their stories.

He helped open the door for black entrepreneurs in Dallas through the Wyly Foundation, which provided mentoring and capital via foundations, bigger businesses and cooperating banks. He sought out the most talented people he could find to bring this idea to fruition. The first was Alan Steelman, the 25-year-old executive director of the Republican Party in Dallas (and later a three-term 5th District congressman). Second was Walt Durham, who formed Minority Business Advisors in Dallas to provide knowledge and contacts to aspiring business people.

Wyly hired Steelman as executive director of his foundation. They began with the idea of making capital available to black entrepreneurs. But capital alone was not enough without the knowledge of how to use it. So, working with Durham, they hit the streets and gathered a group of successful Dallas-area businessmen willing to be mentors. Wyly also enlisted local banks and small-business investment corporations (SBICs) for small business loans and equity investment.

His efforts first came to the attention of Richard Nixon during his 1968 run for the White House. Nixon had looked at the chaos, rioting and militancy building up in the black community, and in his speeches he began to talk about "bridging the gap" with the black community and fostering "black capitalism."

Some thought this a cynical play for the black vote, but whatever Nixon's motives, Wyly enthusiastically embraced the concept, and after his Republican presidential candidate, Senator Chuck Percy from Illinois, lost out in the nominating process, he backed Nixon. He knew his team had something to offer the nation, and wondered, *What if we could nationalize the Dallas model?*

Wyly soon got his chance to find out after he was asked to be fund-raising chairman in Texas for Nixon's presidential campaign. After he set a $2 million fund-raising record for Texas—the first time Texas Republicans had raised as much as New York and California—Nixon wanted to meet him. When they sat down together, Wyly shared his ideas about black entrepreneurship, and explained how the Dallas model worked. Nixon was intrigued.

A few months later, Nixon won the election handily, and knew that his slice of the black vote had been an important part of his victory. Once he was in the White House, he launched the first of many initiatives on behalf of low-income blacks and other poor people in business and education. In a single executive order, signed March 5, 1969—just six weeks into his presidency—he created two important entities. One was the President's Advisory Council on Minority Business Enterprise (PACMBE), an independent group of presidential appointees charged with making recommendations on how to stimulate business in black, Cuban, Mexican and other minority communities. The other was the Office of Minority Business Enterprise (OMBE), a new arm of the Department of Commerce.

Wyly, just 34 at the time, applauded these bold initiatives—and was surprised when the president appointed him chairman of the President's Advisory Council. He immediately brought in Steelman as his executive director. Steelman, in turn, brought in John Topping, a Dartmouth and Yale Law guy, and a respected lawyer with the Navy's Advocate General. Wyly also invited Joe Kirven to be on the commission.

The White House staff recruited top executives across the nation, people with the clout to make things happen. The 70-member council had some of the most powerful CEOs in American industry, including J. Willard Marriott, Jr., of Marriott Hotels; James Roche, chairman of General Motors; and Lester Burcham, chairman of F.W. Woolworth. Washington beltway kingpins included Berkeley Burrell, head of the National Business League (and Wyly's vice-chairman); Benjamin Fernandez, head of National Economic Development Association; and W. P. Gullander, president of the National Association of Manufacturers.

"I looked around the room in awe," Wyly recalls, still impressed by his collection of mountain-movers. "I was the youngest guy there, and I was the leader, and the one with clout at the White House."

And then the hard work began.

Their charter was "... to create a blueprint for a national strategy that would assure that minorities assumed a significant role in developing, owning and managing viable businesses during the 1970s, not 40 years

SAM E. WYLY

Wyly Named By Nixon to Commission

WASHINGTON (AP) — Sam E. Wyly, 35-year-old chairman of the board of University Computing Co., Dallas, and a native of Delhi, La., has been appointed by President Nixon as a member of the President's commission on the White House fellowships.

The commission selects annually a group of young people to serve as White House fellows to gain experience in government by working under members of the White House staff and members of the Cabinet.

Wyly is a 1956 graduate of Louisiana Tech and founded his company eight years ago. The company now rates as one of the fastest growing companies in the world.

He was earlier this year selected as one of the 10 outstanding young men of America by the U.S. Junior Chamber of Commerce, and he and his brother, Charles, were hon-

Wyly met Richard Nixon on the campaign trail, and pitched him his ideas for helping black Americans. When Nixon got into the White House, he put Wyly in charge of the program to help black entrepreneurs.

Right: Wyly preparing a presentation for the White House, 1970. Future Congressman Alan Steelman is standing behind the podium.

Below: Candidate Nixon barnstorming in Texas, trying to win the 1968 presidency. Wyly introduced Nixon in five cities, in one day. With Charles and Sam Wyly as fund-raisers, it was the first time that Texas matched New York and California in political money for the Republican party in the president's race.

Opposite, top: Inside the Oval Office, Nixon and Wyly discuss Wyly's project. First on the left is Donald Rumsfeld, who then headed the War on Poverty. Later, as Secretary of Defense, he would lead the War on Terror in Iraq and Afghanistan.

Opposite, bottom: President Richard Nixon (seated on the right side of the table) introduced Sam Wyly (beneath flip chart in back) to his Cabinet in 1969.

WYLY SHARES PODIUM with Richard Nixon at recent Dallas fund-raising dinner at which he presided.

power. Its training center, the Academy of Computer Sciences, is 10 times larger than was projected six months ago.

Last year Sam Wyly clinched a $1.2 stock bonus and his salary was doubled by the board of directors when he acquired two British computer service firms which had $1.5 million in combined sales. UCC was one of the first computer companies to establish a foothold in the United Kingdom, a nation just beginning to catch up with the fast-growing U.S. market.

The firm's beginning was in 1963 when Sam Wyly was 28. The young computer - oriented accountant decided to form a large-scale computer center to serve the scientific community gathering in Dallas with Texas Instruments, Collins Radio, Southern Methodist University, the Graduate Research Center of the Southwest (now Texas University Center for Advanced Studies at Dallas) and others.

With a new state corporate charter in July 1963, Wyly arranged to purchase a used Control Data 1604 computer for $650,000. (It sold for $1.5 million new). When the computer was delivered in October 1963, he traded computer time to SMU for a place to house it.

"We had no contracts but we had a high expectancy for business," Wyly said. Soon he had contracts with Texas Instruments, Sun Oil Co. and SMU.

From there the UCC story is just plain phenomenal and some people still can't believe University Computing is real.

When UCC stock went on the open market at $4.50 a share in September 1965 and proceeded to move up to $20 during a "bad market year" (1966), the financial community turned its head.

And then when a second block of that stock hit the market at $20 a share a year later and skyrocketed to $80 a share by mid-May 1967, it was impossible for businessmen not to take note.

That was only the beginning. Today the stock is selling over-the-counter above $130 a share and had hit a high of $155 earlier this year, but dropped back during July and August. In less than three years, the price of University Computing stock rose from $1.50 a share (adjusted for splits) to the $155 high. The stock market valued this newcomer at more than $600 million. (Price / earnings ratio: 100/1)

Earlier this year to gain capital strength, the firm bought 25 per cent of Gulf Insurance Group, a well-established Dallas company. And other acquisitions are being planned.

The computer service route is rugged and there are a lot of drop-outs, Wyly asserted.

"It takes a lot of money to play the computer services game and the risks are high," he explained. "The last few years are littered with the carcasses of failures. There has been an unusually high mortality rate among computer service firms for varied reasons."

But, with the guidance and easy manner of Sam Wyly and his finance-minded brother Charles Wyly Jr., who joined him in early 1964, University Computing overcame these risks and prospered. Charles is executive vice-president and chief financial officer.

"The key was to provide a place where highly talented people can work comfortably and productively. Since we have a great deal of faith in the individual, we seek capable technical people, then give them goals and plenty of freedom," Wyly added.

Wyly admits that he is satisfied with UCC's progress so far. But, UCC continues to grow stronger and plan far ahead.

"What are we going to do new?" is a familiar query at University Computing's corporate headquarters in the Frito-Lay Tower. If it's not Sam Wyly asking the question it's his brother or one of the other youthful executives.

Meanwhile, not too far away a large number of UCC's 1,700 employees work freely in a high-rise world headquarters building. Inscribed "UCC . . . . Computer Utility," the $2 million structure houses over $5 million worth of computer equipment. The ominous appearing edifice is a vital link for the 30 UCC offices around the world. UCC operates in all 50 states and 12 countries.

hence." His President's Council worked for almost a year, and then Wyly presented a revolutionary report to President Nixon and his Cabinet. One goal was to establish Minority Enterprise Small Business Investment Companies (MESBICs) in 100 cities. Dallas was to be first.

Wyly knew they needed to start with a big success, and thought he had all the tools he needed to do just that. But this was politics, and D.C., and Wyly quickly ran into obstacles. The first one was the government's organization chart. Commerce Secretary Maurice Stans wanted Wyly's team to report to him, but Steelman, Topping and Wyly wanted direct access to Nixon and his White House staff, so they pushed back. They got what they wanted, but that didn't stop the obstruction from the permanent bureaucrats.

Wyly hired Walt Durham in the Dallas MESBIC. Durham already knew which aspiring entrepreneur would lead their pilot program. Mildren Montgomery was a lot like Joe Kirven—he was a black Dallas businessman who, at six-foot-two and with a degree in biology, was impressive and articulate. A longtime plant manager for Garland Foods, a large meatpacker, he knew the company inside and out. When Garland Foods filed for bankruptcy, Montgomery came up with a plan to get it back in the black. But he needed to borrow $1 million dollars to do it.

Wyly was sure Montgomery could turn the company around just by supplying supermarkets, but knew Garland would shine like a bright star of hope if it got a fat government contract as well.

His brain trust quickly found its target: a big contract for canned hams—the principal product of Garland Foods—had come up for bid from the Defense Department. If Montgomery could land it, Garland Foods—and the federal program to help black businesses—would be up and running.

For months, Durham worked on locking up the canned hams contract with the Department of Defense. The bidding had been open, but he managed to work out a gentleman's agreement with the Small Business Administration in D.C. that the contract would go to Garland Foods.

As Durham and his staff were planning Garland's formal coming-out party—a ceremony that included dignitaries, elected officials and high-profile business sponsors—he received a phone call from his SBA contact. "The Defense Department is not going to give Montgomery the canned hams," he told Durham. "Defense Secretary Laird not only said, 'No,' he said, *'Hell, no!'*"

Durham was stunned. When he asked why Laird had shot them down, his contact said Garland Foods' quoted labor prices were not union prices, and that there were doubts about Garland passing a health inspection.

When Durham explained that Texas was a right-to-work state, so higher union prices weren't a factor, and that Garland had never failed a health inspection, his contact told him, "There is nothing I can do."

These "reasons" smelled to Wyly and Durham like there was a bunch of insiders protecting their turf. They surmised that some prickly egos at the Defense Department didn't like being told where to buy their canned hams, and neither knew nor cared what was at stake for the President's Advisory program. But Wyly knew that Nixon cared, knew that the president needed a prominent success story for his black capitalism programs, and Wyly knew how to "sell" to the man at the top.

Wyly sent a letter to Nixon that said, in effect: "If you really do support the idea of minority enterprise, President Nixon, you will so indicate by telling Defense Secretary Laird to buy those hams."

Nixon read the letter, then sent the message to Laird: "Just buy the damned hams!"

Montgomery got the contract.

It was an important victory that reaped many rewards. Garland Foods became one of the successful companies to come out of the program, and MESBICs helped thousands of black and other minority entrepreneurs over the next 30 years. While new public and private programs have been enacted since then, some MESBICs remain in operation to this day. Based on the Wyly Foundation model, Congress ultimately authorized more than 200 MESBICs around the country to provide venture capital and support to minority-owned businesses. General Motors Chairman James M. Roche committed to creating 250 minority automobile dealers over a 10-year period. Finally, MESBICs were able to raise more than $1 billion in capital from major corporations for deposits into minority-owned banks to make loans and form business ventures in minority communities.

On election night 1968 Wyly watched the votes come in with Nixon and his top staff at the Waldorf Astoria hotel in New York.

Right: Big men on campus: Alums Sam and Charles Wyly were honored at Louisiana Tech's homecoming game in 1968 after they announced the donation to fund a new multipurpose building at their alma mater.

Below: Named in memory of their father, the Charles Wyly, Sr., Tower of Learning was constructed in 1972, and at 16 floors remains the tallest building in Ruston, Louisiana. "Take Highway 80—not I-20," says Sam. "It's amazing to see it rising out of the Piney Woods."

Below, right: Charles and his wife, Dee, enjoy the festivities at a pregame mixer.

For a kid who grew up in the segregated South, Sam Wyly considered the program his best Return On Investment (ROI).

Another social cause Sam Wyly and his brother were passionate about—and another one that gave them an excellent ROI—was informed public debate, something that went back to their days at the *Delhi Dispatch*, the weekly newspaper run by their parents. With all the tumult churning up the nation in 1968, Sam was dismayed to see so much anger and vitriol being broadcast on the evening news, but so little useful, objective reporting. At that time, there were three TV networks—CBS, ABC and NBC—and each did a nightly national newscast. Every major city also had at least one TV station that broadcast a local news show once or sometimes twice a day, but Sam saw their newscasts as pretty much the same thing, with only the names changed to protect the uninterested. Then a man named Bob Wilson walked into his office one day in 1968 and brought him a game-changing alternative.

The 27-year-old Wilson, despite his Boston Irish accent, had recently been named head of the Dallas public television station, KERA, Channel 13. "The station was in such bad shape," Wilson recalls. "It was just not inviting." Charged with improving the station's programming, Wilson hit the road and visited the country's top PBS stations to see what they were doing. He returned with a plan, but ran into dead ends when he tried to enlist people to help him.

Wilson was in a position similar to the one Wyly had been in when he started with Honeywell—both of them looked out over all of the chaos in their field and saw nothing but opportunity. Wilson's first priority was to beef up the quality and integrity of news analysis at the station. But the station's reputation was so bad that he could not get much financial support from the community.

Wilson paid a visit to Wyly and Alan Steelman, who was in charge of the Wyly Foundation. Wilson told them that he had been given the reins to make the Dallas PBS channel better, to make it important, to make it something people in Dallas could be proud of, and, just as important, to make it something they'd want to watch.

Wilson told Wyly and Steelman that he wanted to focus first on news, and explained his plan: During a newspaper strike, San Francisco's PBS station had hired some print journalists to come on the air and discuss the issues of the day, and the shows had worked well. Wilson wanted to do a program called *Newsroom* that would enable him to report the news, conduct live interviews and bring in print journalists for analysis. All of that meant raising a lot of money, local money. He said he could get a foundation grant for most of his budget if he could get a lead Dallas donor. Sam had one question, "Who's going to run it?"

Wilson said, "Jim Lehrer."

Wyly smiled. "If you can get Lehrer, you got me," he said. "He's a fair reporter. He's objective. He wasn't like CBS's Mike Wallace, trying to nail me to the wall when I was pushing Chuck Percy for vice president. You get Jim Lehrer, and you got me."

Jim Lehrer was the young city editor of the *Dallas Times-Herald* at the time. Lehrer knew doing television would be a risky roll of the dice, but he told Wilson he was interested—however, only if journalistic integrity could be maintained. Lehrer wanted to control the show's content, which meant he did not want donors dictating things to him. "I think a lot of businesspeople don't understand journalism, and in those days they expected journalists to be obedient above all," Wilson says. "While Jim was respectful, he did not feel any charge to be obedient to some cracker."

In one of the best investments Wyly ever made, he helped the Dallas PBS station start a news show hosted by Jim Lehrer, which went on to be the *NewsHour* millions of Americans still use as their trusted source for news. "Without Sam Wyly, there would be no *NewsHour*," Lehrer says.

When Wyly and Wilson spoke with Lehrer about doing this new news show, he was the same low-key, non-abrasive, direct, completely informed guy that newshounds have seen on PBS for the past 40 years. He was a long way from the angry ranters who filled the airwaves back then—and clutter them still. Beyond that, he was stunningly objective in his reporting. To this day, Lehrer does not vote because he doesn't want anyone to imagine he leans one way or another politically, which is just one of the many reasons he still is the preferred choice of both Republicans and Democrats to moderate presidential debates.

Raised in a newspaper family, Wyly agreed with Wilson and Lehrer that objectivity was of paramount importance, and the Wyly Foundation gave Wilson $50,000 to launch a weekly *Newsroom* show out of Dallas on PBS. It was an instant hit, and it changed the way news was presented in this country. (At Sam's 70th birthday party, Lehrer said, "Without Sam Wyly, there would be no *NewsHour*.")

That $50,000 donation opened the door for the Ford Foundation to pledge $2 million over four years to fund a nightly *Newsroom* program in 1972, with Lehrer as executive editor. The show eventually moved to Washington, D.C., and became the *MacNeil/Lehrer Report* with Robert MacNeil cohosting from 1975 to 1995. When MacNeil retired in 1995, the show was renamed *NewsHour With Jim Lehrer*.

"That one-program-a-week-type thing was a key influence on Ford's decision to give us the big grant for the nightly news program, because we had proved that we could find local support for what we were doing," says Wilson.

Wilson's show was a big success, but not even objectivity was good enough for some people. Early on, Wilson says he got a call from the head of the Mercantile Bank in Dallas, who strongly objected to both the people and the content on *Newsroom*. "He had called the station and said he wanted to see me," Wilson recalls. "I go down to his office and I'm in this room that's as big as a stadium, and he says, 'Two things have to happen. You have to leave town and Jim Lehrer has to leave town.' And that was kind of scary." Wilson says the man threatened to use his financial pull to end funding for the program.

At the time, Wilson had a small son, and was about to have another (those boys grew up to be Hollywood stars Owen and Luke Wilson), and he wasn't eager to lose his job or move to another city, so he tried to weather this banker's gale of vitriol against the "liberal bias" of Jim Lehrer and *Newsroom*. "For a while it was an intimidating rant," Wilson says, "but something soon became clear—I realized that this guy was not very smart. His father had been a smart and very respected banker, but the son was kind of dumb. He said he had called all the Ford dealers in town about canceling support for *Newsroom*, not realizing that the Ford Foundation was completely independent from Ford Motor Company and its dealers. When he said that, I knew maybe this guy wasn't going to be a formidable opponent."

He wasn't, and both Wilson and Lehrer kept their jobs and gave America better newscasts, if not always better news.

Wyly loved the idea of providing power to the American engine. It gave him a sense of higher involvement in the pageant. It was energy-makers who kept the lights on, the homes warm, the cars running, the tractors plowing, the factories producing and America moving. Before it was over, Earth Resources Company would even change the way a city worked.

MINING YOUR OWN BUSINESS

In the 1960s, UCC had been one of the fastest-growing companies in America. The stock market priced it at increasingly higher valuations in relation to revenues and profits and other measures of intrinsic value. Some folks said, "Don't put all your eggs in one basket," while others counseled, "Put all your eggs in one basket . . . and watch that basket." So Wyly started cashing out small chunks of his UCC stock each year, and used that money to diversify his assets. "Listening to the rumblings in the bushes, I began to think that with accelerating inflation we should own some assets that could benefit from inflation," he says. "Of course, I had no way of knowing that in just a few years inflation would go through the roof, that mortgage interest rates would hit 20 percent or that the First National Bank in Dallas would have to go get 'Eurodollars' to survive the tight money cure for inflation. But I sensed that there was potential trouble coming for paper assets like stocks and bonds, and looked at hard assets like oil, gold, silver and real estate."

In 1966, Wyly had met Dan Krausse at a meeting of the Young Presidents' Organization in Fort Worth, Texas, and thought he was the "smartest guy in the room." Krausse had worked at Halliburton and had run a refinery in the heart of West Texas, and by 1968 was the president of Champlin Petroleum. But he'd hit the ceiling in that family-dominated business, and Wyly knew Krausse was "looking for his own canoe to row again," so he made him an offer: "You're a good manager, Dan, and we want to use our University Computing–created wealth to buy a company for you to run." He told Krausse that he and his brother, Charles, would hock some UCC stock to collateralize a loan to pay for something he could manage.

They decided to go into mining because Bob Burch, their Kidder, Peabody banker, had said that Wall Street would fund a mining company but not a refinery. And to Sam, gold and silver were enchanting. Prospecting for ores was risky, but that didn't deter the Wyly brothers in those heady days when they seemed to hit a home run every time they picked up a bat. Thanks to University Computing, they were rich with collateral and ready to make another bet. Krausse's background was in refining, but they were confident that he could recruit good talent to run another kind of geo-logic business.

Just before Memorial Day in 1968, after examining several prospective ven-tures, Krausse and the Wyly brothers gave a fascinating presentation to Citibank. The proposal was to acquire an oil refinery to provide a reliable cash flow and then use that money to fund a minerals exploration and development program. This would be what Sam called "an earth resources company."

Citibank bought in, and the Wylys moved quickly. In July 1968, they used $20 million in University Computing stock as collateral for a $10 million loan from Citibank, and bought Delta Refining, an oil refinery in Memphis on the banks of the Mississippi River that was for sale by Eugene Constantine, a Dallas oilman, and also Vitro Minerals, a Golden, Colorado–based mining company with a coal mine in Alaska and "hard rock" prospects in the Rocky Mountains. They merged the two companies and created Earth Resources Company.

The Wylys persuaded Kidder, Peabody to take Earth Resources public only seven months later. That public offering cost 25 percent of the equity in the com-pany but raised $13 million, and within six months they had paid off their loan. "We had put a big chunk of UCC stock at risk," Sam recalls, "but we got it free and clear quicker than most big corporations can sneeze!" Now they had no debt, $13 million of equity, and an annual cash flow of $3.5 million. Time to start prospecting.

In early 1969, Krausse flew to Alaska to see the coal mine they owned that was supplying about half of the coal consumed by the city of Fairbanks and the interior of Alaska. He quickly saw that the energy infrastructure there was primitive and expensive, two conditions that set off the alarm bells of opportunity for a smart entrepreneur. The mine was shipping its coal 90 miles by rail to Fairbanks, while heating oil and gasoline were being shipped up from California to a port on the south coast of Alaska, then trucked north 450 miles, making them the most expensive petroleum products in the United States.

The only reason the Wylys even had this coal mine was because it had come with the package of gold, silver and copper mining prospects in the Golden, Colorado, company they had bought.

Atlantic Richfield had just then announced a major discovery of oil in Prudhoe Bay, on the North Slope of Alaska. It was the biggest find ever in the U.S.—bigger than Beaumont, Texas's famed Spindle Top, which at its peak was pumping more oil than all the rest of the world combined. Arco announced that it was going to build a pipeline to move that oil to market, and it was going to go *through* Fairbanks.

Krausse knew retail marketers in Alaska had no North Slope production, but did have high prices and high profit margins. Earth Resources figured a joint venture could link the supply and demand—a North Slope producer, one of the branded marketers (the biggest one in Alaska being Unocal) and them. And his team knew how to build and run small, efficient refineries, and do it better than the big guys, because of their Delta Refining plant in Memphis.

They pitched the plan to Arco and Unocal, both of which passed. So they thought, *Fine, we'll do it ourselves*. The state's governor said Alaska would be delighted to have a refinery in the interior, which would reduce the cost of shipping petroleum products up from the southern coast, so Earth Resources started building a refinery beside the planned pipeline near Fairbanks, halfway between the Prudhoe Bay oil field in the north and the Port of Valdez in the south. The crude from Valdez would be shipped to California on tankers. (Later, a tanker named *Exxon Valdez* would make headlines with an oil spill—the biggest U.S. oil spill until the catastrophic blowout at BP's Deepwater Horizon well in the Gulf of Mexico in 2010.)

As a business opportunity, it was almost perfect.

Almost. Environmentalists rose en masse after Arco announced that it was going to build that pipeline, and lobbied successfully to shut down construction on it. It did not require a big imagination to appreciate their argument: The 799-mile-long pipeline would bisect America's most pristine state, crossing three

When the giant Prudhoe Bay oil field in Alaska was discovered, Wyly swooped in and built an oil refinery that was perfectly positioned to exploit the new Trans-Alaska Pipeline (1) and the increased local demand for oil.

North Pole, Alaska (2). Following the discovery of the giant Prudhoe Bay oil field, Wyly decided to build an oil refinery in Fairbanks, Alaska.

Earth Resource's Mississippi River barge fleet (3) provided its Memphis refinery (4) economical access to crude oil supplies, foreign as well as domestic.

When it absolutely, positively has to burn a lot of jet fuel: Earth Resources got lucky when Federal Express decided to base its hub in Memphis; Earth Resources ran a pipeline from its refinery to the FedEx airstrip and made millions. FedEx started out with a fleet of Falcon jets to circumvent federal cargo regulations (5).

mountain ranges and more than 800 rivers and streams. And the route was crisscrossed with earthquake faults.

But there was another factor at play here for Earth Resources. As expensive as oil was for them, Alaskans preferred it to coal. Coal reserves in Alaska were vast, but that did not matter to the people living there—only six percent of the state's energy consumption used coal. And for the green movement, coal was dirtier than oil. So Earth Resources sold its coal mine in 1971, recognizing that if it was to grow it had to provide the form of energy the people preferred. There was new work to do.

In 1975, the Trans-Alaska Oil Pipeline finally got the go-ahead. It became inevitable after the Arab oil embargo during the 1973 Arab-Israeli war, when oil jumped from $3 to $12 a barrel. America's crippling dependence on foreign oil became clear as prices doubled at the gas pump. As soon as the pipeline was approved, construction began on the Earth Resources Fairbanks Refinery in North Pole, Alaska. On May 31, 1977, the Trans-Alaska Oil Pipeline opened, and the refinery was ready to process the first barrel of crude oil ever pumped from the North Slope. The pipeline would go on to pump an average of a million barrels a day, and now provides about 17 percent of the domestic oil supply.

There were benefits that not even Sam Wyly had anticipated. Suddenly Fairbanks Airport began getting more of the Boeing 747 traffic between the United States and the Far East because New York-to-Tokyo flights could now fuel up in Fairbanks, and since the Arctic Circle route was shorter, routes were changed. Earth Resources was soon refining 40,000 barrels of oil a day, selling to both the Alaskan market and the airlines, and it was the only game in town. For everyone involved—the entrepreneurs, the investors and the community—it was an ideal business. And when Wyly saw the way it created prosperity for Fairbanks, he felt proud. *This*, he thought, *is what entrepreneurship should do.*

The Alaska adventure was a boon for Earth Resources, but it was the Delta Refinery in Memphis that eventually became the heart of the company. When Earth Resources acquired the refinery in 1968, it had a capacity of about 25,000 barrels a day, but the Wylys were committed to expanding that. They did so quickly, took risks others were afraid to take and were able to supply their products at lower costs than the big companies thanks to less overhead, more efficient technology and their strategic location on the Mississippi River, along which crude oil could be brought up on low-cost barges from fields in South Louisiana and the Gulf of Mexico.

Then came what Wyly called "a super-serendipity moment." In 1973, a start-up airborne delivery service called Federal Express relocated to Memphis from Little Rock, Arkansas, because some Little Rock airport officials refused to provide facilities for the Falcon jets used by this small, young company. This nimble, smaller jet enabled FedEx to get into business under a loophole in federal laws and regulations that protected the U.S. Post Office monopoly on "carrying the mail." (Given that FedEx today employs 275,000 people, including more than 25,000 in Memphis, Little Rock probably regrets that decision.)

The Wylys and Krausse recognized the opening immediately. Earth Resources built a pipeline to deliver jet fuel from the Delta Refinery directly to the Memphis airport. In a way, FedEx was another Fairbanks for the company—it was the first to promise overnight delivery of small packages anywhere in the U.S. and made a lot of money.

Since there were always more cars on the road every year, growth was a given in the oil business. The country was converting to lead-free gas to curtail the poison spewing out of tailpipes, but it would be a long and expensive process. The Earth Resources executives debated the question: "Should we convert to lead-free gas at our refinery when we don't yet have to?" Converting the Delta Refinery to produce unleaded gasoline would be a huge capital project for this small enterprise. "Would the early market for unleaded gasoline be large enough to pay back the cost of capital?" "Do we bet our net worth on it?"

But economics was not the only consideration for Sam Wyly. While some of their competitors sued the Environmental Protection Agency (EPA) to halt the lead phase-out coming in 1982, the Wyly team decided to be leaders. They would convert now. It was a risky move, in part because Delta was recording record profits, and in large part because of the Arab oil embargo that began on October 19, 1973. It marked a sea change in Earth Resources' operations and profitability. Oil prices began escalating, and President Nixon abruptly abandoned his free-market philosophy and slapped price controls on crude oil. By 1974, crude had jumped from $3 a barrel to $12, and Earth Resources was awash in cash thanks to Delta.

The company grew mainly via internal expansion—the only substantial

Earth Resources Company 1969 Annual Report

Throughout this report, you will see depicted community and people oriented activities. Matching personal and corporate goals is what makes ERC a "People Company". We are committed to serve our people and our community and hope that you — the Shareholders — enjoy these private scenes we share with you.

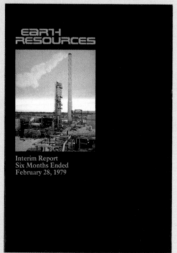

EARTH RESOURCES

Interim Report
Six Months Ended
February 28, 1979

EARTH RESOURCES

Interim Report
Nine Months Ended
May 31, 1979

EARTH RESOURCES

n Refinery,
Silver Mine
roduction

EARTH RESOURCES COMPANY
1980 ANNUAL REPORT

The annual reports for Earth Resources reflected Wyly's commitment to making a profit while making a difference in the world by respecting the planet.

acquisition after the simultaneous purchase of Delta Refining and the mining
company was the purchase of the Red Ace
chain of gas stations owned by Jimmy
Perkins of Nashville and his family. Wyly
paid them $5 million in Earth Resources
stock, and Jimmy became a vice president
for Earth Resources, and managed all the
service stations.

They changed the names of the stations to Delta and developed a logo and
marketing campaign so local consumers would identify the stations with
products produced in Memphis. Then
they set out to double their number of
locations and triple their volume sold,

In an obvious move to close the circle on the
oil-supply chain, Wyly bought the Red Ace gas
stations in the mid-'70s, changed the name to
Delta and had close to 200 stations in the South.

competing with national brands such as Gulf and Texaco, whose gas was priced
at 2¢ more per gallon at the pump (though lots of it came from the very same
Delta Refinery).

They knew their primary *business* here was retail gasoline marketing, and didn't
want to tie up millions of dollars in real estate, so they leased station sites instead
of buying them. The result was a 30-plus percent return on investment. To stay on
top of opportunity and expansion, they figured out how to get a new location open
90 days after signing a lease by using modular station designs. Delta stations also
were among the first to combine convenience store sales with gasoline sales as the
7-Eleven chain later did nationwide.

The Delta Division was on its way to having 330 stations in five states, with
1,800 employees; and thanks to its tight management and the oil crises in 1973
and 1979, it was profitable beyond all their earlier expectations.

Even with all of the excitement, growth and money from refining and retailing,
Wyly and Krausse never forgot that they were also gold and silver miners and that
their prospectors were geologists working out of Golden, Colorado, home of the

Colorado School of Mines. They were equally proficient with handpicks and electron microscopy, but their goals were the same as those of the grizzled old prospectors, the '49ers of the California gold rush and the silver miners who founded Aspen, Colorado, in the 1880s. Even though oil was evolving into Earth Resources's biggest economic engine, Sam Wyly's heart was still in the mother lode game.

Earth Resources redeveloped the century-old Nacimiento Copper Mine in northern New Mexico, west of Santa Fe, which generated decent yields for a few years, but when the price of copper dropped in 1979, the mine lost money and the company ultimately had to shut it down and take its losses. That is one of two times Wyly felt a kinship with all of the prospectors who had come before him. The other was in 1977, when his geologists and explorationists called in from a field phone to say they had found "something big!" They had discovered a significant silver lode in southwest Idaho, on the Oregon border. They named it The DeLamar Mine, for the 19th-century Idaho mining millionaire Captain Joseph DeLamar.

Almost from the moment the company took the first soil sample at the DeLamar Mine, silver prices began to climb. Some Dallas neighbors of Wyly's, the Hunt brothers, sons of one of Texas's really big rich oilmen, began buying silver in 1973 as a hedge against inflation. (Nelson Bunker Hunt was the wildcatter who had discovered oil in Libya; but in 1969, Colonel Muammar Gaddafi's army coup had nationalized the oil industry, so he tried his luck with silver.) At the time, silver was $1.95 an ounce, but the price climbed steadily, hitting $8 in early 1979, as the Hunts bought more and more silver and stashed it in Switzerland for fear the U.S. government would confiscate it. In 1979, Bunker and Herbert got together with some wealthy Saudis and bought enough silver to corner the market—200 million ounces, half the world's deliverable supply. The price of silver on the last day of 1979 was $34.45 an ounce. Within a few weeks, it hit $54—well up from the $1.95 it was at when Wyly began his silver mining venture.

Thanks to the Hunts, Earth Resources was making money hand over fist. Production at the DeLamar Mine was up to 235,000 ounces per month of silver equivalent (silver plus silver value of the gold produced). A third of the value taken from the mine—18,600 ounces—was gold. The mine had revenues of $1.3 million a month, and was judged to have 25 years of proven, unrecovered reserves.

By the end of the '70s, Earth Resources had sold off its copper and coal mines.

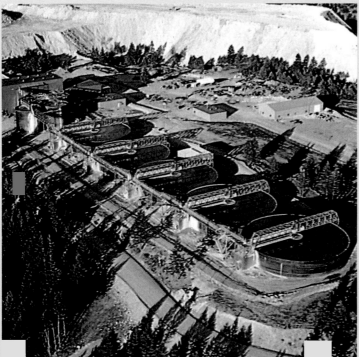

Earth Resources named its new silver mine near Silver City, Idaho, after former sea captain Joseph Raphael DeLamar, a mining magnate who opened the district in 1888 and oversaw a quick boom and bust. DeLamar came from Holland, found gold and silver out West, built a $6 million fortune, then moved to New York and bought a mansion on Long Island, where the elite continued to refer to him as "DeLamar of Idaho."

For Wyly, along with the basic thrill of hitting pay dirt, the new open pit DeLamar silver mine, which started operations in 1977, represented a hedge against inflation. Wyly's investment looked really good when the Hunt brothers started buying silver in an attempt to corner the market.

The company Wyly had begun with $10 million in 1968 had generated $744 million in revenue that year, up from $406 million the year before, with a net income of $34 million, up from $16 million the prior year. In 1980, the company took in $1 billion in revenue, and was selling 32,000 barrels of gasoline a day out of Delta Refining. The refinery at North Pole in Alaska had doubled its per-share earnings from $2.52 to $5.07 in 12 months.

That's when Sam Wyly decided it was time to cash out.

A lot of factors figured into what became a pitched battle for control of Earth Resources. One of them was Wyly's desire, beginning in 1979, to sell the DeLamar Silver Mine. His first thought was *Sell it to the Hunts.* He also began to contemplate spinning off the DeLamar Silver Mine as a public company, and asked his Drexel Burnham pals if they could market a new kind of junk bond, convertible into silver rather than stock.

They said, "Yes, we can."

What he really wanted to do was what any entrepreneur always wants to do, which is maximize the value of his company. With a spin-off, he and the other shareholders would have two stocks in place of one. One would be a bet on silver, the other a bet on oil. Markets like pure plays, just as they love hedges on inflation and companies that can be leveraged up. Earth Resources's stock was trading in the low 20s and Wyly thought it was extremely undervalued.

The silver standard: Wyly keeps this silver-bar paperweight from DeLamar Silver Mine in southwestern Idaho on his desk at home. The DeLamar Silver Mine produced 17 million ounces of silver and 230,000 ounces of gold between 1977 and late 1987. At today's prices, this would make the value of production $662 million.

He met with the Hunt brothers to talk about their buying the DeLamar mine. They told him they would buy the production of the mines for the life of the mines at a guaranteed price of $15 an ounce, with an additional price of half the difference of anything over that. With 25 years of production left, it sounded like a great opportunity, but Krausse didn't want to sell to the Hunts. "Okay," Wyly said, "then why don't we spin off the DeLamar mine?"

Krausse was against that, too, and that irritated Wyly, who decided to go over his CEO's head—he took his plan to his board for a vote, and he lost the vote by 4–3. "They are mesmerized by the profits from silver and oil and just don't understand Economics 101," a frustrated Wyly said at the time. "When prices go up ten to one, demand will drop and prices will come crashing down."

Wyly regarded Dan Krausse as a good manager who had done a great job for 12 years, but felt he was now acting like a parent who kept trying to raise his children long after they had grown up. Earth Resources had flourished under Krausse's leadership, but it was time for him to go. Every instinct Wyly had cultivated about markets over the past 20 years told him a crash was coming, and now was the time to cash out.

He feared his CEO was making the wrong decision here because his ego was in the way, so he tried another tack. "Let's sell it all, both oil and silver," he told Krausse. Again, a 4–3 board vote shot down his proposal. Wyly then decided to make it a decision by the owners of the company—not the board. A competitive shareholder vote would either settle the question or get the company sold in the process. In other words, Wyly started a proxy fight with his own company, to get it sold or merged. Hot markets don't last forever, so Wyly hired a mergers and acquisitions (M&A) banker to shop the company.

There were two suitors. Roy M. Huffington, Inc. (Huffco), was a privately held Houston company that had struck oil and gas in Indonesia and wanted into the U.S. market. Huffington (his son Michael later lost a $60 million bid to become a U.S. senator from California, and his daughter-in-law, Arianna, later started the *Huffington Post*) offered $50 a share, which would have been $350 million—about $2 billion in today's dollars. This was the proposal Krausse and the board liked, because Krausse would become CEO of the combined companies.

The second interested company was MAPCO, a publicly owned pipeline company in Tulsa. It saw Earth Resources as its chance to move into refining and distribution and become a more balanced energy company, and offered $52 a share.

There were secret meetings, angry words and closed-door votes, and the Earth Resources boardroom began to feel like a mahogany-lined OK Corral. On October 30, the MAPCO board upped its offer to $57 a share—a $400 million deal, and $40 over the price of the stock a year earlier. In response, Krausse's people recommended the $50 offer from Huffco, but when Earth Resources' stock rose to $55.25 a share, Huffco's offer was collapsed and MAPCO (and the Wyly camp) won the battle.

There were hard feelings in the aftermath. MAPCO was angry at Krausse for trying to force the Huffco deal through, and relegated him to a consultant's job, far out of the leadership role he had coveted, until his three-year employment agreement ended. Despite the fight with Krausse, who had done a good job for Wyly for a long time, Sam knew he had made the right move. "This was a time when the euphoria had gone out of all of the electronics companies and out of all the computer companies, but the euphoria was still with the oil companies," he recalls. "That year the oil companies made a third of the profit of all the companies in America. That was why I sold out of Earth Resources. We were making money like bandits in everything Earth Resources did. The gas stations, the Mississippi River barges, the trucks—everything made huge money. We started with Earth Resources when oil was $2.80 a barrel and sold it when it was forty bucks a barrel. I knew that was going to drop."

He called it correctly. Oil prices began falling in 1981 after President Reagan abolished all remaining price and allocation controls, and conservation and efficiency efforts reduced demand. They dropped all the way down to $9 a barrel by 1997, and would not get back to $40 until 2008.

The Great (Investment) North: Wyly on-site during construction of the refinery in North Pole, Alaska, near Fairbanks.

EXPLOIT THE CHAOS

The Sterling Software team (from left): Don Thomson, Sterling Williams, Bob Donachie, Sam Wyly, Charles Wyly, Harold Ergott and Phil Moore.

By 1981, Sam Wyly had been out of University Computing Company for three years. He had taken time to contemplate what had gone wrong at Datran, as well as what had gone right at University Computing's other efforts, and applied those lessons to his new task, which would focus on one thing that had gone *very* right: software.

    Wyly, the perpetual student, also decided that he wanted to learn more about his business career from a scholarly standpoint. He began to read a lot to more fully understand the booms and busts he'd been through. He did research, hoping to learn how the booming '60s became the busted '70s—both macroeconomically and microeconomically—and how this recent history aligned with his longer-run view of history. He also reaffirmed his belief that "success is the quality of the journey."

    When he asked himself, *What do I know for sure?* the answer was obvious: he knew software had to be his next big venture. The company he wanted to build would be a born-again University Computing, but focused solely on software products. And this time he wanted to do it bigger and better. The computer market had changed radically in the past decade—by 1981, even IBM conceded that it had to change tactics, and began charging competitive rates for its software. That year,

it sold $2.4 billion worth of software.[1] By 1985, that had shot up to $5 billion. IBM was ready to play hardball a new way, on a new field. Meanwhile, the integrated circuit—the microchip—had been invented by engineers at Texas Instruments and Intel, who shared a Nobel Prize for their work. The microchip would be the heart of the small, affordable personal computers coming soon.

The big question for Wyly was: what kind of software products should he sell, and for which computers? He knew there were three generic categories of software—systems software (which facilitated and controlled the processes of the computers themselves), applications software (which performed specific tasks such as accounting or word processing), and application-enabling and support software (such as code generators or database management systems). Systems software, used to improve a computer's internal performance, had been a big success for University Computing. Wyly wanted to duplicate that model, but there were new questions to answer, ones that University Computing had never faced.

Wyly, along with everyone else in the field, didn't know whether personal computer software was going to become a meaningful business, but the market seemed to be leaning that way. That market, pioneered by Apple and a hundred other start-ups that ultimately failed, was jolted when IBM announced its IBM Personal Computer on August 12, 1981—the company had outsourced the operating software to a tiny new outfit called Microsoft and the microchip to Intel, another company in its infancy. The leading PC hardware-makers back then were Tandy, Commodore and Steve Jobs's Apple. Tandy got off to a fast start selling to

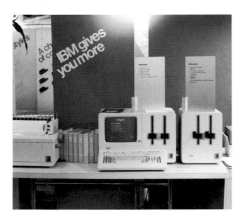

Opposite, left: Ken Olsen, Founder of Digital Equipment Corporation, in 1996. He shrank the computer, and put out a $1 million machine for $100,000. In 1986, *Fortune* called him arguably the most successful entrepreneur in the history of American business. Opposite, right: Nobel Prize winner Jack Kirby invented the integrated circuit at Texas Instruments in 1958, setting in motion Moore's law, that computer power would double every two years. Left: And voilà! IBM brought the PC to the masses in 1981.

hobbyists and tinkerers through its Radio Shack stores, but both it and Commodore were already headed for oblivion. Apple had started well, but most of the world was moving toward the "IBM standard" for PCs.

Some giddy market analysts pronounced the mainframe computer dead and said all computing would soon be done on desktops. More temperate observers—Wyly among them—believed that while PCs would be used more and more, mainframes were not going to vanish any time soon, and he wanted to focus on them, because big computers meant big companies and big margins. He believed that the voracious appetite for technology in the capital markets, which had disappeared in the 1970s (and doomed Datran), would come back in the 1980s. People, Wyly thought, would again get excited about all the great computer innovations. He thought the business was on the cusp of another dramatic shift, like what had happened in the 1960s to the benefit of University Computing, and in the 1920s for radios, and the 1850s for railroads.

He needed a brilliant team that believed in his vision.

As was his habit, Wyly turned to people he knew and trusted. He was not averse to hiring from outside—"We are all outsiders," he said—if someone's experience and performance fit his objectives, but he loved to work with people whose skills he had witnessed, whose performance ability was proven and who were comfortable with his management style. His first pick again was Don Thomson, the versatile manager who would be his chief strategist. He knew Thomson had a three-year attention span—but also that this, along with a championship team and an unstoppable attitude, would allow plenty of time to get rolling.

The two men began massaging ideas for the new company and contemplating who would make up the rest of their team. They pulled Phil Moore, the former manager of development for University Computing's banking software, into the brainstorming process. The team agreed quickly on the best target market: they would build primarily, but not exclusively, a systems software product business for IBM mainframe computers and operating systems. It was an easy call because IBM, the most valuable company in the world, with 70 percent of the U.S. mainframe market and 50 percent of the global market, dominated.

Systems software also would give the new company penetration into big and medium-sized companies across all industries instead of just niches. It was a sprawling, highly competitive and potentially lucrative universe. Rapid changes in technology and markets were creating the kind of chaos that Wyly loved to exploit. Wyly knew Big Blue's aggressive new strategy meant that, after years of underpricing software to help it sell more hardware, it would be charging more competitive rates, which meant there would be some serious sticker shock for its long-standing customers, who would probably soon be willing to give a longer look at alternatives. And, too, IBM had become a vast bureaucracy—he knew that top managers could take two years to make a simple decision. To a former too-small nose guard who had been quick, nimble and smart enough to beat bigger opponents, this felt like a great opportunity.

Wyly's next major strategic decision was to build this new company on mostly acquisitions, not inventions. This was the opposite tack to what he had taken at University Computing, but it would make it possible to get to the market faster, and get revenue flowing. They knew that developing complex mainframe software could take years and cost millions. The key to fast growth and profitability here, they determined, was to identify and acquire software products in high-growth niches early—not unlike how today's Cisco has been buying upwards of 150 small, and not-so-small, companies.

Wyly decided to capitalize the company by adapting a technique used in the oil business in Texas called a "roll-up": Someone with producing wells would convince other operators to bundle their wells with his own so they would have a big enough company to get public equity capital. This would enable them to grow with the cash they'd raised and use their public stock to acquire more producing wells, or to drill new wells in proven fields or wildcat in hopes of discovering a new oil field. "Why can't we do the same kind of thing for a software company?" Wyly asked his lawyer.

"Yeah, you could probably do that," he answered. "I don't think anybody has ever done it in software, but then nobody had ever done some of these other deals we've done either."

Wyly's vision was to make this new venture a kind of holding company, investing in both majority and minority positions in software companies. It would buy parts of smaller companies—or even just shares of products—and roll up their ownership into one large enterprise. His company would ask for the option to buy out a target company with either cash or stock. The aim was to offer the smaller companies the benefits of a big company—money, marketing support and industry expertise—in a volatile, wickedly competitive industry.

Now he needed a CEO.

His first and only candidate was Sterling Williams, who had been Wyly's top sales rep and then a profit center manager at University Computing back in the '70s. And Williams was available—after a set-to with the new top manager at University Computing, he had left in 1978, shortly after Wyly had departed. Williams had later been recruited to run a software company, which he had got up to $10 million in annual profit, but when it was bought

Sterling Williams (above, with wife Barbara, on a cruise to Santa Catalina Island in California) led Sterling Software, which Wyly named after him. It was the first of two Wyly companies that would bear Williams's name.

by the French giant Schlumberger, he'd gone looking for work and had called Wyly.

"I hear you're starting up that new software company," Williams said.

"That's right, and I want you to come down here and run it."

"What about my options in Schlumberger?" asked Williams.

"Cash them out. Grab the money and run."

"Why should I do that?" Williams asked, thinking that stock would keep rising. Wyly gave him a 30-second investment lesson: "Schlumberger is part of the oil price bubble that is doomed to end in destitution. Go to Value Line—it lists the market value of all the companies in the world and Schlumberger is the number three most valuable. They are a good oil field services company with a charming French name, but are they worth almost as much as IBM or Exxon? No way. This is a bubble."

Williams later said, "It was the shortest job interview of my life," and signed on for this new venture. (Wyly was right about the Schlumberger stock—after hitting a peak in 1980, oil prices and oil stocks began a six-year decline, culminating in a 46 percent collapse in 1986.[2])

Wyly, Thomson, Williams and the rest of his team now set about compiling a list of potential acquisitions, but there were hundreds of attractive companies and they needed a complete overview of the industry, as well as access to decision-makers. On April 16,

"One of the best brains we had in Sterling Software," Wyly said of Werner Frank, who was a genuine rocket scientist.

1981, Wyly and Phil Moore, another recruit from his UCC days, flew to San Antonio to meet with Larry Welke, the software industry publisher who knew almost every player in the business. The occasion of their meeting was Welke's annual ICP Million Dollar Awards—the software industry's Oscars—and more than 200 of the industry's most successful companies were there.

"Phil and I sat down with Larry and asked what opportunities there were for acquisitions," recalls Wyly. The subject of this conversation was in itself revolutionary, because company buyouts had been rare in the software industry. Most vendors built products that complemented theirs, and most growth was done through sales. All of that was about to change: two of the companies at that 1981 conference—Wyly's not-yet-named company and the Long Island, New York–based Computer Associates—would buy more than 100 companies by the end of the decade.

On May 19, 1981, a month after meeting with Welke, Wyly made his initial acquisition, for $800,000. He bought 40 percent of Directions, a banking software company owned by Ed Lott, who had sold his previous company to University Computing. Directions became the anchor of their banking software division.

This deal diverged from Wyly's strategic plan for building a systems software enterprise, but he had several reasons for buying into Directions. One was the quality of Lott's software. Another was Phil Moore's experience in banking software. Wyly also knew Lott had earned the respect of the senior executives of the 100 biggest banks in America, who were certain to be systems software customers. His Irish sense of humor was a bonus.

The team now set to work formalizing their process for rolling up new products and companies: The products had to be old enough to be proven commodities, but young enough to have a fecund future. And taken together, they had to make a coherent portfolio, not a hodgepodge of disparate ventures. One of the tools they used to evaluate prospects was a matrix called Grad's Grid, devised by former IBMer turned independent consultant Burt Grad, a relentlessly smart, high-energy Derringer of a man who had been in the computing world since the '50s. Wyly and Williams hired him as a consultant and made him a key member of their brain trust.

Grad says he devised his grid because his mind had always worked that way. "I had done work twenty years before in decision tables at General Electric," Grad says. "For whatever reason, my world sets up in rows and columns." Thinking that

Burt Grad developed a matrix called Grad's Grid that Sterling Software relied on to identify attractive targets in its aggressive acquisition strategy. The grid compared essential features of companies and products and mapped their compatibility with Sterling's goals and technology.

		BUSINESS STRUCTURE MATRIX			12/15/81
		Mainframe (IBM)	Distributed Systems	Mini Computers	Micro Computers
Systems Programs		OS DOS		PICK UNIX PASCAL	CP/M PASCAL MS/DOS UNIX
	Control Systems	Operating Systems Utilities Data Base Data Commun.			
	Development Methodology	RAMIS FOCUS MARK V DMS	DMS	RPG TAPS	DBMS's BASIC
Cross-Industry Applications Programs		Scientific Text processing Education/Trning Graphics Mfg. Control		Accounting Payroll/Per- sonnel Order entry Inv. control Graphics Word processing	VISICALC Accounting Packages

Industry Application Programs		For each industry
		segment --
		. administration/
		    accounting
		. operations
		. processes
				For OEM's --
				by vendor;
				by industry
				(or sub-
				    industry);
				by geography	

way, he was able to find order in any chaos. Among his credits was the complex categorization for Welke's massive *ICP Software Directory*, which covered more than 6,000 categorized and cross-indexed software products. Grad's Grid showed product types, hardware platforms, required operating systems, industry applicability, product features and more. Simply by coloring in the squares in the matrix, potential acquisitions could be quickly identified or eliminated. "There would be a portion of the matrix which we were definitely not interested in," says Grad. "And there would be a portion of the matrix where we would apply strategic opportunism."

"Strategic opportunism," in Wyly's mind, meant: *Pounce!*

"Burt is an encyclopedia," Wyly said of Burt Grad, the Sterling Software consultant. "He knows everything."

Grad's grids did not replace due diligence or personal interaction with the principals—these were handled once a deal was officially being considered—but they allowed the team to rapidly identify companies that might be good roll-up candidates.

In November 1981, Sterling Williams called Don Thomson. They were going to go to an industry conference in Las Vegas to check out potential acquisitions. "Don, we need a name for our company because we've got to register," Williams said. "We've got to have it on our name badges."

Sterling said, "Let's name it Wyly Software."

Thomson called Wyly to clear that, but Wyly said, without hesitation, "No. It is going to be called Sterling Software."

Thomson thought for a moment. "SSI—that's great!"

"Nope," Wyly said. "I hate acronyms. We're going to call it Sterling Software."

Thomson hung up and called Williams back. "Sam says the company is going to be called Sterling Software."

"*What?*" Williams said.

"And not SSI or any other acronym. It will be Sterling Software."

Williams thought for a minute, then said, "That's pretty neat."

Wyly later explained that he liked "Sterling" because it was the name of money used in Great Britain from the days when the sun never set on the British Empire and it was the most trusted currency in the world. He also told his team something his mother had told him when he was a boy. "We don't buy plated silver," she said. "We buy sterling silver because it's the highest quality."

"Sterling," he told his team, "is a quality name—in silver, in currency, in Williamses—and we will make it a quality name in software."

Wyly wanted to grow Sterling Software intelligently but quickly, and he needed a lot more cash than his family had. By 1982, the Dow Jones average had finally gotten back to where it had been 14 years earlier, but on an inflation-adjusted basis, from 1968 to 1982 over half the value of the USA's stock market's capital had been destroyed by inflation.

One timely precedent for Sterling Software had already been established in the software industry—in 1978, John Cullinane's database software company had surprised the industry when he took his company public. It was the first purely software products company to become publicly owned, and would become the first with a $1 billion valuation. It planted the idea of public money in the heads of a lot of software company executives who had started their businesses in a spare bedroom, and in the heads of their investors. Four years later, Apple would be valued at $2.5 billion.

Wyly was a veteran of public companies and knew the equity markets could change the landscape in a hurry. He sensed an opening here, one that would be useful in capitalizing Sterling Software, but he did not know how long the window would stay open.

Two companies would be particularly formidable foes. One was Computer Associates, and the other, ironically, was Wyly's original company, University Computing, now led by Greg Liemandt, the third CEO since Wyly had left. Liemandt was a non-computer guy out of General Electric's conglomerate world,

Sam Wyly Starts $300M Comm Carrier Venture

By Johanna Ambrosio

The latest long-distance resale carrier to take advantage of new markets created by the AT&T divestiture is a $300-million start-up being formed by well-known entrepreneur Sam Wyly.

The firm expects to begin offering its digital voice and data services within six months and will be competitive in terms of both price and service quality with AT&T and other common carriers, Wyly said. The Dallas-based company is currently known as Wyly Telecommunications, but its name soon will be changed to Netamerica.

Previous Wyly ventures include the Wyly Corp. and its University Computing Co. subsidiary, a software and computer services firm, in which he sold his majority share in 1977, and Sterling Software Inc., formed last year to acquire applications and systems packages. All are based in Dallas.

Netamerica, under development for two years, will offer services such as 56K-bit-per-second dial-up and facsimile transmission capabilities via a combination of satellite and terrestrial facilities. The firm will initially target Fortune 1,000 firms and smaller resale carriers, but will eventually go after vertical industries as well.

"We'll be emphasizing those services where the digital network has an advantage over analog in speed, quality or price," Wyly said.

The firm also intends to market communications hardware and is currently negotiating with suppliers. Its in-house engineering staff is also researching projects such as how to tie

Above: NetAmerica was Wyly's second quixotic attempt to build a "telephone company for computers," this time using satellites, but it, too, crashed on the rocks of laws that protected the AT&T monopoly. In 1981, the NetAmerica team (above, front row) included Wyly, Ray Cotten (left) and Ed Jungerman, two veterans of Datran. Cotten was the marketing genius; Jungerman was the engineering genius.

Left: Wyly and Bill Hunt, NetAmerica's CEO, celebrating the bust-up of the telephone monopoly that had stifled competition—and innovation—for decades.

NET AMERICA

**Toll-quality satellite network services
at down-to-earth wholesale prices
for large-scale users**

- A satellite-based switched digital
  backbone network.
- Rates based on the user's *total* volume.
- Unique transmission plan with echo
  cancellation.
- Digital technology virtually end-to-end.

wherein growth came from buyouts. And he knew from watching the University Computing software numbers that systems software was the way to go. Since its best moneymakers were the software products developed under Wyly, Sam was now competing against himself.

Working with a small Dallas underwriter, Wyly took Sterling Software public in May of 1983, selling 1.7 million shares at $9, netting $14 million. Once again, his timing had been perfect. Thirty days later, the market for tech stocks collapsed. There were 85 tech IPOs in 1983; the next year there were only eight. In addition to adding more products with the proceeds, the owners of some of the acquired companies became "owners" in Sterling Software.

Software companies sell intellectual property—program code—and this raised vital questions for Sterling about how many and which employees of an acquired company to keep. By the mid-'80s, software company acquisitions were being done in one of two ways: one, most employees in an acquired company were dismissed, while the acquirer kept just the contracts and the monthly revenue; or two, key employees stayed and continued to sell and support the same products. Sterling Software chose the latter model, and usually retained most of the top professionals and managers.

Wyly wanted to maintain strong customer technical service, something he'd learned at IBM and University Computing. Sterling's acquisitions would not be gutted of their technical and support staffs just because customers were contractually "locked in" to their installed products by their own years-long investments of time and money.

Wyly watched with bemusement as the ruthless strip-the-acquisition approach being used with lucrative results by his competitor Computer Associates ripped through company after company. With its first acquisition—Capex—chairman Charles Wang either laid off all the employees or saw them quit rather than work in his autocratic regime. Software workers worldwide trembled at any rumor CA was seeking to buy them.

CA's model was to quickly cut expenses, absorb most of the new work with existing staff and vigorously collect maintenance fees (including suing customers for them). This approach bumped short-term profits, which Wall Street applauded, but it made many customers feel abused.

Conversely, Sterling was growing through high-quality acquisitions, and its development dollars were being used to enhance and integrate what it acquired, with superior management at all levels. It retained top sales and support specialists from the acquired companies, looking for all the best talent in the newly combined company. And customers were lavished with services, not threats.

Sterling Software was really a business-building concept, not a cost-cutting concept. That said, there is always going to be some overlapping work in a merger, and some job redundancy was inevitable. Wyly was determined to make changes that strengthened the business, and to also improve the lives of his new people. After identifying the best products and best people, Sterling dealt quickly and candidly with those who did not have a job going forward.

"You have to be honest about it with everybody," he says. "And if you aren't, then all your people will know it and you will have a poisoned environment. That's when you begin to fail. And we were not going to fail."

Endnotes

1   The 1981 financial data came from IBM, but from 1979—when the first estimate was made of the company's software products revenue for the ICP 50, the top 50 software companies ranked by revenue and published by ICP, Inc.—the data had to be gathered from seven different sources because IBM did not bother to issue an aggregated portrait of its software sales. That changed by 1985, when its software activities became strategic.

2   Oil price statistics from the Energy Information Administration's Annual Energy Review for 2006, page 174.

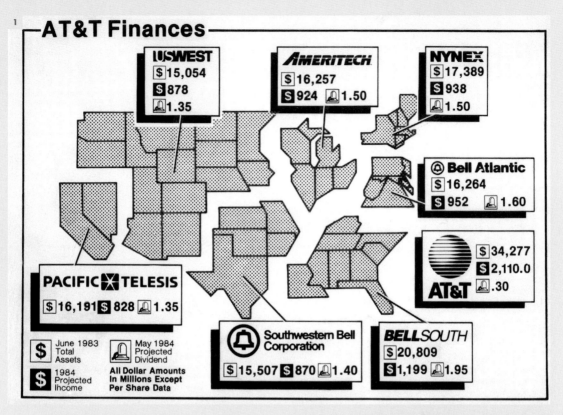

AT&T Finances

USWEST
$ 15,054
$ 878
1.35

AMERITECH
$ 16,257
$ 924   1.50

NYNEX
$ 17,389
$ 938
1.50

Bell Atlantic
$ 16,264
$ 952   1.60

AT&T
$ 34,277
$ 2,110.0
.30

PACIFIC TELESIS
$ 16,191 $ 828 1.35

$ June 1983 Total Assets

May 1984 Projected Dividend

$ 1984 Projected Income

All Dollar Amounts In Millions Except Per Share Data

Southwestern Bell Corporation
$ 15,507 $ 870 1.40

BELLSOUTH
$ 20,809
$ 1,199 1.95

Ding, dong, Ma Bell is dead! In 1982, AT&T agreed to break itself up into eight entities (1). This bust-up led directly to the birth of the Internet, the telecommunications revolution and more. It was truly "last call" at Illinois Bell's Chicago service center (2), where discarded phones piled up as customers lined up for their last chance to exchange, repair or buy phones before Illinois Bell broke off from AT&T on January 1, 1983. Trading of stock for US West (3) and other divested AT&T companies began in November of that year. Southwestern Bell (SBC) later bought Pacific Telephone, plus AT&T. Then AT&T, at the time called SBC, bought Sterling Commerce for $4 billion. Then they took AT&T as their name. Today only AT&T and Verizon survive.

MUDSLINGING CO
SOFTWARE COUN

After being snubbed by Informatics Chairman Walter F. Bauer, Wyly raised his bid to $130 million and vowed, "We are not ever going away."

STE LI G'S WYLY, A VET   A CO PO ATE SC A

CHAPTER ELEVEN

HOW JONAH SWALLOWED THE WHALE

At the end of 1984, Sterling Software's annual revenue was just less than $20 million, good numbers in a densely populated young industry, but not among its top 25 in revenue. There were a lot of opportunities—more than 6,000 software products listed in the January 1985 *ICP Software Directory*—but getting the right product mix, Wyly said, "was a matter of seeking simplicity in complexity. Remember how to KISS? 'Keep It Simple, Stupid.'"

Before making an acquisition, the Sterling team evaluated the features and functions of each product, the skills of the technical and sales people, and then the numbers. If Sterling only wanted a single product, it sometimes had to buy the whole company to get it. To grow, Wyly had to get workers with intimate knowledge of their product, market and customer base. To cause the least disruption possible to customers, he was determined to keep good teams intact. It was conventional wisdom in software that you couldn't do a hostile takeover because "the brains go home every night in the elevator." Everyone knew that key employees would abandon unwelcome new ownership in a heartbeat, and were only too happy to reunite elsewhere in the technology corridors of Austin, Boston or California.

No rule was followed more religiously. The software industry was now 25 years old, and there had never been a single hostile takeover.

But once again, Wyly was going to shake things up.

Wyly had been thinking about how to become 10 times bigger, and he decided the best way was not by swallowing lots of little Jonahs, but by having little Jonah swallow the whale.

Founded in 1962 in Woodland Hills, California, Informatics General Corporation had grown into a $200 million industry powerhouse with 10,000 customers. Its flagship product was MARK IV, a file management and report generation product launched in November 1967. It had been an instant hit, and by 1985, it had cumulative sales of $100 million. Wyly saw the MARK IV as a cash cow that had no potential for growth; and buried deep within Informatics was the product that mesmerized him: OrderNet. It went unmentioned in the company's PR material and was unknown and unloved at corporate headquarters. Its job was to facilitate online purchase orders and invoices. It was a document transmission package that harkened back to Wyly's old Datran dream of merging computers and telephones. He was going to swallow the whale just to get that one product.

Wyly and his team had looked at Informatics from every angle, and run all the numbers many times. Burt Grad knew the company and Walter Bauer, its stern, bureaucratic CEO, well. Also Informatics' cofounder, Werner Frank, a powerful intellect, had joined Wyly's team after being pushed out of Informatics two years earlier.

Wyly knew Bauer did not want to sell Informatics and turn in his crown, but he knew the software industry was evolving from old programmers who had started in garages to professional managers running publicly owned companies with governance responsibilities to shareholders. Merrill Lynch's all-star analyst, Steve McClellan, described Bauer as stodgy. "Walter F. Bauer, the longtime chairman . . . has managed the firm too autocratically and too monotonously for too long," said McClellan. "As long as Bauer remains in charge, don't look for big dynamics here."

Werner Frank (right) is congratulated by Larry Welke, who ran the first publication to pay any serious attention to software products. The first issue of Welke's *ICP Quarterly*, in January 1967, had 110 products from 50 sellers, all banking- and accounting-related. By 1975, the *ICP Software Directory*, as it came to be called, would list 3,000 products from 800 vendors in 350 categories. After personal computers were launched, the industry exploded. Welke's annual ICP Million Dollar Awards—shown here in year 1978 when Frank was still with Informatics—were the Oscars of the software industry.

Wyly agreed. His team had been looking at public data on Informatics for months, and had created rough mathematical models on both relevant and irrelevant business lines. He already knew pretty much what he would keep and what he would liquidate. He also knew that insider control of Informatics was vulnerable—its stock was depressed and erratic, and it was underperforming by lots of standards. So Wyly kept tabs on the company, and waited.

Early in 1985, Bauer himself made a move. On January 7, he called Werner Frank to float the idea of selling to Sterling Software a product line called ANSWER. Frank and Sterling Williams met Bauer at the Regency Club in Los Angeles a month later. After some preliminary supper patter about the ANSWER products, the conversation took an abrupt swing when Bauer revealed the true reason he had asked for this meeting: he wanted to buy Sterling Software. His dinner partners were stunned.

Williams recoiled at the idea, even though Bauer said he wanted Williams to be president of the combined companies, under him. Williams said later, with a smile, "I was getting bribed before dessert."

The next morning, Wyly got a fax:

"Sam,

 I met with Walter and here is what he said:

• It turned out he didn't want us to buy his products.

• He wanted to buy our products.

• Then he really wanted to buy our company.

• But he really wanted to buy our company and have me run it.

• And I'm not even sure he wanted to buy the company. I think he was really recruiting at the end of the day.

So, what do you think we ought to do? —Sterling"

Wyly quickly wrote three words on top of the memo and faxed it back to Williams in Los Angeles: "Let's buy *them*!"

Williams reminded him that there had never been a hostile takeover in the software industry.

"This is different," Wyly told him. "The company has some superb talent that has just never been enabled. Only Bauer and a few people in their headquarters will view us as 'conquerors.' Down in the trenches, the people who produce and sell the products will view us as 'liberators.'"

Sterling Software's pockets were not as deep as Informatics', but ever since the founding of University Computing in 1963, Wyly had believed capitalization was merely a matter of persistence and creativity. As long as the borrower had collateral, character and bank credit, capital could be created. And he knew a publicly traded stock was also currency.

Tech stocks were down and money was hard to come by from conventional lenders in 1985—some commercial banks were even canceling bank credit lines. Sterling had $12 million cash from its IPO, plus a secondary stock sale it had closed a few months after, when the price was more than twice what it had been at the IPO. But it was going to have to find another $140 million cash.

Wyly's team began to outline a strategy for a "hostile" leveraged buyout. First he wanted a toehold and a hedge. He knew that buying Informatics stock would put it "in play," and that Sterling might then lose the deal to someone who could pay more. If that happened, they would still make a profit on the "toehold" stock they had purchased— hopefully enough to pay the legal and banker fees they would incur in the takeover bid, and at some higher (future) price for the stock, it would be wiser—and more profitable—to lose rather than win this war.

Sterling bought 4.9 percent of Informatics' stock— any more than that would have triggered a filing threshold—and then Williams asked Wyly the $140 million question: "Where are we going to get all that money?"

"We'll get it from Drexel. Mike Milken will sign a letter that says Drexel is 'highly confident' they can sell our bonds once we combine the two companies. That letter will be all we need to motivate a majority of the stockholders to tender their shares into our offer. It won't matter if Bauer and his board oppose it. Once we have

Wyly's version of "In case of emergency, break glass"—Drexel helped him raise cash for many acquisitions, a few takeovers and an IPO.

shares tendered equal to 51 percent or more, Drexel's bond buyers will put up the cash we need to close the purchase. That's how it will all come together."

It was now time to talk to Walter Bauer. Wyly bought another five percent of the company over a five-day period, and then he and some lawyers flew out to California. Wyly set up a breakfast meeting for just Bauer, Sterling and himself. Bauer, who believed the meeting was to negotiate the offer he had made to buy Sterling Software, opened with, "Gee, our stock's really been doing well lately."

Wyly smiled, and said, "We know why—we've just finished buying nine-point-nine percent of your company yesterday, and we intend to buy the rest."

Bauer was suddenly the palest man in Southern California.

Later that day, he invited Williams and Wyly over to his home, with lawyers this time, and Bauer's lawyer made the usual speech that Informatics did not wish to sell, and Wyly's lawyer reiterated that Sterling intended to buy the company. It was time to man the battle stations—Sterling's announcement of its 9.9 percent was published and the war was on.

"We literally moved from Dallas to a hotel in West Los Angeles and set up a war room," recalls Werner Frank. "We brought in equipment and telephone lines and lived there for a month."

It was at this point that Burt Grad, the consultant, found himself to be very popular—and very uncomfortable. "I got five different calls," he says. "One from Sterling—could I work with them? No. Informatics is my client. One from Informatics—could I work with them? No, because Sterling is my client. I got a call from General Atlantic, who wanted to be the 'white knight'—the one to buy the company because Bauer didn't want to sell to Sam. I got called by Morgan Stanley, who wanted in on any deal, somehow or the other. But I had to stay out of it."

"It was white-collar warfare," recalls Frank. "Hiring lawyers, accountants, bankers, financial analysts, private detectives, doing some cloak-and-dagger stuff—nothing illegal. There were lawsuits and countersuits. Then other people tried to take advantage of the situation, both inside and outside the company."

Informatics' lawyers pushed for a management buyout. One of the employees invited to bet some of his savings on this scheme was Warner Blow, who ran a division in Cleveland, Ohio. Blow signed on for the plan because he didn't want to be owned by Sterling. He knew that Sterling Software was a software products enterprise and his OrderNet was a document services unit, so he had a nagging fear that his unit would be cast adrift in the takeover. He imagined that his division would be sold off or shut down. He had no idea that Wyly was doing this whole takeover more to get OrderNet than any other product.

Other people in the industry were opposed to Wyly's hostile takeover, even if they didn't have a dog in this fight. Some saw Walter Bauer as a symbol of paternal leadership in the industry. Some said, "Shouldn't he be accorded more respect? If this could happen to him, are any of us safe?"

But to Wyly, this wasn't about respect, this was about business, about getting the most from your products and your people, and he knew he was the man to do that for Informatics. Drexel quickly committed the $140 million Wyly needed. The barbarians were at the gates.

On March 22, Sterling Software offered a deal at $23 a share. As expected, Informatics' board rejected it. The share price then began to rise, as other buyers swooped in. On April 16, Transcontinental and Maxxam both declared that they each owned 331,500 shares.

A week later, another 200,000 shares were bought. It seemed possible that a second and third bidder were collaborating to buy Informatics—or at least drive up the price. Wyly wondered, *Do they have a legitimate interest in acquiring Informatics? Do they have the ability? Have they been invited in by Bauer and promised greenmail just to run up the price in the hope of making Sterling Software go away, or pay more? Or are arbitragers buying the stock to sell into my deal and make a quick buck?*

A few weeks later, the Sterling Software team met with some of Informatics' largest shareholders. The best ownership for Informatics, the Sterling team said, would be experienced software people who could move the company forward, not just sell off its assets for a quick killing. And Sterling would raise the price to $27 if these big owners would commit to tender.

After that meeting, the two independent directors at Informatics began to tell Bauer: "We don't hear any other bid. The Sterling deal is financed. The bankers would not fund your management buyout. Think about our downside risks!" That turned the battle, and won the war.

On June 22, Informatics agreed to the Sterling buyout and Sterling commenced purchasing Informatics shares under its tender offer of $27. On August 8, Maxxam

Informatics Rejects Sterling Software Takeover Proposal

DTH 4-25

Sterling Software files suit against Informatics

By KATHRYN JONES
Staff Writer

Refusing to give up its take-over attempt of Informatics General Corp., Dallas-based Sterling Software has filed suit against the much larger California software company to force it to provide Sterling with a list of its shareholders.

In a filing with the Securities and Exchange Commission, Sterling said it filed suit in Delaware state court after Informatics rebuffed a request for a list of its shareholders.

Meanwhile, a proxy fight is shaping up for Informatics' May 9 annual meeting. Sterling said it is considering a proxy contest, but only if Informatics refuses to be acquired. Informatics, based in Woodland Hills, Calif., plans to ask shareholders at the meeting to approve anti-takeover and anti-greenmail provisions.

Sterling already owns about 9.3 percent of Informatics. Earlier this week, the company raised its offer to acquire Informatics to $26 share in cash, up $1 from its previous offer of $25 for the estimated 5 million outstanding shares of common stock, or about $125 million.

In attempting to gobble up the larger company, Sterling hopes to broaden its line of systems software for large International Business Machines Corp. computers and banking software.

Informatics, which develops software for retail, business and legal applications, had $4.4 million in profits and $212 million in revenues last year. Sterling reported $1.4 million in profits on revenues of $18.7 million.

Hostile takeovers were rare in the software business, but Wyly thought Informatics was being badly run, was underperforming and would be a great fit for Sterling. For four long months, he waged a bidding contest to make sure Informatics shareholders knew the true story of what Sterling was offering, and what they would be missing if they stayed with their current leadership. Each side bought full-page page ads in *The Wall Street Journal* to denounce the other. In the end, the board capitulated and Sterling got the company.

Informatics ripe for a takeover

But Sterling bid termed 'inadequate' by directors

By ANDREA ADELSON
Daily News Staff Writer

Haunted by lackluster profits and with its stock slumping last year, Informatics General Corp. fits the classic example of a takeover target waiting to happen.

The Woodland Hills-based software concern, with 400 of its 2,600 employees in the San Fernando Valley, has a bankroll of $37 million and little debt, a sure temptation for a takeover specialist looking to buy a company with its own cash.

Surprisingly, no corporate raider had moved until Sterling Software Inc. came calling last week. But Informatics board last Monday scoffed at the Dallas-based firm's $25 a share offer, calling it "inadequate." The company then formed a committee to search for "alternatives to maximize shareholder values" — boardroom parlance for a better deal.

So far, the company hasn't disclosed if any rescuing "white knights" have come forward. Informatics hasn't even put out a memo to employees on what Sterling proposed, according to a source close to the company.

But Sterling Chairman Sam Wyly said in an interview from his Malibu Colony home he won't be easily put off. An entrepreneur who has started three companies since 1963, Wyly is well connected among Wall Street's investment community.

And he appears to possess the bankroll to sweeten his initial $125 million offer. Wyly's name surfaced last week among other financial heavyweights backing Texas T. Boone Pickens' takeover try for Unocal Corp. Wyly put up $5 million and Sterling chipped in an equal amount for Pickens' "junk bonds."

The looming takeover skirmish for Informatics is likely to unfold at the annual shareholders meeting on May 9, sources said. Informatics' board isn't scheduled to convene before then, company spokesman Chris Richter said.

At first glance, the proposed marriage looks like a mismatch. Sterling, with revenues of $19 million, is trying to buy out a company that had sales of $193 million.

But the faceoff between Wyly and Informatics Chairman Walter Bauer doesn't seem so strange to analysts and former Informatics executives. Bauer declined to be interviewed for this article.

Informatics is one of only a few companies in the software industry with broad experience, creating programs for big and small computers and for a range of uses, said Jack Keen, vice president of the Manhattan View-based market research firm Input. The "smorgasbord approach," as Keen called it, is a trait the highly specialized software industry has so far shunned.

Informatics pursuit of customized programming and systems for customers ranging from NASA to Transamerica Corp. will be viewed as a strength when the market becomes more sophisticated and demands a range of solutions, Keen said. "People underestimate Informatics because it has had its up and down," he said.

Ray Hannon, a spokesman for Sterling in Dallas, had the same sentiment. "We see in this merger strength for both sides," he said.

While Sterling may be the minnow trying to swallow a whale, Keen believes Wyly holds an important means to snag its prize. "The key is the people who are running Sterling," Keen said.

Among those is Wyly himself, an entrepreneur and financial wizard. Second is Sterling's president, Sterling Williams, who helped build Wyly's first company into a $200 million-a-year company. Lastly is Werner Frank, who helped found Informatics but left a top post at the company after a lower-ranking executive was named president. He joined Sterling last October after a stint as a consultant.

In an interview, Frank refused to say what role he may play in a merged company. He heads Sterling's systems software group, which is located in Calabasas.

Sterling was created through the acquisition of six smaller firms in the last two years. One of those is Dylakor in Granada Hills.

Wyly's career began in 1963 when he founded University Computer Co. Ultimately the company was bought by three investors and now exists as Uccel Corp. In the early 1970s, he founded Datran, a data communications company that failed in 1976.

Datran's legacy, however, was a $50 million judgement won from American Telephone & Telegraph in 1980. Datran's antitrust suit was instrumental in AT&T's breakup.

The company Wyly is seeking was founded in 1962 by Bauer, Frank, Richard Hill, John Postley and Frank Wagner, all colleagues at Ramo-Wooldridge, an aerospace firm that became TRW Inc. of Redondo Beach. Bauer, who has the additional posts of president and chief executive, is the only founder still actively involved.

Hill is Honeywell Corp.'s liaison to Microelectronics and Computer Technology Corp., the Austin computer consortium. Postley heads a software company of the same name in Van Nuys. Wagner, retired, and a Pacific Palisades resident, is editing a book written by an Informatics archivist outlining the company's history 20 years.

STERLING'S BID FOR INFORMATICS GENERAL

SAM WYLY

WALTER F. BAUER

Informatics' financial picture
Dollar amounts in millions, except per share earnings. Years ended Dec. 31.

	1984		1984
$191.5	Operating revenues		$152.1
$5.9	Revenues from investments		$3.2
$6.3	Income (cont. operations)		$5.7
$1.12	Per share earnings		$1.10
$6.9	Long-term debt		$6.3
$81.9	Cash on hand		$1.3
$36.7	Short term investments		$46.5
2,600	Number of employees		2,600

Sterling ready to sweeten bid, filings show

By Jim Mitchell
Staff Writer of The News

Sterling Software Inc., whose offer to buy Informatics General Corp. was rejected last week, apparently is prepared to sweeten its offer to purchase the Woodland Hills, Calif., computer products and services firm.

In filings with the Securities and Exchange Commission, Dallas-based Sterling also said it will attempt to have two of its officers elected to Informatics board of directors and plans to oppose anti-takeover measures Informatics wants to add to its charter.

Sterling was informed by its financial adviser, Drexel Burnham Lambert Inc., that it is "highly confident that it can arrange financing for Sterling Software's merger with Informatics General for $26 a share."

That would be $1 a share more than Sterling had offered Informatics in discussions earlier this month. The new offer is valued at about $130 million, about $5 million more than Sterling had offered.

On Tuesday, Sterling and Informatics officials would not comment on the matter. Since mid-March, Sterling quietly has acquired about 9.3 percent of the estimated 5 million outstanding shares of Informatics common stock.

Formed in the early 1980s, Sterling Software employs about 200 people. In the fiscal year ended Sept. 30, 1984, Sterling earned $1.4 million or 25 cents a share on revenue of $18.7 million. During the first quarter of its 1985 fiscal year, Sterling earned $247,000 or 6 cents a share on revenue of $4.9 million.

Sterling officials said acquiring Informatics would broaden Sterling's software product line. About 75 percent of Sterling's business comes from systems software for large-scale IBM computers. Specialized software for banking applications make up the remainder of Sterling's business.

Established in 1962, Informatics employs about 2,800 people. In 198(—) the company earned $4.42 million or 82 cents a share on revenue of $212 million. Its product line includes software for retail, business and legal applications.

Informatics plans to ask shareholders at the company's May 9 annual meeting to approve anti-takeover and anti-greenmail provisions.

THE WALL STREET JOURNAL, FRIDAY, MAY

informatics
general corporation.

Important Notice to Shareholders of Informatics General Corporation from your Board's Special Committee

Your Board of Directors has unanimously determined that the unsolicited merger proposal announced by Sterling Software, Inc. is inadequate.

Sterling has made only a conditional merger proposal for Informatics at $26 per share. Sterling has begun a solicitation of proxies in opposition to the proposal to amend Informatics Certificate of Incorporation. Sterling is also proposing that you vote for the election of Mr. Sam Wyly and Mr. Sterling Williams to the Board of Directors of your Company so that they may seek to effect an acquisition of Informatics on their terms, which the Board and Smith Barney, Harris Upham & Co. Incorporated, a leading investment bank, believe are inadequate.

We strongly urge you to vote FOR the Board's candidates and FOR the proposed charter amendment.

Informatics studies takeover options

Informatics General Corp. said Wednesday it is exploring several alternatives to Dallas-based Sterling Software's bid to acquire the company, including a possible acquisition by an investment group that includes Informatics management and a possible sale to a "substantial corporation."

Sterling Software To Buy Informatics For $126 Million

A Sterling Performance In The Repackaging Of Informatics

Sterling reaches merger agreement with Informatics

By Jim Mitchell
Staff Writer of The News

Sterling Software Inc. has reached an agreement to acquire Informatics General Corp. in a transaction valued at $135 million, ending a several-month takeover battle.

"The acquisition of Informatics is consistent with Sterling's long-term strategy of acquiring companies in the software industry which have a significant potential for growth and increased market share," said Sam Wyly, Sterling's chairman, in a formal statement that accompanied the merger announcement.

Under the agreement, Sterling will acquire all of the outstanding shares of the Woodland Hills, Calif., computer products and services firm for $27 a share. The agreement is contingent on Sterling being able to arrange financing for the acquisition by July 17 and to begin the tender offer by June 27, the companies said. Informatics' board has recommended that shareholders tender their shares to Sterling.

Sterling Williams, president of Sterling Software, will become Informatics' chief executive officer. Walter Bauer will remain Informatics' chairman.

Dallas-based Sterling Software had quietly begun acquiring Informatics' common stock on March 13 and now holds about 9.3 percent of the estimated 5 million outstanding shares of Informatics common stock.

Informatics' board had rejected earlier offers of $25 a share and $26 a share from Sterling, contending that the offers were not in the best interests of the

Sterling Williams, president of Sterling Software, will become Informatics' chief executive officer. Walter Bauer will remain Informatics' chairman.

company or its shareholders. Sterling then launched an unsuccessful proxy fight for control of Informatics board.

As the battle became heated, both companies exchanged full-page advertisements in national publications.

Formed in the early 1980s, Sterling Software employs about 200 people. In the fiscal year ended Sept. 30, 1984, Sterling earned $1.4 million, or 25 cents a share, on revenue of $18.7 million. During the first six months of its 1985 fiscal year, Sterling earned $888,000, or 20 cents a share, on revenue of $10.9 million.

Sterling officials said acquiring Informatics would broaden Sterling's software product line. About 75 percent of Sterling's business comes from systems software for large-scale IBM computers. Specialized software for banking applications makes up the remainder of Sterling's business.

Established in 1962, Informatics employs about 2,800 people. In 1984, the company earned $4.42 million, or 82 cents a share, on revenue of $212 million. Its product line includes software for retail, business and legal applications.

Sterling to Shut Headquarters of Informatics

and Transcontinental tendered their stock. At one o'clock in the afternoon of August 13, the deal closed. Jonah had swallowed the whale.

As Wyly had predicted, there was no mass exodus of employees. A few years after the takeover, he was visiting the Columbus, Ohio–based OrderNet when he stepped into an elevator with one of the former Informatics software developers, who now worked for him.

"Sam, do you know how many people were working here when you bought us?"

"I don't know. Two or three dozen?" he guessed.

"About thirty. And do you know how many we hired this year?"

"No," said Wyly.

"Three hundred!"

A few years later, OrderNet was at the heart of Sterling Software's e-commerce spin-off, Sterling Commerce.

Sterling Software was four years old but already one of the top players. Sam Wyly was back.

Now that Sterling Software had swallowed its whale, it had to digest it in a hurry. Wyly figured they had one year to look good before the crows would start pecking them to death about "overambitious takeover" and "ghosts of Datran." High-yield bonds had landed him the company, but he knew that refinancing with conventional money was the only way to keep from being eaten up by interest payments simultaneously. They first must reduce the debt as much as possible by selling off products that didn't fit.

Determining which were keepers was only the beginning. In Wyly's model, they also had to treat well—meaning as decently and generously as possible—those they had to lay off. It was a pricey decision, but that humane policy sent a message throughout the software industry. In Wyly's words: "If you are going to be bought, better it be done by those good guys at Sterling than those ogres at Computer Associates."

Most Informatics employees stayed. But at the San Fernando Valley headquarters, Wyly made offers to only three of the 85 people. Two said no. Jeanette Myers decided to give the new owners a shot, and moved to Texas. Within a few years, a *Dallas Morning News* story wrote that she was the highest paid female executive in Dallas. Of the 1,500 people down in the divisions making and selling software and services, nobody was laid off. As Sterling's managing practices and growth incentives were put in place, more jobs were created.

With Informatics—as with the 34 other companies, both small and large, that he acquired over the next 18 years—Wyly worked hard to retain the expertise and enthusiasm within the acquired product group. Focused teams ran their individual units as virtual owners. They had centralized strategic and financial planning, and accountability for performance standards. But tactical and operational decisions were completely local, close to the customer.

Wyly knew making that formula work wouldn't always be easy, and now he had to get hundreds of new employees to embrace it. When he spoke with his division managers, he liked to use the example of Ed Lott. He told them that when Lott was thinking about selling his banking software company to Wyly, he had qualms. "I went into a big company once before and I saw the loss of some of the excitement in my people," Lott had told him. "Our office wasn't full on Saturday anymore, and that disappointed me."

Wyly made it very clear that the attitude was different at Sterling Software, and cited his experience with the Bonanza Steakhouse chain. "The franchisees who owned the restaurants would have their families in working if the cook or dishwasher didn't show up, and they were making money," he said. "Meanwhile the company-owned stores were losing money, and they were cooking the same steaks. We want that same 'we own the store!' spirit in Sterling Software."

Sterling introduced the Informatics' managers—who had been used to Walter Bauer's top-down, centralized organization—to this bottom-up, highly interactive, entrepreneurial model. For many, it was a shock.

When Warner Blow first presented his plans for the OrderNet division at the strategic planning sessions, he felt overwhelmed. But eventually, he got the hang of it. "We didn't know what good management was until you guys bought us," Blow later told Wyly. "You monitored us ruthlessly every quarter. There was no place to hide. At first we thought this was tough. But then we realized how good this was because it brought out the best in us."

Sterling always erred on the side of entrepreneurial structure and economy, versus the temptation of overworking what Wyly called "that infamous word of M&A investment bankers—'synergy.'" And he didn't start buying businesses just to be buying businesses—he never forgot that 100 percent of those deals were successful for the bankers, lawyers and auditors involved because of their big fees, but 60 percent of them were failures for the buyer.

He only rarely stepped in. As a breeder of entrepreneurs, he was committed to not interfering. And in most instances, he found that people rose to the level of belief that he had in them. He found that managing a collection of entrepreneurial businesses was like conducting an orchestra. It meant uniting different musicians—often the original owners, with their unique eccentricities—into a symphonic whole.

As it sought more companies to acquire, it was clear Sterling needed a credible spokesman to explain its entrepreneurial business-units concept, because most target companies had never heard of anything like it. And many had reservations, including fears about what would happen to their employees. Wyly wanted someone to talk to the key people, to allay any fears, and to explain that the employee carnage they had seen elsewhere wasn't the way Sterling did things.

He turned to Ed Lott, who had thrived in this entrepreneurial model after selling his company to Sterling. Lott focused on the key people—the gifted developers, sales reps and tech support. "In fact" says Lott, "in some cases we were influenced more by the talent than we were by the product." He developed a polished presentation designed to frighten as much as seduce, telling prospects that acquisition was now a fundamental part of a rapidly changing industry. A lot of software companies had gotten big and gone public and were using the cash to acquire other companies. As their resources increased, those competitors could make life difficult for the smaller software competitor.

Lott explained that in this new world each of them had three options: One, they could keep their company and run it and realize their equity value by paying dividends to themselves. Two, they could sell out. Or three, they could go public. If they took it public, Lott said, they were taking a chance. It might look like a bigger payoff down the road than they would get with Sterling, but they were going to take a much bigger risk and their role was going to change radically.

In that new role, they would no longer be the technology guys they had been, where many had found fulfillment in the role of craftsman, creating beautiful code. They would have to deal with grumpy investors and a parade of investor intermediaries. Did they, Lott asked, really enjoy spending their time with lawyers, auditors and PR people? Did they look forward to rehashing with today's Wall Street security analyst the same litany they had gone over with yesterday's analyst? In the end, taking your company public had all the appeal of warts. But Lott had the solution: "If you want to sell," he said, "we are the guys to sell to." He took prospects through his background, and pointed to others who had merged with Sterling Software. The creative people were still there, he told them, and still creating.

If the targets of a buyout were worried for their vendors and their employees, they weren't alone. Customers had become accustomed to dealing with an eclectic but highly attentive patchwork of smaller vendors, and if a customer had a problem that wasn't getting solved, he could often call the president of the software company and get some serious attention applied to his problem instantly. Some owners even answered their own phones. Some took calls at home.

The advent of larger public companies changed all that. More start-ups were being funded by venture capital funds that wanted what was called "an exit," which meant the business—after a get-ready period—either was taken public or sold to a "strategic buyer," such as Sterling Software.

The question for customers became whether, in a large company, they could maintain the intimate client relationship they had enjoyed in the "old days." Wyly was determined that Sterling's customers would not become abstract account numbers. He constantly cited Peter Drucker on this point: "What is the purpose of a business? To create customers!"

Having grown up in computer services, Wyly's team understood that the sale was just the beginning, not the end, of the relationship with a customer.

Sterling rarely cut any technical workers, and usually hired more. Their competitor Computer Associates, conversely, was more interested in impressing Wall Street's short-term bottomline watchers. So they bought, cut vast numbers of employees and raised prices. This often set Wall Street's heart aflutter, but alienated customers.

Meanwhile, Sterling also gave executives of acquired companies a charter to pursue their own acquisitions. Divisions drew up wish lists. Early on the acquisitions were small. The larger ones would come later—Fran Tarkenton's KnowledgeWare, Bob Cook's VM Software and the software division of Texas Instruments.

Between February and June of 1986, Sterling Software sold three of the old Informatics divisions for a total of $34 million in cash. They paid off all the takeover debt with that cash plus $115 million in new debt that had a much lower cost of capital. The market began to see that Wyly's team was doing what it had said it would do, and the stock price rose.

By summer's end, Sterling Software was reorganized and refinanced—with much work still to do—but it was already a very different company from that of a year earlier. Its offerings now ran on all three generations of IBM-based hardware, from mainframes to midrange to microcomputers, and spanned the software spectrum from systems software to applications software to microcomputer software.

Sterling was now competing against the best niche players, but also against two huge companies—IBM and Computer Associates—that had a similar strategy: "Be everything to everyone." Wyly knew that was an impossible goal, because the industry was too diverse, and he steeled his resolve to strive instead for focused excellence.

In 1985, the top 200 software companies had $32 billion in aggregate software product and services revenue (in a $45 billion industry), but no one monopolized the field.[1] Even the mighty IBM had less than a $5 billion share of that, most of which was confined to operating systems products and database systems. Sterling's strategy had been the right one: to specialize, to invest in niches.

Despite the large playing field, most competitors still kept a wary eye on IBM. A Fujitsu executive put it this way: "In the world of information processing market, we have to respect IBM. We are like the hunter who approaches the lion. Suddenly the beast kneels down. 'Are you afraid?' the hunter asks. 'No,' the lion replies, 'I'm just praying before eating.'"

Sterling's competitive response was to ignore IBM and CA, and develop its niche expertise in ways that they never could. Over time, Wyly believed all would see that the lion had no teeth, and *should* be reciting its prayers.

Endnotes

1   Financial data from June/July 1986 issue of *Business Software Review* magazine, "ICP 200 Report," published by ICP, Inc., Indianapolis, IN.

SAM WYLY: WILL THE HUNTER BECOME THE HUNTED?

Now his Sterling Software may be ripe for a hostile bid

WYLY: THE FINANCIER'S ROAD TO RICHES HAS FEATURED SOME SPECTACULAR WRECKS

Financier Sam Wyly made computer industry history two years ago when he proved that undervalued software companies were as vulnerable to raiders as other businesses. After Wyly took over Informatics General Corp., revenues at his Sterling Software Inc. increased tenfold, to $239 million, and its stock tripled, to 21. Promising encores, Wyly designed a system for ranking the acquisition appeal of some 200 software makers. Today one company stands out as the perfect takeover candidate: Sterling Software. While the average software stock is trading at 25 times earnings, Sterling's multiple is 11.

Part of Wyly's problem has been the booming stock market. Software stocks rose just as he perfected his strategy and now trade at 15 to 20 times cash flow. Laments Wyly: "You can't add a 40% premium and call it a bargain." Once investors realized this, Sterling's stock declined and so did its ability to acquire. Last fall the Dallas company lost out to other suitors in bids for a software division of Martin Marietta and for Integrated Software Systems Corp., a California graphics company.

Another part of Sterling's problem is

Wyly. The 53-year-old financier's road to riches has featured some spectacular wrecks: One Chapter 11 bankruptcy, plus a 1979 consent order settling SEC charges that he maneuvered illegally to secure a badly needed recapitalization. Thus, investors weren't forgiving when Sterling's earnings fell 15% in the quarter ended Mar. 31, to $1.2 million on revenues of $46 million. The decline was caused in part when International Business Machines Corp. scrapped four of its nine programming contracts with Sterling. After that, Sterling's stock fell from 15 to 9.

ADROIT. All of this has led to some elaborate efforts to make Sterling takeover-proof. When a $15 million buyback failed to prop up the stock last February, Wyly decided to exchange high-yielding preferred stock for 5 million of Sterling's 8.5 million common shares. Doubts about Sterling's ability to pay the dividend forced Wyly to scale back the offer to 2.5 million shares. Still, only 1.6 million were exchanged. Meanwhile, Wyly and his brother, Charles, Sterling's vice-chairman, swapped their preferred stock for a new preferred issue that gives them more votes. Combined, the two ma-

neuvers give the Wylys 34% of the vote on an unfriendly takeover.

By all accounts, Wyly has managed Informatics adroitly. The trouble with software takeovers is that programmers, the main asset, tend to leave. But Wyly knew that Informatics had popular products and a stable revenue stream of annual maintenance and support fees. So in one division, for example, Wyly scaled back development, cut employment by 40%, to 180 workers, and found new markets for existing products. "Sterling made a lot of profit that first year," says a former executive. "It wasn't magic. It was cost control." Sterling's earnings decline has raised doubts about continued growth, but Wyly insists the company has its problems under control.

Still, Wyly's erratic record leaves some investors skeptical. A former computer salesman, he talked Southern Methodist University into housing a Control Data Corp. mainframe in 1963 and started a company called University Computing. He got free rent, free electricity, and cheap student labor; the school got to use the mainframe. Some 16 years later, University nearly went broke trying to wrest a piece of the data transmission market from American Telephone & Telegraph Co., and Wyly was ousted. University is now UCCEL, a crosstown software rival bought on June 1 by Computer Associates International Inc. Wyly dropped $10 million of his own on a second challenge to AT&T before trying safer ventures.

DEALMAKING PROWESS. Now his portfolio includes USACafes, a limited partnership franchisor of Bonanza steakhouses, plus Michaels Stores, an arts and crafts retailer, upscale Frost Brothers department stores in San Antonio, and Torie Steele Boutiques in Beverly Hills. Named after his wife, that chain recently has added branches in Dallas. And on June 22, Wyly bought Delman/I. Miller Inc., an upscale New York-based purveyor of women's shoes.

Indeed, it's Wyly's dealmaking prowess that keeps critics from writing off Sterling. His exchange offer appears to have bought him a little time to make good as a software raider. It pushed up Sterling stock only 17%, to $10.75, but company insiders claim that a rebound in earnings next year—perhaps occasioned by the return of some IBM business—will boost the stock more. A lot is riding on whether they're right. For one thing, Wyly has the option to call the new preferred in three years at an equivalent of $12 per common share—a bargain if the stock climbs higher. If it doesn't, Wyly may have to abandon his dream of becoming a software mogul.

By Todd Mason in Dallas

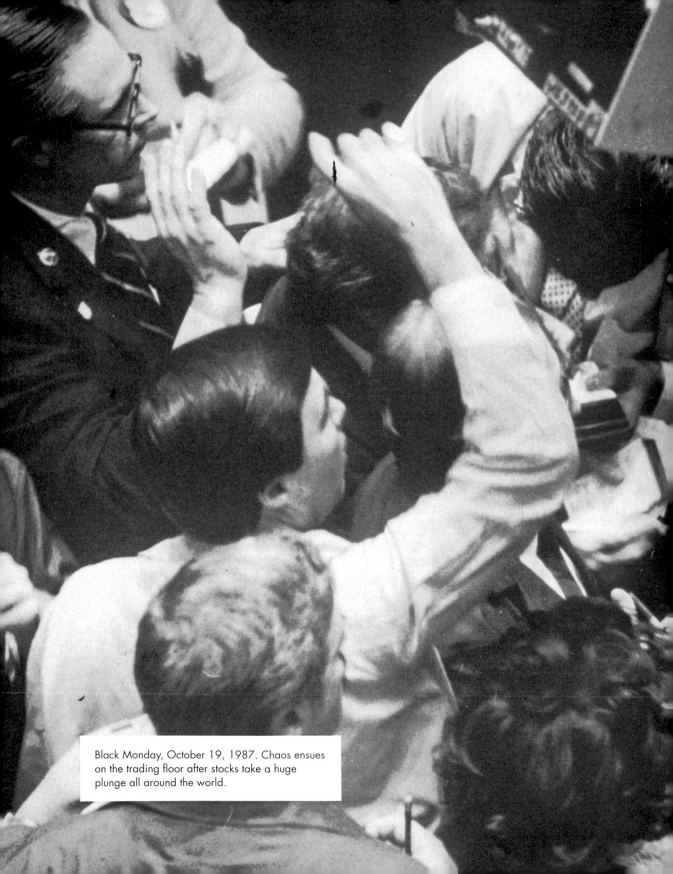

Black Monday, October 19, 1987. Chaos ensues on the trading floor after stocks take a huge plunge all around the world.

CHAPTER TWELVE

WHEN ALL AROUND YOU ARE LOSING THEIR HEADS

In June of 1987, after six years of building his new company, Wyly was eagerly anticipating a long vacation in Italy, his first real stretch of R&R since he'd founded Sterling. But a chance to turn a $200 million company into a $2 billion company doesn't come along every day, so he decided that Milan would have to wait.

As a company built on strategic acquisitions, Sterling Software was always looking for the next one. It used Grad's Grid to assess potential buys that aligned with its growth-value strategy, and kept an eye out for undervalued properties. Early that summer, it found a really interesting one: a diversified computer equipment manufacturer called Control Data, one of the Seven Dwarfs, the company that had made the first computer Wyly bought for University Computing.

Control Data Company (CDC) was about 10 times larger than Sterling, but this didn't deter them. The company had been founded in Minneapolis by engineers from Univac who had helped Univac build the first commercial computers in June of 1957; its initial funding had come from the sale of 600,000 shares of stock for a dollar each. Some CDC folks went on to historic achievements, including its founder, Bill Norris, and one of the founding engineers, and Seymour Cray, who built the Cray Supercomputer for weather forecasting and war games. In the 1960s, CDC built the fastest computers in the world, giant supercomputers for engineers (one of which Wyly had bought secondhand, on a shoestring, to start University Computing), but now it was mainly known as a manufacturer of printer and storage hardware. It still made supercomputers, and it also owned Arbitron, a television ratings service that competed with A. C. Nielsen.

But CDC was adrift: it was in its third year of reporting bad numbers; its stock price was down, even though the tech market was rising; and it was getting whipped by the minicomputer-makers, such as DEC, from below and the IBM mainframers from above.

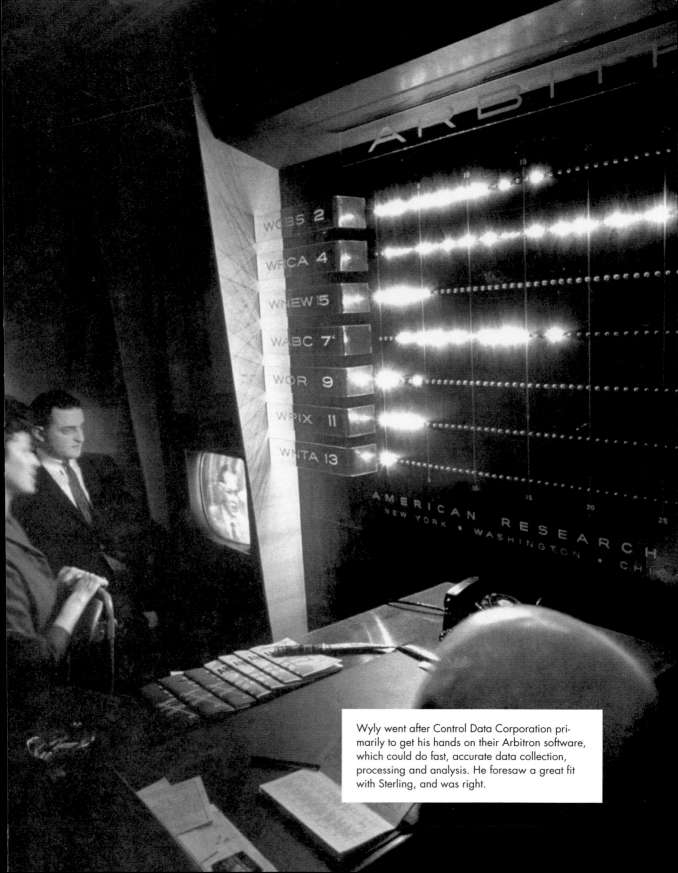

Wyly went after Control Data Corporation primarily to get his hands on their Arbitron software, which could do fast, accurate data collection, processing and analysis. He foresaw a great fit with Sterling, and was right.

But there was much about Control Data that Wyly liked: for one, its managers were spunky. When IBM abused its near-monopoly power, they'd taken on Big Blue's pin-striped legal legions with an antitrust suit. Another thing he liked was that in the 1973 settlement of that suit, CDC took over Service Bureau Corporation (SBC), the first place both Sam and Charles Wyly had worked out of college. Buying it would have been a little like going to the class reunion with the prom queen who had ignored you so many years ago, and whose rejection had stoked the competitive fire that pushed you to success.

The idea of owning his first employer tickled Sam Wyly, but it was not an entirely nostalgic notion—SBC was still a high-quality, growing business, second in the market only to Automatic Data Processing (now ADP) in payroll processing.

Even though CDC had 14 divisions, Grad's Grid showed little fit with Sterling Software's mission statement. CDC sold some software, mostly to run on its own computers, which Wyly did not think would survive. But he began to outline a plan: He would keep at most three of its divisions, and maybe just one. The real reason to buy Control Data was the entrepreneurial opportunity to capitalize on the gap between the market value of its different businesses and the market value of its stock. "We looked at each of the pieces," he recalls. "Then we decided which pieces we wanted and which pieces we didn't want and what we thought the value of the total would be if we sold off all the divisions, except SBC."

It had computer services contracts with the federal government that could be combined with Sterling's Air Force businesses. And it had Arbitron, which in addition to media ratings also offered data processing services. It thrived on fast, accurate data collection, analysis and distribution, a field of technology Sterling Software knew well. "I finally had to put aside any idea of the business I was in—that is, software products and services, as then defined—when I thought about Arbitron," Wyly says. "Instead, I just asked myself, 'Is it a good business?' I wanted to own good businesses. I knew that if we acquired Control Data, we would have totally abandoned the notion that we were a purely software products company. Sterling Software would become Sterling Services."

Wyly asked Don Thomson to review CDC's numbers. "What is the value of, and market for, each division of the company?" Wyly asked him. "And how much money will be left over if we turn every division into cash?"

Both Thomson and Williams concluded they could make money on the deal. "We thought we could buy the company for two billion dollars," Williams recalls. "And we thought we could sell its parts for three billion dollars."

That was all Wyly needed to hear: He assembled his takeover team, which dubbed their secret mission "Project T," for "target." For a toehold, Sterling Software spent $15 million for just less than five percent of CDC stock at $23 a share. Initially, Wyly estimated that his winning bid would end at $30.

The Project T team met day and night, and eventually included 50 people, all sworn to secrecy . . . although Wyly had little faith that a group that large, with all those lawyers and bankers, could keep anything secret. They enlisted experts on every CDC business, and had specialists identifying potential buyers for each division so they could move quickly if they made the acquisition.

For his bankers and lawyers on this deal, Wyly wanted the best in the business. He wanted the guys who had pioneered hostile takeovers when the big-name Wall Street bankers were afraid to do so because they might offend some of their blue-chip clients. He got Drexel Burnham behind the acquisition—they liked Arbitron and SBC as keepers as much as he did. For his lawyer, he wanted Joe Flom, the "Pit Bull," whom he had hired once before for Earth Resources. Flom had built Skadden Arps into the number one takeover legal firm in the '80s. It was to law what Drexel was to investment banking, equal parts icon and pariah. Flom had been an outsider and misfit most of his life and preferred that type for colleagues and clients. Born poor in Brooklyn in 1923, he got into Harvard Law School without a college degree, and unlike the "white-shoe" lawyers who found the takeover business distasteful, he was a street fighter eager to throw the first punch. During proxy fights he was happiest in the "snake pit," where the votes were counted; and by instinct and inclination, he was usually on the attack side of a takeover.

Wyly also liked Flom because he was a notoriously hard worker. When someone suggested that his biggest deals had been a right-time–right-place bit of luck, Flom said, "It's funny, but the harder I work, the luckier I get."

Wyly's team met with Flom in his conference room at the Skadden Arps offices in New York City.

"We want to own Control Data," Wyly told him.

Above: CDC, founded by some of the geniuses behind Univac, had done a lot of great things, and a lot of brilliant people worked there. In the early '60s, it made some of the fastest computers of the day—such as this Control Data 6600 console from 1963—but Wyly sensed the company was adrift and needed to be shaken up.

Right: Joe Flom was the top lawyer to get if you were in a takeover so hostile that it resembled a street fight, and Wyly hired him for his CDC campaign, in part to make sure the other side couldn't hire him.

Flom asked, "Do you have the money?"

"No," Wyly replied.

"Okay. That will be $175,000."

Wyly immediately uncapped a pen and wrote the check to cover Flom's retainer. Meeting over.

Sterling Software continued to buy Control Data's stock all summer, but it was getting more expensive by the day, as the price shares kept climbing and climbing. This was good for the shares Sterling now owned, but it was bad news for all the shares it still needed to buy. Toward the end of July, the price hit $30, the ceiling Wyly had set for his tender offer, but by the time a premium was added to the offer, he might now have to pay $36 or $37 a share. "The investment bankers kept saying, 'We've still got a deal here,'" Wyly recalls. "We can make this happen—it's just gonna cost you $40."

And then it went up to $45, in part because most stocks were going up in the bull market of 1986 and 1987, particularly tech stocks. Control Data stock was a boat on a rising tide, Wyly decided, but what bothered him most was that few people seemed to think that tide would ebb, even though he knew it always did. The Dow had been rising steadily, almost doubling from 1,500 in January of 1986 to 2,700 in August of 1987. In August 26, 1987, *The Wall Street Journal* wrote, "In a market like this, every story is a positive one. Any news is good news. It's pretty much taken for granted now that the market is going to go up." The market peaked the day before that *Journal* story ran. That's when the announcement came that University Computing had been sold to Computer Associates at a 50 percent premium over the market. *A price of 45 times earnings!* Wyly thought. He still had some University stock—his "nostalgia" shares—but even nostalgia has its price. He called his broker and said, "Cash me out. I'm done."

Sterling Williams was getting antsy, too. "Can we really buy this thing?" he asked Wyly. "And can we really run it once we do?" At this point, they were three months into their secret siege and Wyly was beginning to feel that there was no longer a single rational reason to proceed. But after putting so much time, money and thought into the takeover, the emotional side of him—the bulldog in him—still wanted to get across the goal line, still wanted to score that touchdown. And then his brother, Charles, walked into his office and said, "Sam, you look troubled."

"Yeah. This isn't working. We've got all these people working on it, and we've got all this stock. But we're not in the business of owning stock, and I can't figure out how to make this deal work."

"Sam," Charles told him, "we don't *have* to do anything."

Sam sat up straight in his chair. Do nothing? Yes! After months of running on adrenaline, of having bankers and lawyers tell him, "We can still pull this off!" the option of doing nothing had been forgotten. "Right," Sam told his brother. "We don't have to do anything. I'm shutting this down."

Over the next 10 days they sold off 20 million shares of CDC stock for about $36 a share. The profit on it was phenomenal, more than enough to pay for the 50 people who had worked on Project T; and it also covered the cost of Joe Flom, whose solitary act on Sterling's behalf had been to cash that check for his $175,000 retainer.

That game was over. Wyly flew to Milan for his long-delayed vacation, where he spent some time with his two youngest children, Andrew and Christiana, who attended boarding school there. In the morning, he'd put them on the little yellow school bus with all the Italian kids and then he would amble down to the corner cappuccino bar, and cross the street to the small news shop for the *International Herald Tribune* to see what was going on in the world. It was a blissful three weeks.

When he returned to the United States in mid-October, he spent a day sitting in on his eldest son Evan's class at Harvard Business School in Boston, then went to New York City for dinner with Richard Hanlon, a journalist by way of London and Dallas whom he had hired to do investor relations work for Sterling. Hanlon had set up meetings for Wyly with several Wall Street analysts, who followed software companies over the next two days. Sterling Williams had long ago taken over the road shows for Sterling Software, but Hanlon thought it would be a good idea for Sam to get reacquainted with key people on The Street.

Wyly was eager to do some serious one-on-one with some of the smartest guys on Wall Street, but as he went through his meetings on Thursday, he sensed that the men across the table were awfully distracted. In fact, some of them seemed to be turning pale. Periodically, one of them would get up from the table, step out of the room and return even more ashen. It was like a contagion.

After Wyly pulled the plug on Project T, the top-secret plan that had consumed him for the past four months, he finally spent a mellowing few weeks in Milan with his youngest children, Christiana (left) and Andrew. He didn't know it at the time, but he had narrowly avoided a disaster of monumental proportions.

It was worse on Friday. At noon he went down to the Merrill Lynch offices at the World Financial Center, where he met Merrill's top computer software analyst, Steve McClellan. That massive office was buzzing with fear and anxiety, like a war room receiving urgent missives from troops under siege. The whole place reeked of calamity. Finally, someone whispered something in McClellan's ear and he got up and left the room.

He returned a few minutes later and said that all of his software stocks were being trashed. A few had been cut in half in two days.

Wyly flew home to Dallas that weekend. When the markets opened on Monday, the 19th of October, the bloodbath the analysts had felt coming on Thursday and Friday was fully upon them. It was Black Monday—and the wrath of the market had hit the tech guys first. Wyly did what everybody did that day, which was watch in mute amazement as the Dow dropped 508 points, losing 23 percent of the wealth of the U.S. stock market in one trading session.

As he watched the conflagration, he thought back to his decision of four weeks earlier, when he had backed off the Control Data takeover. The shares Sterling had just sold at $36 were now at $13. He had narrowly escaped a disaster of monumental proportions. Had he bought CDC, it might have pulled him down like a brick tied to a rubber duckie.

In a postmortem with Charles and Sterling Williams, Wyly quoted this passage from Ralph Waldo Emerson:

> A foolish consistency is the hobgoblin of little minds, adored by little statesmen and philosophers and divines. With consistency a great soul has simply nothing to do. He may as well concern himself with his shadow on the wall. Speak what you think now in hard words and tomorrow speak what tomorrow thinks in hard words again, though it contradict everything you said today.

Grateful that Sterling had dodged a cannonball, he asked himself, "In the face of all this fear and panic, what do I now know for sure?" His answer was "I know we will not default on paying our Sterling Software preferred stock," so he bought some that had been dumped into the market at an 18 percent yield. Other than that, he hunkered down. Wyly still believed there was opportunity to be found in chaos, but was a shrewd enough student of history to know that sometimes the smartest move is to simply take your money off the table. "Persistence is a good quality," he says, "but sometimes changing your mind is greater wisdom."

Almost on a dare, Wyly bought the tiny, Dallas-based Michaels arts-and-crafts chain in 1983. Before he was done, Michaels had 1,000 stores nationwide and 44,000 employees.

LET A THOUSAND SUPER-ENTREPRENEURS BLOOM

Sam Wyly was by now a fully formed, fully engaged entrepreneur, looking for opportunities in all fields. He knew and loved computers, but he now had the tools—the experience, the executives and the management strategy—to succeed in a variety of businesses, which was fortunate, because his next venture offered more variety than anything he'd touched thus far. In the fall of 1982, a modest seven-store Texas arts-and-crafts chain out of Dallas was put up for sale. Like Bonanza, which Sam Wyly had "inherited" by guaranteeing a $1 million bank loan, the Michaels Arts & Crafts chain came his way for an odd reason. Other buyers had been offered the company, but passed because of the constant warfare between its father-and-son founders.

The Michaels chain began in Dallas in 1973 as a converted five-and-ten-cent store that was owned by an entrepreneur, Jim Dupey, and run by his son, Michael. Over the next 10 years, Michael opened several more stores, mostly in Texas. He was clearly a savant at merchandising crafts, but didn't have the expertise to manage his growing company, so his father became frustrated with the company's performance, and put it up for sale. But he waited and waited for a buyer, because everybody realized that Michael Dupey was the vital talent, and would quit to become a competitor of whomever bought it.

Despite that monumental obstacle, when Sam Wyly and Don Thomson got their first look at the books, they saw a small company with huge potential. "Numbers talk to me," Thomson liked to say, and while they told him Michaels needed work, they also told him these stores—if successfully replicated and professionally managed—could have a big future. And Wyly always had a weakness for a company with spectacular potential, even if that's *all* he knew about it.

Michael Dupey—the namesake behind the original Michaels chain—was a savant in the crafts world, great at spotting trends or creating them. Wyly and Thomson were much less impressed, however, with his ability to run a company. Dupey had a big personality that stood out in the quiet world of arts and crafts. When he traveled to wholesale shows to buy items for the stores, he was by far the biggest buyer there and a much-watched trend-spotter. If he thought some new yarn, ceramic, scrap-booking idea or teenage girls' "Twista-Beads" was going to be the next big thing, he would buy it en masse for his stores, sometimes setting off a buying frenzy. The vendors loved him, and he loved the limelight. "He had a limo take his people all around town," says Jeff Wandell, an Illinois floral store owner and acquaintance for more than 25 years. "He always had lots of people from his stores following him. He had just this gigantic entou-rage, and he would be there in his shorts and his tennis shoes and [fishnet] athletic shirts. He would walk up and down the aisles with all of these store people behind him, and the sales people in the booths would just be frothing at the mouth to get to talk to him. It was quite a scene." But while Dupey's star status soared, Michaels' busi-ness operations were taking hits. One problem was Dupey's some-times confrontational management style. While people used the word "genius" to describe his merchan-dising ideas, he had an unpredictable temperament. Sam Wyly was about to learn that in order to take advantage of the genius—and he had to—he also had to deal with the firebrand.

The Inventory from hell: there are more than 40,000 items in a Michaels store, and there are more than 1,000 stores in the U.S.

And that was pretty much all he knew about Michaels. Wyly and Thomson had never heard of the chain before being solicited as potential buyers, but when Thomson mentioned the store to his wife, he was told that she and their daughters visited the stores often and loved them. Sam heard the same from the women in his family. The stores provided the raw materials for creative people—yarns, paints, canvases, beads, floral products, picture frames, a custom framing service, mosaic tiles, more than 11,000 items—and Mike Dupey had an uncanny sense for trends. What he didn't have was the experience or temperament to run a retail chain.

Thomson knew the operational problems at Michaels could be corrected by professional managers, and he wanted to buy the company. Wyly agreed that the numbers seemed promising, but he always asked the long-view questions—"Can we successfully duplicate the Michaels concept in a chain? Can we earn public capital to expand? Go national? Go international? Build shareholder value? Build *extreme* value?"

Wyly also was interested in growth by acquisitions. Twenty years into his entrepreneurial career, he had made a lot of them. If Michaels could grow by acquiring similar store chains, and converting them to the Michaels' layout, product mix and brand, the way Wyly had grown University Computing and was growing Sterling Software, he knew they could quickly build a U.S. dominant superstore chain. The arts-and-crafts field was wide open for a national name.

As the stores grew in number, they would need to replace their manual stock-keeping and accounting operations with computerized inventory and management reporting. With tens of thousands of pieces of merchandise handled every day, accounting, inventory keeping, ordering and tracking done manually would be a huge expense. They needed the speed, accuracy and flexibility that came with computers and their software systems. But that did not worry him—his concern was the same one everyone else who looked at Michaels had: he knew the chain would need its merchandising genius, Michael Dupey. Wyly could get professional managers, but Dupey knew the marketplace, and the artisans and crafters, like nobody else. He was that "talent that goes home each night."

On February 25, 1983, Wyly acquired the seven Michaels Stores and five Ben Franklin Stores for $8 million cash, even though he had never been inside a single store, and later laughed, "If I had spent time in the stores trying to understand what customers [over 90 percent women] did with all these products, I would never have bought it!"

The day the deal was announced, Michael Dupey quit—and never spoke to his father again. Wyly quickly arranged a sit-down with the angry son, and proposed this deal: in exchange for staying with the company, Wyly would grant him exclusive, royalty-free rights to develop Michaels Stores in the eight counties around Dallas, and own the warehouse for the chain, also in Dallas. One month after the sale closed, Michael was back at Michaels.

Sales for the stores in 1983 were $20.7 million, with net income hitting $2.1 million. For Michael Dupey, it was a record. For Wyly, it was just a start—he knew his team had to open stores in many cities if they were going to become as powerful in the market as he wanted them to be. He also knew that opening new stores was a tedious, expensive and mistake-prone process of scouting locations, assessing demographics, negotiating leases and cultivating customer bases—unless someone has already done it for you. So he again hammered out a plan to grow by acquisition.

On February 3, 1984, the company's name was formally changed to Michaels Stores, Inc. On May 6, Michaels Stores, Inc., began trading on the American Stock Exchange, with the Wyly family as the largest shareholders. At that time, the Wall Street underwriters—those still standing after the Crash of 1970 and the miserable market of the '70s—were afraid to underwrite the offering, so Sam and Charles Wyly agreed to buy any shares not bought by the public. Sam became chairman of the company, Charles was vice-chairman and Jim Kelly, who had run a very good store in Hurst, Texas, became president. Dupey was Michaels' chief merchant, traveling the world for products and ideas. He was the creative power, and he owned and operated the chain's only warehouse. Wyly carved out a small space in the warehouse for corporate headquarters, but for the time being, he left the accounting and most of the buying to each store. He wanted to keep the benefits of local entrepreneurship on-site as long as he could.

Wyly put most of the money from the stock offering into buyouts of local chains; this was the start of what would total more than $100 million in acquisitions over the first five years. He wanted the stores to be unlike anything people had seen before. And he wanted them to be profitable.

At first, Wyly let store managers do their local operating, accounting and buying, and he recruited new talent by offering them 15 percent of a store's profit—similar to what Sam Walton had done to get Wal-Mart started. Word soon got around that this crazy computer guy in Dallas was making local managers rich, and some very good managers came knocking at his door. (Wyly always had great respect for Walton's business acumen. One of the Michaels executives came to him one day and said, "Wal-Mart has started a chain like ours, named it Helen's Arts and Craft Stores for Sam Walton's wife, and opened in Monroe, Louisiana; Fort Smith, Arkansas; and Springfield, Missouri. I want to open across the street from each one and run them out of business." Wyly immediately told him: "No. Absolutely not! The last thing in the world I want to do is make Sam Walton mad!")

Franchising had worked well for Bonanza, but there were vast differences between steakhouses and crafts stores. Each Michaels sold a core of like merchandise but had a great deal of latitude to stock what they thought would work in their markets. The downside was that this meant sacrificing the cost savings that came with centralized buying.

At Bonanza, there were no chefs, and only a few inventory items—steaks, salad ingredients, sides, beverages, condiments. A Michaels store had 11,000 items on its shelves (eventually, 41,000), and Wyly knew that with that much inventory (in 200, 400, 600 or 1000 stores), there were millions of dollars in savings and more sales per store possible if inventory could be more centrally managed, so he decided that company-owned stores was the way to go, not franchising.

By 1984, his grand plan was rolling—total square feet of retail space almost tripled, sales reached $46.3 million, a 123 percent increase, and total stores stood at 33. On May 16, 1985, Michaels sold 1.5 million new shares to the public.

Part of the proceeds went to standardizing operations in all of the stores so that, for one thing, Michaels could maximize bulk discounts. Net sales rose dramatically, and more and more vendors—from Chattanooga to China—wanted to get their new products into Michaels Stores. Despite the puny profit line, no one was bailing out. There was a sense among the Wyly team that they were on to something.

———

Despite all this good news, Michaels was heading for a divorce—by 1986, the "marriage" with Michael Dupey was on the rocks. The power he had negotiated with Wyly made him not just the face of the company, but its de facto CEO, and he had control of key merchandising decisions that affected Wyly's bottom line. He was running his own stores in Texas plus charging Michaels a 12 percent premium for the warehousing, and it was becoming increasingly hard to make the margins Michaels Stores, Inc., needed for its growth all over the U.S.

Wyly decided he could live without his "star," and Dupey was booted. Wyly's team installed a professional management model that could be replicated as they added stores. The start-up era was over at Michaels. The professionals had moved in.

In 1986, sales for Michaels Stores broke the $100 million mark for the first time; net income came in at $3.3 million. At year's end, there were 51 stores in 12 states—not too bad for the seven-store, $8 million purchase of a few years earlier.

Wyly made a big acquisition in September 1987, a 30-store chain in Southern California called Moskatel's. California was the nation's largest consumer market and, specifically, the largest arts-and-crafts market. Seventeen of the stores were in greater Los Angeles, and the stores in Tarzana and in Sacramento were each earning almost $1 million a year profit.

A month later, management began to increase the sophistication of Michaels' buying tactics, in part because the product line was being added to rapidly, moving from the original 11,000 items up to 31,000. This required a meticulous accounting of every item from every vendor, all measured against budgets and discount thresholds. Trying to also hold on to the entrepreneurial benefit of a decentralized structure of management, Wyly came up with a second stage in the evolution of the organization, a "lead store manager" concept: highly successful store managers would not only run their own stores but also oversee and assist up to 10 others nearby. It rewarded the best rainmakers financially, and gave them a career track beyond a single store. These lead store managers were dubbed "super-entrepreneurs."

Michaels now had 96 stores in 14 states, and sales rose to $167.2 million, with a net income of $4.9 million. And then the economy blew up, again. The stock market crashed in October of 1987, but Wyly decided to keep his foot on the gas, so as not to slow down the company growth.

Wall Street asked, "Are you recession-proof?"

He answered, "Not recession-proof, but recession-resistant!"

In late 1987, Wyly got a call from the CFO of Wal-Mart, who said, "We are a low-margin, high-turnover concept. Arts and crafts is a high-margin, low-turnover concept. Would you like to buy our three Helen's stores at book value?"

In less than 20 seconds, Wyly said, "Yes."

It was a good deal for Wyly—all three of those locations proved to be continually profitable, but the best part of it was that Wal-Mart was out of the crafts business.

Despite all this success, Wyly knew that if Michaels Stores were going to be the industry touchstone, inventory tracking and replenishment needed to be state-of-the-art. Most of that was being done by hand, and most of the managers, especially the super-entre-preneurs, had become highly adept at calculating how much of what item would sell, but it was obvious that this rapidly increasing number of SKUs was eventually going to overwhelm them.

About that time, Wyly was out in his holiday home in Malibu Colony, California, when he called Warner Blow, who had been running OrderNet (which would become Sterling

The Michaels team was careful to place stores away from prime commercial real estate strips, and it was quick to move a store if a nearby location was better and it could offload what was left on its 10-year lease.

Commerce). Blow knew more about systems that connect wholesalers and retailers than anyone on Earth. "Come on out to Malibu," Wyly said. "I want to talk to you."

They went to a Wendy's for coffee and Wyly started laying out his vision of what he wanted. He got a napkin and drew his ideal flowchart for information at Michaels. Point-of-sale terminals at the cash register would scan the bar code on an item; check the stock level; reorder the stock if it had fallen beneath a designated threshold; issue the invoices; and prepare a management report that could give a live, real-time view of how the item—and the company—was doing. Blow took some paper out and started scribbling.

"You don't need to do that," Wyly said. "I'll give you my notes." Then he handed him the napkin, which Blow kept for years.

Wyly wanted a turnkey system—hardware and software bundled together, requiring only a "key" to turn it all on—from his Creative Data Systems up in Cleveland that was being managed by Blow. He thought the installation would go smoothly, but it was a bad fit from the start, as prepackaged systems sometimes are. Eventually, they scrapped that whole thing in favor of one they had inherited from the Moskatel's chain, even though it fell short of what Wyly wanted.

It was years before the system Wyly drew on that napkin was fully realized, but Michaels began installing the point-of-sale (POS) terminals in stores, which was more or less the first leg of the information marathon. They were designed to track all 31,000 SKUs in each store, provide better information on sales, on margins and on the success (or failure) of promotions, and facilitate better inventory control.

It was vital information, but while the POS terminals marked a good start at managing the chaos, they lacked the capability to automatically monitor and replenish stock. The thorny problem was made worse by the rapid growth of Michaels. Another problem: they were dealing with so many suppliers globally, both small and large, who had differing computers and communications protocols (or none at all) that it was impossible to link them all into a single system. Michaels did not have the clout of a Wal-Mart to dictate to vendors exactly the input required by its standardized data systems.

Still searching for a software solution, Wyly made the company stronger the old-fashioned way: by making a great hire. He had heard about a young man from New Jersey doing phenomenal work for Family Dollar stores. "When I got to Family

Dollar they had one hundred and eighty stores," Doug Sullivan says. When he and Wyly spoke, 11 years later, the chain had 1,400 stores. "It was a tremendous education in retail and in real estate," Sullivan recalls. "Those guys were masters. They were hard-nosed negotiators, very, very tough. By the time I left we were putting in two hundred new stores a year."

Sullivan joined Michaels as a senior vice president, and he got pitched into the cold water right away. In his first staff meeting, the CFO casually said, "Well, we just went over our bank borrowing limit on Friday, but I don't think they can do anything to us. They'd have to repossess all the glue guns that we own as collateral for the loan."

"Financially," Sullivan recalls, "we were very much on the edge."

Despite that, Michaels had attracted interest from one of the first leveraged buyout (LBO) shops, Grauer & Wheat. Doug Wheat was a Dallas lawyer Wyly knew from an earlier deal. Peter Grauer had been with Donaldson, Lufkin and Jenrette, the first stockbroker-underwriter to go from being a private partnership to a publicly owned company. He was named chairman of Bloomberg LP in 2001.

On August 10, 1989, Michaels Stores, Inc., agreed to be acquired for about $130 million in a leveraged buyout that would take the company private. The transaction was valued around $220 million, a price that drove the stock price up from $5 to $9. And then Michaels got hit by a freight train. First, the company made a bad call on its Christmas inventory—the make-or-break sales of the year. All those customers who usually bought a lot of crafts at Christmas, even in tight times, got caught up in the economic crunch and didn't spend as much as expected, so Michaels had to take a write-down on its inventory. Its stock fell from $8 a share to $6.75 the day the news broke in December.

Then it took another hit. Doug Wheat called to tell Wyly that they could not raise the money for their deal. Nearly all LBO financing was drying up because Drexel and all the other big Wall Street banks that had copied the Drexel formula were being smashed in the junk bond scandals that erupted in the late '80s (leading to Drexel Burnham's Chapter 11 bankruptcy in February 1990). Michaels' earnings dropped from $5.2 million in 1986 to a dismal $13,000, even as annual revenues rose 20 percent to $290 million.

This meant Wyly and his team had to cut back their growth, hunker down

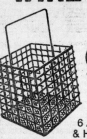

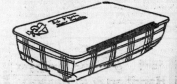

and focus on surviving. It was a brutal time—the 10 biggest banks in Texas went bust, along with 500 smaller ones and 95 percent of the savings and loan banks. Brand-new skyscrapers in downtown Dallas stood empty. To turn Michaels around in these tough times, Wyly knew he needed a magician. Fortunately, he had the home phone number of one in his Rolodex, and Don Thomson took over in August 1990.

Thomson and Wyly went looking for Michael Dupey, who was now operating his own 24-unit arts-and-crafts chain, which he had named MJDesigns, since Wyly owned the Michaels brand name. They knew Dupey was still the ultimate merchandising genius (though he was still having trouble with his bottom line), so he was brought in as a special consultant. As always, Thomson did a brilliant job of scrambling out of a hole—he established more unity between stores and headquarters, and marketing was beefed up and made more targeted. In fact, Michaels was on their way to becoming one of the biggest local advertisers in hometown newspapers, something that continues to this day. Michaels began sponsoring its own show on Lifetime Television Network, a 30-minute Saturday morning program called *The Michaels Arts & Crafts Show*. By year's end, it was generating 1,000 letters a week.

Michaels Stores' total sales grew 25 percent to $362 million in 1990, and net income bounced back to $5.8 million. Seventeen new stores were added that year, bringing the total to 136 in 19 states. But Wyly knew the company was leaving money on the table until the technology system was nailed down.

Then he received terrible news. Don Thomson, a chronic smoker, had been diagnosed with what the doctors believed to be a terminal illness. He cut back to just a few hours of work a day, and began working from home. Wyly made Thomson president emeritus—even a part-time genius is still a genius—but again the company had to adapt. Wyly split the operational responsibilities. Doug Sullivan, who had been running real estate, was given store operations, distribution, marketing, real estate, legal and human resources. Don Morris, the CFO, kept the books and oversaw computer technology.

In 1991, Wyly recruited Jack Bush—who had been in merchandising roles with Sears and was at the time president of an ailing discount store chain that had got plowed under by the invading juggernauts of Wal-Mart and Target—to be president. He'd offered Bush that same job 12 months earlier, and Bush had turned him down, but two things had changed since then: Wyly had a whole new company to show Bush; and Bush had made himself into an arts-and-crafts guy, doing a lot of homework visiting arts-and-crafts stores. "This time," Bush said later, "I saw an absolute sleeping giant."

Jack Bush came aboard on August 1, 1991, and a week later, he gathered his store managers together in Dallas. "In arts and crafts we will be the biggest retailer," he told them. "We will be number one. When people say 'arts and crafts,' they will then say 'Michaels.' Just like Home Depot dominates home improvement and Wal-Mart dominates discounting. We'll be the most innovative, creative retailer in the country, the number one gift place in the country, and the number one custom framer in the country. In five years we'll double our sales."

He was obsessed with providing exemplary customer service, which had been inconsistent during Michaels' fast growth. (In his intelligence gathering prior to meeting with Wyly before he took the job, he had visited a dozen stores and spotted a few things that needed to be fixed immediately. One example: "Out of 12 stores," Bush told his managers, "I was acknowledged by just one person.") He often walked through stores all over the U.S., and also sent anonymous "mystery shoppers" to gather intelligence. One bit of information he didn't need to get from his spies was that Michaels was still weak in information systems. "I couldn't even get the sales for the last week," he told Wyly. "I had to phone the stores in order to get samples of the sales."

Always pushing customer service, Bush had his battalion of mystery shoppers visit each store five times and send back progress reports; full-time district managers now visited every one of their stores weekly; customers completed several hundred thousand evaluation cards each year. He established a bonus system for managers partly based upon their customer service. Near the entrance to every store he put greeters who were working on crafts projects. Each store had 250 storyboards describing how to do various projects.

Bush—a superb merchandiser with an eye for appealing ideas—had only been on the job for three weeks when he told Wyly and Thomson he wanted to fire Dupey. Bush said Dupey had too much power, and too few good answers. He also saw that Michaels was buying too much of its imports through either domestic wholesalers or through Dupey's warehouse, which was a lot more expensive than buying direct from China or Chattanooga. Bush told Thomson, "He's got to go."

"I hired him," Thomson replied, "so if you don't mind, I'll tell him he's leaving." He did it that day.

At the end of September—60 days after Bush started—the monthly sales numbers stunned everyone: a 19 percent increase. In October, a 21 percent gain; in November, a 41 percent gain. In early December, Bush got a call from *The Wall Street Journal*, and the reporter—seeing the stock price had more than doubled to $12—asked, "What's going on at Michaels?"

"Don't ask me," Bush said. "Ask the customers. If you want to write about us, go out and interview some customers." A short time later, *Individual Investor* tabbed Michaels as the stock pick for the next year, and by Christmas the stock hit $15.

Wyly decided this was a good time to have a secondary stock offering in order to build equity and reduce debt. "We went to the market the week after Christmas, and while we were telling our story the stock jumped to $19 a share," he says. "We harvested about $65 million, paid off our senior subordinated notes that had been costing us 15.8 percent, and we put $27 million in the bank."

Michaels, which had been teetering on the brink 12 months earlier, was now the number one specialty retailer in the arts-and-crafts world—and still growing fast, with rapidly improving margins.

In 1992, arts and crafts was a $7 billion industry, and Michaels was the largest chain, with three times the revenue of its second-largest competitor. And it was about to roll out another big cannon: they decided to invest heavily in custom picture-framing. They were already offering that service, but their framing guru, Mike Greenwood, convinced Wyly that it could be done better, so Wyly gave him the go-ahead.

Framing was a different animal from the rest of the arts-and-crafts business. It was labor-intensive. It was all done in the stores. If a store manager hired specialized labor, it cost too much, but if he had his staff do it, each job took too long. Greenwood figured out how to centralize the process in a few locations and redesigned the service so that workers did it all in-house (but not in each store) and reduced the cost by a third, plus got the customer's frame in hand more quickly.

He knew a handwritten order came out wrong half of the time, whereas automated ones were almost always right, so he spent $50,000 on a computerized system.

Once he had all his improvement in place, Greenwood invited Bush and Bob

If you're running an arts-and-crafts empire, you'd better make sure your annual reports are artistic.

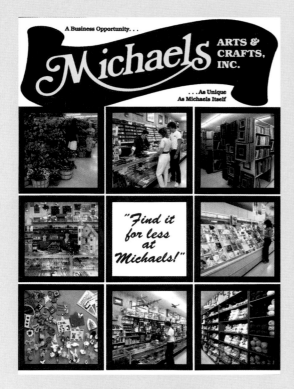

Rudman, the head of merchandising, out see the new system in action. He welcomed them to the shop and proudly told them, "Now here's what happens: You push this button and the orders print out on these little labels. Then that label gets attached to the molding and then the mat warden gets it processed and sent out." He pushed the button for the first orders and, to his horror, saw the computers were printing gibberish.

Fortunately, neither Bush nor Rudman caught that. "I just kept on talking," Greenwood says. "I took them through the process and never told them that the data coming out was crap. They saw the shop operating and they made their speeches to the employees. As soon as they walked out the door, I yelled, 'Shut it down!' I was there until four in the morning getting that computer synced up so that the shop would operate."

Greenwood smoothed out the kinks, and the new framing business paid off quickly, growing from about $500,000 in 1992 to $13 million by 1995—more than all of its direct competitors combined. Wyly knew he now had momentum, and

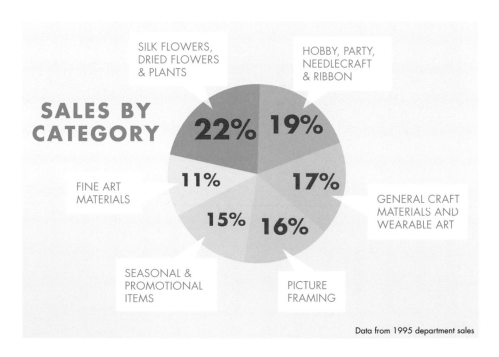

Data from 1995 department sales

**MICHAELS
STORES IN
1991
TOTAL: 141**

**MICHAELS
STORES IN
1994
TOTAL: 254**

**MICHAELS
STORES IN
1997
TOTAL: 449**

Doug Sullivan (left) was the real estate swami who would sometimes evaluate hundreds of locations before leasing a site for a Michaels store.

refused to slow down. He opened new stores in bunches, and no one wanted to cut back because of computer limitations—though, in hindsight, he says, "We should have." The company had its best year to date in 1994 and now had distribution centers in Texas, California, Kentucky and Florida. Revenue came within a sneeze of $1 billion, up 60 percent from the year before. Net income rose to $35.6 million, a 72 percent increase. Shares hit $35.

Greenwood got a boost in 1995 when Michaels acquired Aaron Brothers, Inc.,[1] which had 71 high-end framing stores, mostly in California. "I've done a margin analysis on this and I'll tell you that there is a lot of money here," he told Wyly. "We could make 25 percent of the picture frames that we sell, and capture that margin all the way back up to the tree."

Wyly turned him loose, and by 2006, the chain was selling 2.5 million custom frames annually, which accounted for about 15 percent of Michaels' sales and a bigger chunk of its profits. Over a period of 12 years, Michaels had become the largest chain of arts-and-crafts superstores in the world—in a best-in-class sort of way.

But being best in class didn't guarantee that there would be no more rough patches, and Michaels hit one just a year later, when the economy plummeted in the mid-'90s and the chain was stuck with a massive amount of inventory it couldn't stock or store. Jack Bush had taken Michaels a long way, but Wyly began to feel that the company was going to need an extraordinary new leader with lots of energy to turn it around yet again. When he called Bush in to talk it over, Bush chose to retire. He was now rich, thanks to Michaels' stock.

While Wyly began his search for a new president, he persuaded Doug Sullivan, who had been with Michaels since 1988, to take over as interim president. A few weeks later, Sullivan told Wyly, "I don't see how Michaels is going to survive." Wyly thought, *It's déjà vu all over again. Just like our CFO telling Doug the day he arrived from Family Dollar that the bankers are going to foreclose on our glue guns!*

They decided it was time to take drastic action on the excess inventory and wrote off $65 million of it. The stock plummeted again, so Sullivan and Wyly decided to run the business for cash rather than earnings because the company's bankers were choking up again. By Christmas, they had amassed about $90 million more cash than the year before by driving down inventories, cutting costs, deferring openings of new stores and signing no new leases.

Wyly knew they still had to solve the technology problem, and it was frustrating and embarrassing for him to have this issue still hurting the company, since he had led three of the top software technology companies in the world. "I feel like

Wyly persuaded Michael Rouleau to take charge of Michaels in 1996, and from the day he arrived, the chain never had a bad quarter.

the shoemaker whose kids have no shoes," he said at the time. He decided to stop patching. They yanked out any nonworking systems and spent about $30 million to install advanced IBM point-of-sale machines in the checkout lines of every store. That was the front end—the data input end—of a system that would have to be unlike any other. The back-end problem was next.

In early 1996, Wyly met the man he knew could run the company and who had the knowledge and the determination to force all that technology to work. Michael Rouleau had been working nonstop since the age of 10, and had paid for his college education with money saved from sailing *Edmund Fitzgerald*–style ships for the Merchant Marines on the Great Lakes. In 1960, he got a retail sales job with Dayton Department Stores[2] while still in college. A year later, Dayton launched its Target Stores concept and he was one of their first people. (This was 1962, the same year Kresge, the five-and-ten-cent store, launched K-Mart, and Sam Walton started Wal-Mart.) Rouleau spent 10 years with Target—paying special attention to developing its sophisticated information systems—and over 20 years (in three stints) with Dayton. He then managed Lowe's new "big box" home improvement store chain, which, during his four years there, became the only real competitor to Home Depot.

Wyly invited Rouleau to his home for a chat, and they talked all day. Then Rouleau spent a week scouting a Michaels Store in Winston-Salem, North Carolina. "What I found out over the course of the week was, number one, the store was busy with customers every day," Rouleau later told Wyly. "The second thing was that the registers were always backed up and customers were waiting in long lines getting awful service. And third, the store manager and the assistant manager sat in the back room all day and never came out on the floor except to go home or go to lunch. And fourth, I could see that there wasn't a lot of competition. I didn't need to do all kinds of analysis. After you've been in the business for 38 years, you say, 'Man this is just a miracle waiting to happen.'"

Wyly hired him on April 15, 1996. From that day until the company was sold for $6 billion in 2006, Michaels never had another bad quarter. In the beginning, Rouleau worked seven days a week. It would be a long while before he gave himself a day off.

Five or six weeks into his tenure, Wyly called him. "We have a great opportunity to raise $100 million of capital in the form of long-term bonds. The markets are strong and getting stronger. So, we have to go on a 'road show.' And you are the star of the show."

 "I had to fly all around the country with our brokers for a whole week," says Rouleau. "I had to present this story about Michaels as though I knew everything there ever was to know—after being there such a short time."

He apparently knew enough. "After five days on the road we were oversubscribed on our bond offering," Wyly recalls. "We raised $125 million and probably could have raised $250 million."

Their first major investment was in the information technology system that had thus far eluded them. Rouleau started with the most basic building blocks, putting the point-of-sales terminals in each store. Michaels now had, at long last, advanced POS systems throughout the chain. Rouleau also standardized store layouts to take advantage of all the purchase data the stores were now capturing, including "impulse buy" items at the checkout counter, and regional favorites, such as tropical silk flowers in southern Florida stores. He installed new merchandising systems and transportation and warehousing systems. Using satellite links, they could share data in unprecedented ways. Rouleau's ultimate goal was the automated replenishment of inventory based on historical sales per store (by item, season, discount, promotion, impulse, and regional special items), and he pushed for a management information system that would provide analysis and red flag both on its own, as well as by query. He knew it would make their merchants as well as their troops in the stores smarter.

All his changes resulted in profit growth of 35 percent compounded annually during his first five years at Michaels. The average revenue generated by a store jumped from $2.9 million in 1997 to nearly $4 million by 2002. Over his 10 years as CEO, Rouleau opened more than 500 stores—almost one a week—bringing the total close to 1,000. At that point, there was a sense it was time to take advantage of another cycle in Wall Street's occasional mania to give away free money. LBOs, which historically were priced at four or five times cash flow, were now being priced at seven and eight multiples, with Wyly's exhibit A being the recent sale of Neiman Marcus at eight times. He told his board, "Based on the Neiman buyout, we can get ten times!" And he did.

On March 21, 2006, Michaels was put up for sale, with JPMorgan as the company's agent. Shares jumped 14 percent that day, and three months later, LBO firms Bain Capital and Blackstone Group agreed to buy the chain for $6 billion. On

Twice over the years Wyly and his team at Michaels faced disaster and dissolution but fought on. Several different CEOs, with different skills and personalities, became like those who dreamed of building a car a minute or walking on the moon—they didn't quite know what couldn't be done.

Above: At the company's listing on the NYSE in 2001.

Below: The board in 1999 featured four Wylys: in the front row, Evan, Sam, Charles and Kelly.

October 31—Halloween, one of the stores' busiest holidays—the transaction was closed. For those IPO investors (including the Wyly brothers who had to be the underwriters because the big Wall Street firms would not do so), the initial investment in public stock earned a 60–1 return over 20 years.

Asked to sum up what lessons in entrepreneurship can be drawn from his success with the Michaels Stores, Wyly says, "The best businesses are born out of optimism and tenacity, and the inability to know when all is lost."

Endnotes

1 Aaron Brothers brought a wealth of framing-related experience to the Michaels fold, with stores dating back to the 1940s. After Almore and Len Aaron were discharged from the service in World War II, they returned to Hollywood, California, and opened a photography studio. Noticing that most of their customers' photos ended up gathering dust in drawers, the brothers began selling photo frames. In 1946, Aaron Brothers opened its first frame shop in Hollywood. The store quickly attracted show-business personalities and grew to include 16 more stores in the late 1950s and 1960s. As the "framer to the stars," Aaron Brothers' custom-framing service was born. Al and Len were determined that the business should be fun and adventurous. Art supplies were added in 1969, and by the 1970s, the stores were pioneers in mass-marketing quality prints and paintings. As trends have come and gone, store inventory has expanded to include macramé, decoupage, batik, pottery and candle-making supplies. It all made for an ideal complement to the Michaels Stores empire.

2 While Michael Rouleau eventually got into the Target store concept at Dayton, the company had built a golden reputation over nine decades with a variety of other top-end stores, including B. Dalton Booksellers, Dillard's, Marshall Fields, Mervyn's (making it the seventh-largest retailer in the U.S. acquisition) and many others. Dayton was considered a breeding ground for some of the top executives in retailing. Wyly had become an admirer of Bruce Dayton's since he met the second-generation family CEO at a management council for Presidents (years before he had recruited Rouleau).

Wyly: "Like the ancient Jews in the Bible, we had to go through multiple disasters before reaching the promised land."

CHAPTER FOURTEEN

THE SWEET SPOT AT LAST

In the spring of 1982, *Business Software Review* magazine pro-claimed, "Sam Wyly Is Back," and quoted him saying that "Sterling Software will become a dominant factor in the software industry" by the end of the '80s. He wasn't afraid to make that bold claim because he could see the future lining up just as he had predicted it would. Now all he had to do was make sure he caught a ride on that cresting wave.

He had known since the first days of University Computing that the "sweet spot"—the union of computers and telephone lines—would bring a technological and social revolution that would change the way the world worked and played. And he knew Moore's law would continue to cut the cost of an electronic trans-action in half every two years; and with the millions of desktop computers that would be sold over the next 20 years, the potential market was staggering.

Although Datran had been a $100 million economic loss, Wyly knew it had been a transformative idea, and that "telephone companies for computers" would be coming soon. Datran had made technological advances that would be the foun-dation for today's online universe, but in the mid-'80s the graphical Web-based Internet was still six years away. There still was no simple, efficient way for most businesses to merge their computers and their phones.

Wyly could see that the technology arc was getting steeper: desktop comput-ers were putting computing power on 300,000 desks a week, and the demand arc was following that same rapid ascent as businesses—with all this new computing power on every desk, in every office—demanded much more capability than standalone applications gave them. They needed not just electronic communica-tion capability, but the seamless interaction of the software on their mainframe, midrange and personal computers. The key would be software that not only knew how to transmit data to other machines, but how to interact with their programs—analyze information, render conclusions and take actions.

And Wyly now had that software, hidden in a little office in Cleveland, Ohio.

Back then, OrderNet provided standardized electronic transmission of documents, mostly purchase orders and invoices, but it also greatly facilitated the demand-supply-fulfillment cycles among retailers and wholesalers. From that alone, Wyly forecast an exciting future. If Sterling Software went after industries that had sprawling networks of retailers, wholesalers and manufacturers—for example, grocery store chains, healthcare businesses and transportation—it could establish standards in document transmission. And it was clear to him that purchase orders and invoices were not the only kinds of documents that could be electronically transmitted.

The engineers at tiny OrderNet, the smallest of Sterling Software's divisions (the "pearl of great price" Wyly had sought in his takeover of Informatics), called the technological magic their software did "electronic data interchange," or EDI. It converted business documents (invoices, bills of lading, purchase orders) into standard formats and then sent them over telecommunications networks to the computers of trading partners, whose receiving software converted these digital images back into standard documents. And all of that EDI was done without human intervention.

Automation was the key. Standardized EDI transmissions enabled computers to execute functions traditionally done by humans (with lots of paper copies), and did it hundreds of times faster, with a lot less paperwork. EDI could eliminate the mailing of paper documents and the manual processing of price quotes, purchase orders, invoices, shipping documents and so many other business and governmental transactions. The data was processed and stored automatically, so tasks such as re-keying data and printing documents were eliminated.

To sell this wondrous product, Sterling Software went after industry leaders with vast networks of retail and distribution outlets, companies that would enjoy phenomenal gains in productivity from EDI. The mission was to make OrderNet the EDI standard among leaders in each industry the company went after, figuring that the littler fish would have to follow the lead of the giants.

They targeted five areas: pharmaceutical companies, grocery store chains, transportation companies, hardware chains and large retailers, and selling was done at the top of each organization. The first contract sold was to Topco, a grocery services giant that would be Sterling's entry point for signing up the other major grocery chains. Sterling then signed up the giant Kroger Supermarkets chain and quickly set up EDI for 1,500 stores in 38 states.

The company quickly made a strategic software product buy to go along with OrderNet: Gentran, which would help build the supply chain business. It was a perfect complement to OrderNet's service because it could handle a variety of EDI standards, not just Sterling's. Soon versions of Gentran were ready for both IBM mainframes and midrange computers, with programs for other platforms on the way. This software gave users more self-sufficiency and network independence, and it was a hit. Wyly realized how big a hit when mighty Wal-Mart became a customer.

He was dazzled as he watched his evolving system operate. One very satisfied customer was his Michaels Stores. "We could watch the software guide a colorful silk flower from the moment it was hand-painted by a young Chinese lady," Wyly recalls. "We could watch as the flower moved from her family's hut on one of her country's 42 million half-acre cotton farms to a plant on mainland China and on to a dock at Hong Kong, to a ship that steams across the Pacific Ocean to Long Beach, then across the USA in a freight train to our Pennsylvania distribution center to a truck running along the Old National Road to our Michaels Store in Indianapolis, where our customer, Janet Hamilton, bought that silk flower and took it home." Along the way, the purchase orders, invoices, customs documents, bills of lading and more were all processed automatically.

Wyly saw both great intimacy and import in what the system delivered. "The process was so untouched by intermediaries," he says, "that it's almost as if the young artist handed the painting to Janet herself. And the software we put in place was vital to this long supply chain, which was raising the standard of living and the quality of life all over the world. It was part of the process we had come to call globalization."

Within three years, Sterling Software had 5,000 customers worldwide, including 90 of America's 100 largest industrial corporations and 85 of the top 100 banks. By 1989, OrderNet was the technology standard in many of the world's largest industries.

While the company aggressively beefed up the EDI product line, other Sterling group executives—Werner Frank (Systems Software Group), Ed Lott (Financial Software) and Geno Tolari (Federal Systems)—worked hard with their teams to supplement their product offerings, and by the end of the '80s, all three groups were growing faster than the industry averages and had expanding profit margins. With its $15.1 million in profit, the Systems Software Group was earning almost 25 percent in net income.

The long and complicated supply chain for Michaels' vast inventory was a major challenge for Wyly's management team.

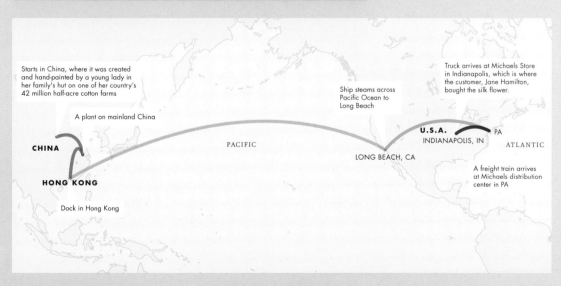

Starts in China, where it was created and hand-painted by a young lady in her family's hut on one of her country's 42 million half-acre cotton farms

A plant on mainland China

CHINA

HONG KONG

Dock in Hong Kong

PACIFIC

Ship steams across Pacific Ocean to Long Beach

LONG BEACH, CA

U.S.A.
INDIANAPOLIS, IN

Truck arrives at Michaels Store in Indianapolis, which is where the customer, Jane Hamilton, bought the silk flower.

PA

ATLANTIC

A freight train arrives at Michaels distribution center in PA

Above, and below: Sterling was an industry leader internationally and extremely profitable, and it had some huge government contracts, including ones with NASA's Ames Research Center near Mountain View, California, and the U.S. Army Commissary.

Below: In 1989, Sterling upgraded the Advanced Computational Facility at NASA's Ames facility from a Cray X-MP/48 to a Cray Y-MP/832, the newest generation of Cray supercomputers.

Those were all stellar performers, but EDI was the sexy product on the covers of trade journals every week and the subject of scores of trade conferences, so Wyly began to wonder if there was a way to better capitalize on all of this attention. *Maybe*, he thought, *two stocks would be worth more than one.*

He knew that EDI had the high profile and the potential for exponential growth. At the same time, he could not ignore the fact that the company's largest sources of income, the Systems Software Group, had serious challenges. One was a rapidly diversifying computer world—more and more, Sterling was running into customers with mixed hardware platforms. The only answer was to expand beyond the once-dominant IBM technology. Sterling bought a product called ZIM, which helped develop applications for multiple hardware platforms: whatever processors and platforms customer companies had, Sterling would accommodate them, and would be the first to do it.

The Systems Software Group began a major initiative in data storage management after IBM announced a new generation of storage software, and rolled out new products from 1991 through 1999, as the group continued both its stunning growth and its 25 percent profit margin.

The rest of the company wasn't doing badly either—Tolari negotiated a $210 million contract with NASA's Ames Research Center in Sunnyvale, California. It was Sterling Software's largest contract ever but got no headlines. When Wyly asked Tolari, "What do we do for the Air Force?" he replied, "I can't tell you."

"Why not?"

"Because their employees won't tell me. They are under a mountain in Colorado—an atomic bomb–proof shelter, and they don't tell anybody what our computer systems do for them."

In 1990, Sterling created the EDI Group. The goal was simple: "Be the number one EDI supplier in the world." The four-pronged attack would be in:

1. Software—Sterling would provide translation software that converted data from internal formats into standard formats for EDI transmission, and interpreted incoming EDI transmissions back to internal formats for processing. This was Gentran, the backbone software.

2. Network services—These included electronic mailboxes, data communications, backup and recovery, in-network translation, internetwork gateways, and

media conversion services. These were the OrderNet services, which provided the flexibility to move among different networks and the security that big company computer users demanded.

3. Database services—These provided a data capture and retrieval capability. With the permission of participants, EDI data that flowed through the network was stored in databases and retrieved to provide market intelligence data. This service was named MARKETQUEST.

4. Education—"EDI University" began to teach customers how to make their relationships with their trading partners more productive.

The key was translation software, the root of the EDI process. The more EDI standards its systems could accommodate for users, the broader the potential base. Sterling bought Metro-Mark Systems, a translation software supplier with a large user base, and in 1990, the EDI Group added 1,000 new customers. Companies were not merely adding the EDI technology, some were beginning to be built *around* it.

EDI was fast becoming a global business—U.S. companies wanted it for their multinational branches and international trading partners, and European and Asian companies needed it to interact with their U.S. constituencies. This was a tricky challenge because of the different ("spoken") languages and differing standards, but Sterling moved quickly. Its first overseas operation was in London; EDI International landed several clients and quickly built strategic alliances with major software and communications companies.

Back in the U.S., they bought Control Data Corporation's EDI business, Redinet, adding 1,100 new customers and another entire industry—automotive—to its client base. This technology was fundamentally altering the ways companies conducted business. Digital supply chain management had arrived.

Banking was a special opportunity, because Sterling already was a major player in that field—95 of the 100 largest banks already used its check-processing software, and Sterling had been doing electronic funds transfer for years. As domestic and international banks moved to the next generation of electronic funds transfer, they were incorporating more document exchange. It was the place to be.

The company finished 1991 with a total revenue of $224.4 million and was the world's largest EDI supplier, but by now the term "EDI" no longer described all of what it was doing. It had become something much, much bigger because of a little-noticed event in Switzerland.

A British engineer and MIT professor named Tim Berners-Lee, who was working at CERN, the European laboratory for particle physics, created the first standards for the World Wide Web on Christmas Day 1990. CERN was searching for a means to make it easier for a few elite scientists to share research. When Berners-Lee came up with a solution to that problem, he opened the door to the Internet, used by 2.1 billion people as of 2011. Adding the World Wide Web to the Internet brought images and a user-friendly interface to what had been a highly technical, text-only network used mainly by academicians and the military. The network of all networks was now on the brink of becoming accessible by anyone anywhere with a phone connection. That paradigm shift was about to occur.

Sterling was booming domestically and globally, and then, on May 10, 1992—Mother's Day—tragedy struck: Don Thomson died. On Saturday, he and Ed Lott had gone to the racetrack in Shreveport and Don had done well at the window. He went to bed happy and didn't wake up. "The best there ever was," said Wyly, echoing the words of the hundreds of people who had worked for Thomson. "Don was the most talented, versatile and instinctive manager I have ever known."

Despite losing one of its most important leaders, Sterling kept pushing forward, trying to anticipate the next breakthrough. It was clear the technology had expanded beyond electronic data interchange—company managers were putting transaction automation into more and more aspects of their enterprises, facilitating every step along the path of a customer's decision to buy something, from availability to ordering to payment to delivery, and a vendor's decision to make or stock something. That meant anticipating supply and demand, speeding the replenishment of stock, transferring funds, and transporting inventory. It meant conducting nearly every aspect of business electronically.

Looking at this trend, they began to wonder if they needed to again change the business's name from EDI. "We weren't just technology," Wyly says. "Our customers said, 'Solve my problem,' and we solved those problems. We needed to be in our customers' conversations without somebody in the room having to stop and explain what this three-letter word for a company means. So we came up with

In the midst of Sterling's booming success around the globe, Don Thomson (right) died in his sleep on May 10, 1992. "The best there ever was," Wyly said. "Don was the most talented, versatile and instinctive manager I have ever known."

the phrase 'electronic commerce.'" A few years later, as the Internet bloomed, IBM began running full-page ads that said, "IBM means e-commerce."

The new Electronic Commerce Group's customer base grew a stunning 80 percent in 1992, to 4,100, and now included more than 100 of the *Fortune 500* companies. By 2010, 18,000 companies in 95 countries were dealing with one another through Sterling Commerce's software and data links.

With this phenomenal growth, Wyly saw another capitalization opportunity. He knew that often two stocks could be worth more than one, and began to think through how best to spin off the Electronic Commerce Group.

There was another important factor for Wyly: he sometimes felt that to Wall Street, Sterling Software was the Rodney Dangerfield of stocks—"I don't get no respect!" was the comedian's punch line. He saw that similar companies had higher price-earnings ratios—even though every Sterling division was strong and profitable, had a record of consistent growth, solid prospects for expansion, products for platforms ranging from mainframes through PCs, and the communications tools to link them. "But many players in the stock markets still viewed Sterling Software as just a mainframe stock," he says. "And while we had a solid reputation, Wall Street gave high multiples to the pure plays."

Several things had set the stage for Sterling's spin-off of Electronic Commerce. In '94, Sterling completed its 24th consecutive quarter of uninterrupted growth, ending the year with $473.4 million in revenue and a net income of $58.3 million, and was one of the 10 largest software companies in the world. The next year marked the launch of the Wall Street boom in tech and telecom stocks, the "dot-com" revolution.

The launch event for this exuberance was the day of Netscape's IPO in 1995. Marc Andreessen and some of the other programmers had created the Mosaic browser at the University of Illinois, where its ownership was in the public domain. They were lured to Silicon Valley by venture capitalist Jim Clark to write an enhanced version—Netscape. Its stock doubled and doubled and doubled again. Old-fashioned telephone companies were now seen as pipelines into homes for computers to talk to computers.

Watching investors snatching up any tech stock on the board, Wyly remembered the staggering but illusory 100–1 multiplication in share value for

During the dot-com craze of the '90s, investors seemed to be ready to buy any pig-in-a-poke company so long as it had ".com" attached to its name. The apex (or was it the low point?) of this bubble was the IPO for Netscape in 1995. Programmer Marc Andreessen (right), who had helped create the browser's predecessor, Mosaic, and venture capitalist Jim Clark (left) celebrated IPO day at headquarters in Silicon Valley. Most analysts argued that the rules had changed, but Wyly sensed an inevitable bust coming.

University Computing from 1965 to 1969. While many Wall Streeters and journalists said the dot-com boom had brought new rules to the market, Wyly remembered the rules that had applied for decades, even centuries. He remembered the Crash of 1970 and the disastrous decade that had followed the first computer boom in the 1960s.

But it wasn't his job to be a Cassandra, to warn investors to put their money away. It was his job to exploit the market, to grab his best chance, to increase value for his shareholders. Dot-com companies that consisted of little more than a Web site were going public with astronomical proceeds, and it was now vividly clear to him that the Electronic Commerce business was most valuable to stockholders if Sterling Software recapitalized into two separate public companies. This would increase shareholders' wealth and expand opportunities for employees.

They changed the name of Electric Commerce in March 1996, completed an initial public offering (IPO) of 18.4 percent of Sterling Commerce and listed it on the New York Stock Exchange. What had begun as the OrderNet "pearl" a decade earlier became one of the larger tech IPOs of the decade, raising $267 million in cash for Sterling Software and $40 million for Sterling Commerce. Wyly's team then distributed the remaining 81.6 percent ownership in Sterling Commerce to Sterling Software shareholders as a tax-free dividend.

Most observers expected Sterling Software's share price to tumble after dividending out Sterling Commerce, but Wyly knew otherwise. "That fear was the result of asking the wrong question," he says.

The right question to ask was: "What will be the *summation* of the market capitalizations of both companies to owners after the creation of two separate publicly owned companies?" Sterling Software's share price didn't drop after the spin-off—values for all shareholders and employee stock options holders were substantially enhanced, many more employees became millionaires, and some of them became multimillionaires.

The timing for this spin-off was as close to perfect as one could get, and both companies were suddenly cash rich. Sterling Software had $700 million in cash entering 1997, and plenty of ideas about how to spend it.

Wyly: "Know your products. Know your niches. Know your customers. Speak personally with everyone."

THE $8 BILLION HARVEST

By late 1995, markets were speculating on who would be the winners in the race to hit Wyly's "sweet spot"—where telephone and computer merged. This mad dash was being accelerated by Moore's law, with costs being cut in half every two years, and the sweet spot now had a name: the Internet. And everybody was throwing money at it—this was the dot-com boom, with its "new economy stocks," with its countless tissue-thin IPOs, overheated (or nonexistent) price-earnings ratios and easy money that had a lot of people thinking tough times might never come again.

There had been only eight tech IPOs in 1985; in 1999, there were 308, which made up over half that year's offerings. If you had a dot-com in your name, it seemed that Wall Street was begging to give you money. By 2010, the numer of tech IPOs was down to 10.

Everywhere Wyly looked, institutions and individuals were frantically chasing instant wealth via the IPO craze. He saw his son's buddy (and pick-up basketball companion at their gym in Dallas) Mark Cuban start Broadcast .com in 1998, quickly grow it to $100 million in sales and then sell it to Yahoo for $5.9 billion in 1999. (Cuban used $180 million of his take to buy the NBA's Dallas Mavericks.)

Analysts smirked that Fed chairman Alan Greenspan was just an old-school party pooper when he warned

When Alan Greenspan (above) warned of "irrational exuberance" in the markets, analysts smirked.

of "irrational exuberance" in the markets. The old guy just didn't get it, they chuckled, didn't understand that the Internet economy had changed everything in fundamental ways. Wyly knew better—his 30 years of experience told him that booms lead to busts as surely as A leads to B . . .

Just prior to spinning off Sterling Commerce, Sterling Software had a market capitalization of $2 billion, and after that dividend, it was still $2 billion. His team had built a world-class business by following a proven strategy, one that involved an old-time tangible presence in Sterling's chosen markets. But he wondered if there was now a new definition of what qualified as a "world-class company." Was Sterling in danger of becoming passé?

This time, when Wyly asked himself, *What do I know for sure?* he knew that he didn't know enough. So he and his team decided to pull back; it would create Internet sites, monitor sales and service on them, listen to customers and strive to learn what they wanted. The niches the company sold into now were alive and well, always being reconfigured, and always looking for better software. "That's why we continued to succeed," says Wyly. "We did not pretend to do everything in software. But we did what we did better than anyone else."

But innovation happened rapidly in technology, and acquisitions and divestitures change companies and markets, sometimes suddenly and often radically. There were always new products, new specializations, new services, new employees and a new base of users—sometimes overnight. And sometimes, Wyly knew, the pioneers are the guys lying in the creek with a chest full of Comanche arrows. He also knew that sometimes what Wall Street analysts thought really did matter. Was Sterling "an unfocused hodgepodge of acquired software in a stagnant market" or "a coherent and evolving product line of complementary systems with a vital future"?

The answer was, Wyly knew, the latter, and the message regularly delivered to his managers was: "Know your products. Know your niches. Know your customers. Speak personally with everyone."

Still, his team had to work hard to persuade investors and customers that Sterling Software was a high-value-added enterprise. While it was a huge thing that its stock price was unfazed after the huge Sterling Commerce dividend, the real test would be in the company's long-term performance. Every year, the company expanded—sometimes by 20 or more products and two or three new niches—so every year it had to tell people all over again what it "did for a living." And in the wake of the spin-off, it was more vital than ever that the investors who rated the company and the customers who bought from it had a clear vision of what the business was.

Wyly and Sterling Williams knew the only solution was the old solution: reorganize with as little disruption for employees and customers as possible, and offer as much clarity as possible to prospective clients. In what had become an almost annual ritual, Sterling Software was again restructured in 1996, this time into six business groups.

Sterling Software's revenue for 1996 was $439 million, proving there was indeed life after Sterling Commerce. While Sterling Software had proved itself again, Sterling Commerce now had to show it could fly on its own, although few doubted it would get airborne. Its first-year revenue of $267 million put it among the 25 largest software enterprises in the U.S.

The Internet was now affecting the commercial practices of almost every business, the potential customer base was skyrocketing and Sterling Commerce launched several major initiatives to exploit it. But it began to see that it would have to reengineer every software product to keep its edge. And it had a lot of them.

When Sterling surveyed its base, it learned that security and privacy were becoming crisis issues for clients because of the vulnerability of the Internet. Companies desperately wanted to be online, but they also wanted to be safe. Stephen Perkins, who headed the company's most prominent unit, the Communications Software Group, was assigned the task of figuring out how to be the first company to meet those challenges.

Perkins loved talking with customers. He and his team would sit and listen to them describe their problems in sometimes numbing detail. But they also constantly asked about future problems and requirements, how they anticipated using the Internet, how it was changing the nature of their businesses, what sort of internal "Intranet" were they building. Did they believe Sun Microsystems' slogan, "The network is the computer"? Then he would craft a solution for them. That's why he always had an answer for today's challenge, and knew what tomorrow's challenge would be.

Texas entrepreneur Sam Wyly has started
two computer companies. The second
is turning out much better for him.

Profiting from mistakes

By Christopher Palmeri

WHEN DALLAS businessmen Sam
Wyly and Sterling Williams decided to
build a new computer software company in 1981, they drew up a list of
more than 100 acquisition candidates. It was quite a list. On it were a
$15 million (sales) company in Seattle
named Microsoft and a $1.2 million
company in Northern California
named Oracle. "We had very good
taste," jokes Williams.

Microsoft and Oracle weren't for
sale, of course, but others were. Wyly
and Williams whittled the list down to
four small software companies and,
with a $2 million investment from the
Wyly family and $15 million raised in
a public stock offering, bought them.
Sterling Software was born.

Sterling hasn't been a Microsoft or
an Oracle, but it hasn't done too
badly. Last year operating earnings
were $49 million on revenues of $412
million. If a recently announced acquisition is completed, Sterling's revenues should jump to $600 million
this year, making it the eleventh-
largest software company in the
world.

Sam Wyly is the consummate entrepreneur. Over the years he has invested in dozens of businesses. Some, like
the arts and crafts chain Michaels
Stores, have been great successes.
Others, like Bonanza steakhouses and
Frost Brothers, a now-defunct retailer
based in the Southwest, have been
disappointments.

In starting Sterling, Wyly and Williams came armed with mistakes they
had made with an earlier computer
company Wyly had started, University Computing Co. The firm grew
rapidly during the Sixties. But in the

STERLING COMMERCE PROFIT
(IN MILLIONS)

$96.4

$71.6

$46.3

1994 1995 1996

STERLING COMMERCE NET INCOME
(IN MILLIONS)

$58.4

$42.9

$27.8

1994 1995 1996

STERLING COMMERCE REVENUE
(IN MILLIONS)

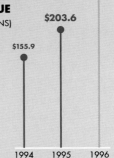

$267.8

$203.6

$155.9

1994 1995 1996

Turning Sterling into gold, one record-breaking year at a time.

The business world has entered the Era of Electronic Commerce. Soon, every company will be part of an interconnecting network of information that links all the players – raw goods suppliers, wholesalers, manufacturers, retailers, bankers, everybody in the chain – into a global trading community. The people at Sterling Commerce pioneered this revolution, remain at its leading edge, and are developing the tools for the *future*.

KAREN CHUVALAS | ACCOUNT MANAGER | COMMERCE SERVICES GROUP

They began by retrofitting older systems with Internet capabilities, but after a while it was clear more was needed. Systems needed to be redesigned from the ground up. This was a daunting commitment few companies had the energy or wherewithal to make—after all, Sterling Commerce provided almost 100 business-to-business electronic commerce products and services. But it got done. Thanks to Perkins and his programming teams, the reengineered software was well designed, and almost immediately, the software family soared to the top of the e-commerce field. E-commerce had become central to almost every kind of business, an essential component of productivity, competitiveness and profits—and the company was willing to spend a lot of money to get it right.

Wyly and his executive ensemble did not, of course, always succeed in building the number one company in its field—and once in a while they flopped—but the dogged pursuit of that goal made all their businesses better. That top-dog status is what they had in mind when they began looking at Texas Instruments Software (TI), the top company in another emerging niche—component-based programming—to add to some application development tools they had already, including software they'd got from "the Scrambler," Minnesota Vikings' quarterback Fran Tarkenton, who had started an Atlanta-based software company called Knowledgeware after his Hall of Fame football career.

Because of the soaring costs of developing applications and a chronic shortage of information technology professionals, businesses were increasingly backlogged on the development of critical systems. They were looking for a way to build and maintain applications—including mission-critical applications—faster, cheaper and more predictably. TI had an answer. TI's component-based development enabled programmers to quickly assemble new software systems by using modules of reusable code that was already in other programs. Basically, it enabled them to create new applications from reusable parts, saving countless man-hours. Today's interactive interfaces, for instance, are built by reusing components to create graphic windows and pull-down menus.

In June of 1997, Sterling Commerce bought TI's software division for $165 million. The move expanded its customer base significantly, and further solidified its leading position in enterprise application development. Wyly knew

TI's software would have to be marketed very intelligently, because in the bohemian world of elite programmers, there could be some resistance to the idea of "recycling code." (Imagine Rembrandt using "reusable scenes" painted by other artists to understand how hostile some programmers were to this technology.) There were a lot of things here that could go south on Wyly, but with some good marketing and better customer relations and salesmanship, those concerns were addressed, and the young component-based development market began to grow quickly. Wyly's team had again gotten in on the ground floor of a tech revolution.

Back in 1965, Wyly had predicted at the spring joint computer conference in Atlantic City that when the computer finally "met" the phone, nothing would ever be the same. By 1998, he realized that that had been a gross understatement—worldwide electronic commerce on the Internet already totaled $22.9 billion, the e-commerce technology that supported it was on fire and every big company in the marketplace was clamoring to get closer to the heat, including giants such as Microsoft and IBM and all the European and American telephone companies. Established, highly successful brick-and-mortar businesses were now deathly afraid of getting "Amazoned"—leveled by a cyberspace company the way Amazon was overwhelming so many bookstores.

Sterling Commerce kept running faster, and thinking bigger. In 1997, it acquired an international electronic commerce distributor that instantly gave the company a strong presence in 16 countries and control over 39 distributors. In 1998, it made acquisitions in Germany, the U.K. and two in Singapore, and a European support center was established in Amsterdam.

The *Computer Industry Almanac* said in April 1998 that there were 150 million Internet users worldwide, and predicted that number would hit 318 million in less than two years. (It hit 2.1 billion worldwide by June 18, 2011, with 272 million in North America.) These swelling numbers presented marketing opportunities, and problems. How do you sway a billion people? Sterling Commerce launched everything it could think of to make sure the world knew it on a first-name basis, from full-page advertising to alliances with respected companies, and created a course that taught programmers how to construct applications using Sterling Software's components. All this paid off immediately.

Wyly knew he was riding a pair of voracious tigers in Sterling Commerce and

● **STERLING COMMERCE OFFICES**   ● **STERLING COMMERCE DISTRIBUTORS**

FIVE-YEAR CUMULATIVE TOTAL RETURN* COMPARISON

Among Sterling Software, Inc.,
and the S&P 500 Index.

*$100 invested on 9/30/93 in stock or
index — including reinvestment of dividends.
Fiscal year ending Septermber 30, 1998.

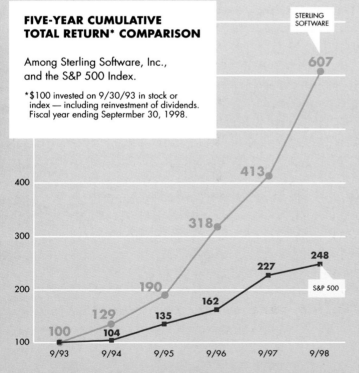

STERLING
SOFTWARE

607

413

318

190

100   129

104   135   162   227   248

S&P 500

400

300

200

100

9/93   9/94   9/95   9/96   9/97   9/98

Sterling Commerce kept running
faster and thinking bigger. In 1997
it acquired an international electronic commerce distributor that
instantly gave the company a strong
presence in 16 countries and control over 39 distributors. In 1998, it
made acquisitions in Germany, the
U.K. and two in Singapore, and a
European support center was established in Amsterdam.

Sterling Software, but he was also worried, because he knew this boom market had not yet caught its breath. Few of the forecasters were accounting for the downturn Wyly knew was inevitable. In the late 1990s, *Forbes* magazine joined Alan Greenspan in warning that a fall was coming, and valuations of the dot-coms, and others in the tech and telecom sector, had exceeded "ridiculous" status. Still, people had buckets of equity cash, so companies were spending freely on computer systems that were now a continually rising share of corporate investment, which meant Sterling's outlook looked great . . . on paper.

By 1999, Sterling Commerce had penetrated every major industry that relied on e-commerce—retailing, banking and financial services, healthcare, transportation, hardlines, government, groceries, telecommunications, manufacturing, entertainment and more. The company's GENTRAN, COMMERCE and CONNECT products were being used by 482 of the *Fortune* 500 companies. Of the top 100 banks, 99 utilized the company's VECTOR systems.

Wyly was proud—he knew that even if the capital markets collapsed, the software sold by the Sterling companies would continue to be purchased for years because it lined up with how businesses were being built for the 21st century. But he still feared that valuations for tech companies were approaching "tulip mania" status and that the whole market was heading for a crash.

His strongest evidence of that was the failure of the IPO of his new clean-energy company, Greenmountain.com, in March 1999 [Chapter 18]. For four years, the dot-com market had seemed limitless, with investors, institutional and otherwise, pouring money into stocks that were considerably less substantial than that of Green Mountain, which he had started up in 1997. But that offering failed, and he filed away his letter from Prudential that had promised, "We will raise you $500 million for Green Mountain." He thought the entire market was overpriced and getting more so all the time, as rationality was being replaced by irrational exuberance. He thought about all this, and finally decided that the game was over. It was time to cash out.

In the fall of 1999, Goldman Sachs was hired to discreetly seek out buyers for Sterling Commerce. The company's growth rate and profit history, combined with the optimistic forecasts for electronic commerce, made it attractive on both the pragmatic and emotional levels. Sterling Software, however, was a tougher sell, because it had "succeeded" itself into something of a box: through its growth-by-acquisition strategy, it had acquired most of its potential buyers, and there were only a few software companies big enough to buy it.

The best fit for Sterling Commerce, IBM, was at that time prohibited from buying Sterling Commerce under its antiquated antitrust settlement of a federal lawsuit. Several of the telephone companies in Europe were interested. Then Goldman Sachs called to say that SBC was interested. Wyly and his team immediately sensed a good match—SBC Communications (the former Texas Bell) was one of the eight companies created when the AT&T telephone monopoly was busted up. It had bought Pacific Bell and wanted electronic commerce technology to combine with its other telecommunications products, so Sterling Commerce would be a strategic acquisition. And SBC had plenty of cash—it had just bought Ameritech in October of 1999 for $77.4 billion in a stock-for-stock merger. It was putting Humpty Dumpty back together again—growing into another huge telephone duopoly—and now wanted to be sure it was "a telephone company for computers," too. Wyly and Williams were optimistic.

Finding a good buyer for Sterling Software, however, was going to be difficult. Sterling's bankers were told, "Go to HP. Go to Compaq. Go to Dell. Go to IBM." And they did, but HP and Dell (hardware companies) were not yet ready to fully commit to the software and services part of the industry (they would by 2008), and Compaq was busy absorbing minicomputer giant Digital Equipment—not knowing that Compaq themselves were going to be ultimately gobbled up by HP. By 2010, all those companies—at least the ones still standing—knew that software was the heart of their businesses, but that realization came to some of them slowly. The only obvious suitor was Computer Associates, but for Wyly that was like making a deal with the devil. CA was everything Wyly's companies despised, the model of "how not to run a computer company."

In early 2000, Wyly's team agreed on terms to sell Sterling Commerce to SBC (today renamed AT&T), with its headquarters moved to Dallas. AT&T partnered with the Wyly Family on a philanthropic project that houses the Opera and the Wyly Theater in a performance arts center in downtown Dallas, but it still didn't have a "home" for Sterling Software. Ultimately Goldman Sachs said, "Look—you know and we know there is only one buyer: Computer Associates." So, holding his nose and his wallet, Wyly told Morgan Stanley to let CA know that just *maybe* Sterling Software could be bought. Ultimately, CA jumped on the hint, desperate to pad its numbers by swallowing up this truly sterling competitor, and desperate to maintain its spiraling growth in order to pump up its bottom line. The company's CEO, Sanjay Kumar, was in Wyly's backyard the next Sunday.

Wyly and his managers ended up closing both deals in one amazing week in March of 2000. Sterling Software was bought with $4 billion in stock, a 30 percent premium over its market price. Knowing (and wary of) the corporate ethos at Computer Associates, Wyly and his board approved a generous severance for employees likely to be laid off by CA's cost-, payroll- and overhead-slashers, and a week later Sterling Commerce was sold to SBC for $3.9 billion in cash, 40 percent premium to the market and 10 times revenue.

Once again, Wyly's timing was eerily apt. That month, the tech bubble popped and the subsequent black hole sucked a lot of wealth into the ether. From 2000 to 2002, the tech- and telecom-heavy NASDAQ index dropped 80 percent. In 2010, it was still 50 percent below what it had been a decade earlier.

Wyly and his public shareholders got out unscathed—and very, very rich. And he remains proud of the company he built: "Ten years later—May 2010—AT&T sold Sterling Commerce to IBM for $1.4 billion, $2.6 billion less than they paid us and our fellow owners. But it was still a roaring success as a company and IBM would keep it as an independent subsidiary."

Endnotes

1   *Computer Industry Almanac* was founded in 1986 and specializes in market research for the personal computer, Internet and related industries. It is published out of Arlington Heights, Illinois.

What's in a name? Sterling Williams and Wyly worked together for 30 years, and their relationship spawned two multibillion-dollar software companies, both of them named after Williams.

Painter Mort Künstler's *Moonlight and Magnolias*—the Wyly family tree meets *Gone With the Wind.*

CHAPTER SIXTEEN

INVESTING THE TIME TO INVEST WISELY

When Sam Wyly's first publicly traded company, University Computing, was enjoying incredible growth in the late '60s, and analysts and investors were speaking of it—and of Wyly— in worshipful tones, a grizzled old trader who'd survived the Great Crash of '29 told him over dinner at a popular Wall Street steakhouse: "Never confuse a bull market for genius."

Wyly's stock in University Computing gave him huge rewards—some of which he'd cashed out year by year at $3, $9, $30, $90 and $150, and reinvested or given away—and then huge disappointments during the recession of the 1970s. Over the next couple of years, he started thinking more seriously about what goes into successfully managing a portfolio of public stocks. He had some theories and some money, so he experimented.

In 1990, he thought he had identified some sound principles for investing, so he started First Dallas (later renamed Maverick), an investment company for his family's money and that of a short list of others. The classic Alfred W. Jones model hedge fund formula is simple: "Basically, you take one dollar of investor capital, then borrow another dollar, and then bet a dollar-fifty on stocks held long and fifty cents on stocks sold short," says Wyly. "We focused on seven industry groups. We bet about seventy-five cents in the USA and about twenty-five cents outside the USA." (Jones called it a "hedged fund," but the press had run with "hedge fund," so that nonsensical term stuck.) It is a simple formula, and it has the added advantage of working. At least it does for Sam Wyly—as of 2011, Maverick had $11 billion in assets, and had survived the nearly apocalyptic Crash of 2008.

How Wyly developed his principles for investing is a lesson in contrarian thinking, and it starts on a cotton farm. He learned the concept of the hedge as a boy in Lake Providence, where cotton farmers would sometimes "sell forward" their spring planting to a merchant for a guaranteed price in the fall. Wyly recalled one season in which his parents decided not to sell forward. "The price in the fall dropped so much that the cotton was hardly worth picking," he says. "My parents wished they had hedged their risk."

IDEAS AT WORK

Maverick Sam Wyly hopes to corral fellow millionaires

Sam Wyly, the Dallas entrepreneur who brought you University Computing, Bonanza restaurants and Sterling Software, has what he thinks is another great idea. And he wants 99 American millionaires to pony up for their share.

CHERYL HALL

Place at least a million in Mr. Wyly's hands, let him invest it for you in high-yielding U.S. corporate or foreign government bonds or an emerging nation's stocks, and pay him 20 percent of the profits that he makes. He says he expects to make plenty.

Audacious. Yes. But what would you expect from the guy who leveraged a $1,000 investment and the idea of selling mainframe computer time into a personal fortune that he estimates at $260 million — depending on the time of day and how you define "his"?

For the past three years, Sam Wyly has played a high-stakes investment game for his family. His strategy: Find high-yielding investments around the world, buy aggressively when others bail out, spread out money to cushion losses and get out when others move in.

■ The Wyly outlook. 7H

He's made money. Every dollar Mr. Wyly invested for his family on April Fools' Day 1990 had multiplied to $2.43 two months ago. Now, in true entrepreneurial spirit, he'd like to make more.

"I'm pretty good at it," says the 58-year-old chairman and controlling stockholder of Sterling Software and Michaels Stores. "It's a game I'd play if I didn't get paid to do it."

With a family ante of $35 million, he's launching Maverick Fund USA — the country's newest hedge fund named to reflect his penchant for separating himself from the herd.

No Treasury bills or 3 percent bank interest for Sam, or his kids and grandkids.

When Iraqi tanks rolled into Kuwait in August 1990, oil soared to $40 from $17 a barrel, the stock market went into free fall and Sam Wyly went on a junk-bond buying spree.

He liked Datapoint. Its bonds were yielding about 50 percent in interest, given their heavily discounted price. He felt the management was inept, but the company's core was worth betting on. If it stayed in business two years, he'd have his money back just from the interest.

His gut feeling was that he wouldn't have to

Please see WYLY on Page 8H.

The Dallas Morning News Richard Michael Pruitt

Investment maverick Sam Wyly says his work is "a game I'd play if I didn't get paid to do it."

Wyly's first rule of investing: "Luck is what happens when preparation meets opportunity."

He also began to appreciate the Original Law of Luck, first advanced by the philosopher and dramatist Seneca 2,000 years ago, which holds that "Luck is what happens when preparation meets opportunity." While a sharp eye for opportunities is imperative, he learned that the best opportunities came to smart people willing to sweat blood in order to find them. Wyly found that rigorously researching companies—their management, their products, their strategies and their markets, and then extrapolating their futures—was a fascinating exercise, and a rewarding one.

Tony Skvarla, a broker at Bear Stearns who did a lot of business with the Wylys, from junk bonds in the '80s up through Maverick and other investments, thinks Wyly shrewdly tailored his investment fund to meet his very specific needs. "When Sam became liquid in the '90s, when he had a lot more cash, I think he wanted to pull back from the business part of business, but putting his money in the stock market meant more risk than he was willing to accept because they weren't companies that he controlled," Skvarla recalls. "That's when he came up with the concept of a truly *hedged* fund, so that he could have considerable sums in the market during good and bad times and not have to face the fear of being down fifty percent at any one time. And, of course, the method he chose with the people he chose to do it worked out extremely well.

"Ironically, making money in the market the way Maverick makes money in the market—with a diversified disciplined approach—isn't what Sam was good at. Sam was good at finding a niche and putting a lot of money into it. Sam is more like [Warren] Buffett that way—he finds a few things he really likes and holds on to them for a long time."

When setting up First Dallas, Wyly figured that whatever skills or training in investing he lacked would be mitigated by the skills and experience of his partner in this new enterprise—his son Evan, who earned an economics degree from Princeton University and an MBA from Harvard Business School, then worked in mergers and investments for Michaels Stores, where he managed an $80 million investment account. (Evan's Princeton thesis was on the AT&T telephone monopoly. He went to New York City to interview their CEO, Charles Brown. After the monopoly was broken, AT&T entered the computer service industry and Sam welcomed it with a speech at the industry's main conference, ADAPSO. His speech, which alluded to Evan's thesis, was entitled, "Welcome to Our World, Charlie Brown!")

Early on, First Dallas focused on macroeconomic plays, such as busted bail-out bonds from Brazil, Argentina and Mexico—high-yield products that corporate America eschewed after Drexel Burnham founder Mike Milken went bankrupt. Finding the hidden opportunity—the ignored, the buried, the obscured, the misread, the misunderstood—was a strategy, not an accident. Wyly liked to quote Sir James Goldsmith's tenet: "If you see the bandwagon, it's too late."[1] Sam Wyly had his own herd instinct—figure out which way the herd was going, then bet the other way.

Early contrarian opportunities came during a time of market chaos. When junk bonds crashed, taking down Drexel Burnham Lambert—a company that had helped Wyly several times—an entire class of investments and investment managers vaporized. After Congress mandated that all U.S. savings and loans divest every junk bond in their portfolios, regardless of return, the Wylys knew that bargains were being created. The negative press coverage made junk bonds radioactive, so Evan and Sam cherry-picked from the abandoned orphans, carefully deducing which companies would not default on their debt. "Good companies such as 7-Eleven were being trashed along with others that really were very, very junky," Wyly recalls.

First Dallas took strong positions in Asian stock markets—Taiwan, Singapore and especially Hong Kong, but *not* Japan. Japan was the bandwagon investment. For example, the price-earnings (P/E) multiple of the Japanese telephone company was 10 times the P/E of AT&T. Instead, Sam and Evan looked for stocks that would benefit from China's growth. (They learned about the Chinese market firsthand in the 1980s, when they imported millions of dollars' worth of arts-and-crafts items for Michaels Stores. But the only way to buy China back then was through Hong Kong–listed companies.) They picked stocks on the Hong Kong exchange for companies that had family ownership control and were buying back their own shares. That investment performed superbly as freer markets continued to open up.

Banks were also exploding chaos overseas. They had been lending to third world countries and calling the loans Lesser Developed Countries (LDC) debt, which was a way to recycle the "petro dollars" created by the huge spikes in oil prices. But Latin America's overwhelming economic problems pushed LDCs out of favor, and hundreds of billions of dollars in debts were at risk because the "sovereign" countries were unable to service them. (The South American continent was stricken by inflation and rising gas prices, and deemed unworthy of credit, which is why the '80s were called "Latin America's lost decade.")

Then, Treasury Secretary Nicholas F. Brady proposed what came to be called the Brady Plan, which allowed American banks to offer debt relief to those debtor nations—additional time to repay, without penalty—in exchange for macroeconomic reforms. The banks got a tradable asset in exchange for an illiquid loan, so they could go ahead and take their loss and get it behind them. As partial collateral, the U.S. government put up Treasury bonds as security for 20 percent (and up to 50 percent) of the face value of the LDC bonds. That meant that even if a country defaulted, the U.S. Treasury collateral was still at least 20 cents on the dollar. Sam and Evan got in early, and when they finally saw the tide coming in and the price of the bonds begin to rise dramatically, they got out.

"We really did a lot on Latin American debt investments," Skvarla says. "We had a guy at Bear Stearns, a rocket scientist who helped create some of this paper who came to work for us, and he explained to us how it worked. And I thought, *Boy, this is something Sam would like.* And I got Sam on the phone, and those two rocket scientists talked to each other and we ended up doing a lot of business together for a few years. I think they made a lot of money.

Charles and Sam endowed chairs at Louisiana Tech (1); Sam on campus (2); Cheryl, Sam's wife, and Lisa, Sam's daughter, at the University of Michigan's dedication of Sam Wyly Hall (3); UM's Sam Wyly Hall (4); Sam with Joe White, dean of Michigan's School of Business (5).

Sam made sharp decisions on the Latin American debt investments. "He assimilated information pretty quickly," Skvarla says. "If he trusted the people and liked the information he was getting, he would act on it. So if you came to him with an idea that really made sense, he would make that decision and do the trade. He is a sponge for knowledge from multiple sources, individuals in varying walks of life, and good at sorting out the ones looking to just make a buck and the ones who really have a good idea and that you can make a buck with, hand in hand."

When Saddam Hussein invaded Kuwait in 1990, oil prices tripled. Many investors figured this would lead to a wider Middle East war, which meant that oil prices were going to continue to soar, and that the stock market was going to dive even further. The Wylys had the opposite read, and poured money into their decliners. That meant there were bargains everywhere if they were right . . . and the grandkids would be taking out college loans if they were wrong. When Desert Storm was launched in January and coalition forces pushed Iraqi troops out of Kuwait, the market rallied. The Wylys' 1991 return on investment: 199 percent.

Companies have taken shareholder investments for centuries (the first stock issuance was by the Dutch East India Company in 1602), but today's hedge funds date back only to about 1949.[2] There were a couple of hundred back in 1968, but most got killed in the market dives in 1969 and 1974. Even late in 1992, there weren't that many hedge funds around, and the success Sam and Evan had had motivated some of their friends to ask if they could invest alongside them. The Wylys were pleased they could help their friends, and they enjoyed turning the management of those portfolios into a business.

Around this time, Sam Wyly got a call from his friend Richard Hanlon, a former writer for *The Economist* and the *Dallas Morning News*, who had worked at UCC in its early days, and then for Legent, a large software company, as the investor relations manager. Hanlon had left Legent to start a consultancy, so when he called, Wyly said, "I want to be your first client. I'll pay you eight thousand bucks a month to help us get a hedge fund rollin'."

"You're on," Hanlon said, then returned to his office and began calling every name in his Rolodex to tell them what Sam Wyly was doing and essentially to ask this question: "Tell me again what a hedge fund is and what it does?"

Wyly had a headhunter feeding him candidates to manage his fund, but Hanlon said, "Let me tell you about the smartest Wall Street software analyst who ever called on me." He was talking about Lee Ainslie, a 29-year-old star at Tiger Management, one of the three biggest and best-known hedge funds at the time, which had been founded by a former Kidder, Peabody guy named Julian Robertson. Wyly's friend Bob Burch was an investor in Tiger. "I know Lee because Tiger happened to be the largest shareholder in Legent," Hanlon told Wyly. "And he took a huge gamble putting Tiger into it. When Legent missed a quarter, and its stock dropped in half, Lee said, 'I am going to meet with you and your CEO and, as a result of the meeting, I am either going to sell everything or double down.' We had that meeting. And he doubled his position."

Hanlon knew Ainslie not only understood how to buy long and sell short but also knew that he communicated his ideas brilliantly, because they spoke every other day while Hanlon was at Legent. During those conversations, Ainslie mined for every conceivable detail about plans, operations, management personnel and any other factor that could affect company performance or stock price.

Instead of the mostly macroinvestments Sam and Evan had made, Ainslie's approach centered on picking individual stocks. He did it the way Wyly had been assessing companies ever since his stock-picking class in college: dig, dig, dig. He would focus on the quality of a business, and also on the integrity of its management team. Through constant interaction he would burrow into companies—including their books, managers, markets, customers, suppliers, boards and competitors—and determine which were likely winners and which were not, then take positions in longs and shorts in every industry sector and every region.

Wyly was interested, so Hanlon got the two men together in New York City. Sam liked him, met his parents and made an offer: 30 percent of the fund to manage at the outset with the expectation that it would grow, with a guarantee of $1 million per year for three years and an ownership opportunity.

Ainslie signed on, and proposed calling their fund Maverick, because it suggested both Texas and someone with a streak of stubborn independence—such as Sam Wyly. The word had entered the English lexicon via Samuel Maverick, a signer of the Texas Declaration of Independence (who escaped the fate of Wyly's Uncle Christopher and the other 187 heroes of the Alamo because Colonel Travis

The Wylys with President George H.W. Bush. Sam's dream when he was a college freshman was to be elected governor of Louisiana, and he never lost his interest in politics; he has been a big donor throughout his adult life, as well as a fund-raiser for candidates and his causes. Bush: "Charles and Sam Wyly backed me in every race I ever ran, and they never asked for anything."

asked him to carry a message seeking reinforcements). In the days of the open range, he became known for not branding his cattle. Cowboys started calling unbranded cows out on the open range "mavericks."

Wyly envisioned Maverick Capital as the perfect union between his entrepreneurial world—building businesses—and the investment world. He knew that most mutual funds and hedge fund portfolio managers didn't really earn their fees because they didn't produce results as good as the market averages, which can be bought for a tiny fee as an index. The first index fund, Vanguard, was created by John Bogle, whose 1951 Princeton thesis declared: "Money managers, as a group, fail to beat the market average." So Bogle created Vanguard to simply mimic the S&P 500 and charged a fee about one-tenth that of active portfolio managers. Wyly had built substantial companies in dissimilar industries for 30 years, and had built or bought whole businesses. Investment gurus Benjamin Graham, Warren Buffett and others had preached: "Pay no more for a share of stock than you would for its *pro rata* part of the whole company." Thirty years of studying business had given Sam Wyly the background. And now he had Lee Ainslie.

By 1995, the fund had $100 million in assets. Eighteen months later, it was up to $400 million, and Sam put Maverick's entire portfolio under Ainslie's control. By 1996, people were trying to poach Ainslie, who told Sam and Evan he was willing to stay, but he wanted to buy out the majority of the Wylys' interest in Maverick. "I understand your point," Wyly told him. "But I really need to think about this."

Ainslie thought to himself, *Oh, gosh, this is going to be two months of back and forth . . .* Instead, Sam and Evan talked about it, slept on it and got back to Ainslie in the morning. "What is most important to us is that our family's stock market type assets are preserved and grown by someone we trust leading a team," the Wylys told him. "And you're that person. So let's make this happen on the terms you proposed." End of discussion. Skvarla says that kind of decisiveness is typical of Wyly, and a big reason for his success. "A lot of guys are smart, but they can't execute," he says. "Sam is smart, and he is not afraid to execute. He is not afraid of making mistakes and just picking himself up and moving on to the next thing."

Evan Wyly, who had cofounded Maverick with his father, was comanaging partner with Ainslie for more than a decade, until 2007.

In 2000, in one of the more spectacular hedge fund collapses up to that time, Julian Robertson liquidated Tiger Management's funds, saying the "irrational market" caused by the Internet craze and "earnings and price considerations taking a backseat to mouse clicks and momentum" had rendered his strategy ineffective. Much more dramatic collapses were to come with the Crash of 2008.

Ainslie led Maverick Capital through those sharky, post-millennium waters—in 2002, the five-year returns for the Standard & Poor's 500 was 20 percent, while Maverick Capital's was 127 percent. At the end of 2010—despite a devastating 2008, when Maverick had its first down year—Maverick delivered a 10-year compound annual return of eight percent compared with a minus-five percent for the S&P 500.

While Wyly was impressed with Maverick's performance during its first 15 years, he was equally proud of what it did during the Crash of 2008, when the fund lost 27 percent, while the S&P 500 lost 37 percent that year. Although they could no longer say, "Never had a down year," their goal of capital preservation paid off in what Wyly called "monstrous market turmoil." He says of that time, "One way to win is to lose less in hard times." Despite the 2008 loss, Maverick's long-short equity strategy still outperformed the Standard & Poor's 500 in 2007–2010 by more

Charles Wyly Senior (1); Evan with his two grandmothers (2); Sam with his daughter Kelly (3); Sam married his third wife, Cheryl, in 1993 at the old plantation mansion in Louisiana, the former home of his great-great-grandfather Edward Sparrow (4); the Wyly "Love Bug" in Malibu gets the once-over by Evan and Lisa (5); Andrew as an extra in a movie about the Alamo (6); Sam with Evan, Lisa and Laurie (7); Evan and his wife, Kim, with the Tesla electric car (8); Sam—softball pitcher (9); Kelly (10); Christiana with Richard Branson at a green conference in Mexico (11).

than 40 points—while many hedge funds collapsed. (In 2008, a record 1,471 were liquidated out of a total of 6,845, according to Chicago-based Hedge Fund Research.) The industry's total capital plummeted by $600 billion to $1.33 trillion as of the end of the first quarter of 2009, during which investors pulled another $104 billion out of them.

By January 1, 2010, the total 10-year change for the S&P 500 was minus-24 percent; and for the NASDAQ Composite, minus-44 percent, according to *The Wall Street Journal* (January 4, 2010). For Maverick, the 10-year change was plus-70 percent.

By the end of 2010, Maverick was managing an $11 billion fund for about 1,000 investors. The company had 155 employees, including 53 investment analysts who monitor 160 to 180 primary companies, a ratio of investments to investment professionals of roughly three to one, which has made Maverick both low-risk and highly rewarding. What began as a way to take care of family money is now one of the world's best hedge funds.

The grandkids' college money is in good hands.

Endnotes

1   The late Sir James Goldsmith was a high-flying British financier turned crusading politician who made his fortune as a corporate raider in the United States in the 1980s. He actually had dual citizenship in both England and France, and tried to sway the politics of both countries, funded by the billions he made in business. The slogan might have been the only thing he and Sam Wyly agreed upon. Goldsmith came to believe that global free trade would lead to societal dysfunctions, while Wyly remains a steadfast Adam Smith free-marketer.

2   In 1949, A. W. Jones established in the United States what is regarded as the first hedge fund. Jones combined two investment tools—short selling and leverage. Both are regarded as risky when practiced in isolation. Jones is credited with showing how these instruments could be combined to limit exposure. He saw that there were two clear sources of market risk: risk from individual stock selection and risk of a drop in the general market. His idea separated the two. He maintained shorted stocks to hedge against a drop in the market. Thus controlling for market risk, he used leverage to improve his returns from picking individual stocks. He went long on stocks that he considered "undervalued" and short on those that were "overvalued." The fund was considered "hedged" to the extent the portfolio was split between stocks that would gain if the market went up, and short positions that would benefit if the market went down. Thus the term "hedge funds."

Marc Klionsky is a master artist from Russia who once painted the official portraits of Soviet leaders before coming to America, where he painted the likes of jazz great Dizzy Gillespie, Saudi Arabia's Ambassador Prince Bandar bin Sultan, publishing magnate Steve Forbes and author and Nobel Peace Prize winner Elie Wiesel. He has also painted everyone in Sam's immediate family, plus grandchildren. Clockwise from top left: Laurie, Lisa, Evan, Kelly, Andrew, Christiana, Cheryl and Sam.

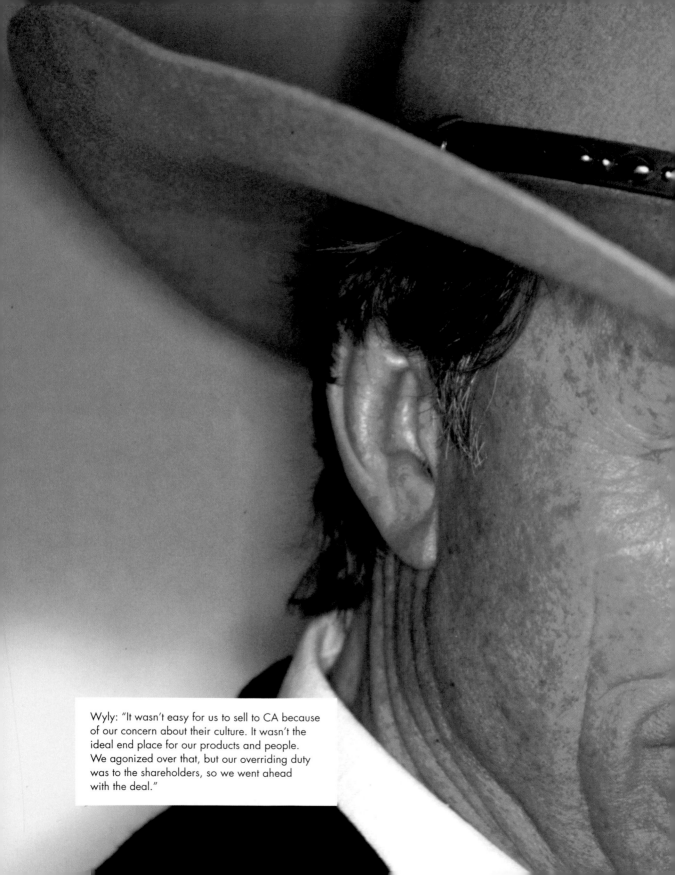

Wyly: "It wasn't easy for us to sell to CA because of our concern about their culture. It wasn't the ideal end place for our products and people. We agonized over that, but our overriding duty was to the shareholders, so we went ahead with the deal."

WE'RE DOING
THIS FOR RAY

After the March 2000 sale of Sterling Software and Sterling Commerce, Sam Wyly had figured he was out of the software business for good. He was now focusing on his new company, Green Mountain, which promoted clean air through clean energy, but by the middle of 2001, he was deeply troubled by the corrupt behavior of Computer Associates' top managers and board of directors. There were many examples of their malfeasance. The most recent: they waited until after midnight before the July 4 holiday weekend to announce that they would fail to meet their quarterly sales projections. The market, justifiably, pummeled them—CA's stock, which traded at $52 on July 3, opened at $29 on July 5.[1] On a rebound a few months later, Wyly sold his CA stock, which he'd acquired through the sale of Sterling Software, at $36.

Wyly had always been wary of CA, and he had wanted cash from them in the Sterling deal, but CA couldn't get their hands on that much money. They did, however, paint a very pretty picture of the company's future, and Wyly was confident that Sterling's products would add to CA's profits, so he took stock and options worth more than $100 million. But over the next year, he began to understand that he'd been duped, and that while CA was claiming $6 billion in revenue it was really pulling in just half that.

By May, he had had enough of what he called their lies and incompetence. The only fix, he concluded, was to throw the rascals out—replace CA's top managers and its blissfully compliant board—so he decided to launch a proxy fight to oust them. He believed that if CA's board and top officers could be changed, it could be a good company, recalling Pete Drucker's nugget that "There is no difference between two companies in the same business other than the quality of management at all levels." And Wyly knew that this company could be managed better, and that he had an impressive record of putting stellar managers in the right situation. Wyly also knew plenty about how CA did business, because he had been competing against the company for so long—he and Charles Wang, CA's founder, had been adversaries in the software business for 25 years, and Wang had paid almost $5 billion for two companies Wyly had started.[2]

Ironically, Wyly had a link to Computer Associates that predated Wang—in the early 1970s, when Wyly was building and acquiring data centers in Europe for University Computing, he sent a young Texan named Sam Goodner to work for him in Amsterdam. Goodner later left University Computing and formed a Swiss company called Computer Associates. In 1974, he hired a young Chinese immigrant living in New York City as CA's distributor in the U.S. Charles Wang's parents had fled to America during Mao's Cultural Revolution in the late '60s, and their eldest son immediately took to business. Charles's brother, Tony, knew securities law, so the two were able to get a public offering for Computer Associates done in the U.S., and they bought out Goodner in 1979.

The company back then had one main software product—a program for sorting data that was better than IBM's. Charles Wang's corporate strategy was to

The untouchable Charles Wang, who ran Computer Associates, was never convicted of any crime despite the endemic corruption of that company.

acquire software companies and then slash their employee rosters until they were scraping bone. Over the next 18 years, CA acquired hundreds of products, and in 1987, in its biggest deal to that point, it issued 100 percent more stock and paid a 50 percent premium over market to acquire Wyly's old company, University Computing. By then, it was no longer controlled by Wyly, who had started Sterling Software and taken it public in 1983. By 2001, CA was the second-largest independent software company in the world, behind only Microsoft.[3]

Despite that apparent success, CA was hated by many of its customers and employees. Customers regularly complained about its support and maintenance, and both customers and employees would be strong-armed contractually by CA and were sued if they tried to escape. One legal target was EDS—the Dallas company founded by Ross Perot, sold to General Motors, and then spun out after a serious "culture clash" in Detroit. Ultimately, it was gobbled up by HP after the Crash of 2008. In preparing for this proxy fight, Wyly commissioned a survey that showed that half of CA's customers would stop doing business with CA if they could get out of their contracts.

Wyly had always been disdainful of Wang's fierce top-down micromanagement style—"This dragon has one head," Wang boasted—which was vastly different from Wyly's management style, which looked for good people and gave them a lot of autonomy; and he had heard the persistent rumors about CA's creative bookkeeping.

All these things were swirling through his mind when he called in his old Sterling Commerce colleague Steve Perkins to help him analyze CA and then come up with a strategy for a proxy battle. "I have been lied to," Wyly told him. "So have all the public stockholders."

The dam of damning words burst on April 29, 2001, when *New York Times* business writer Alex Berensen published an article entitled "A Software Company Runs Out of Tricks." It detailed not only CA's size in 2000—$696 million in reported profits, $6.1 billion in reported sales and a $20.3 billion market cap—but some of the accounting tricks it had used to get there. These included adding days to the close of fiscal quarters—35-day months—so CA could book more revenue and meet the numbers they had given to Wall Street. "This article," Wyly said at the time, "should get a Pulitzer Prize." It didn't, but soon after it was published, CA's long-term CPA firm resigned.

On April 16, 2001, CA (now using a new auditor) reported another version of its numbers, and these told a far grimmer tale: revenue fell almost 60 percent. After reporting a profit of about $700 million in 1999, the company reported a loss of $175 million for 2000. The stock plunged from $75 in January of that year to $18 by December. Wyly believed that the managers were profiting themselves, but not caring for their shareholders. CA's top management were expected to work for all the people who owned stock in the company, but they seemed to be working only for themselves. Shareholders were losing value on their investment, while CA's top people were getting very, very rich.

There was yet another factor driving Wyly to join this battle: products from his former companies, University Computing Company and Sterling Software, were responsible for over 40 percent of CA's product line, and he could not shake a paternal feeling for them. There was yet another paternal tug here: he had also heard that many of his former Sterling employees, including tenured workers with spotless records, were being dismissed for so-called performance reasons and being denied severance; that some contract agreements for ex-Sterling employees were being ignored by CA; and that the poor treatment of both employees and customers was widespread.

There seemed to be endemic deception and thievery at CA, which was pushing customers to extend their licensing and maintenance agreements for as many as 10 years, and booking all of it as license revenue so the company could claim all 10 years of revenue immediately (maintenance revenues were allocated over the years of the contract). In an extraordinarily bold act of rapaciousness, CA's three top officers (with their board's approval) had used those phony sales figures to pay themselves a $1.1 billion bonus in 1998.

These misdeeds were no secret in the business world. In 2000, *Chief Executive* magazine named CA's board of directors one of the "five worst boards in America," and at about the same time, *BusinessWeek* quoted corporate compensation expert Graef Crystal as saying that the way options granted to CA's top three were presented was " . . . designed to be misleading and obfuscating." In April 16, 2001, *BusinessWeek* said, in its survey of the most overpaid executives, "At the bottom of the performance heap, Charles B. Wang of Computer Associates earned $698.2 million from 1998 through 2000 and produced a dismal shareholder return of minus-63%, making last year's loser, [Michael] Eisner of Walt Disney, look like a bargain."

BACK TO COURT

Wyly's War

COMPUTER ASSOCIATES GENERAL COUNSEL STEVEN Woghin was unrepentant in defeat when he signed a shareholder settlement in August 2003, dispensing with charges that executives had cooked the books to bolster their own bonuses. Though CA had agreed to terms that would cost it $174 million in stock—and later would pay another $225 million to shareholders to avoid criminal prosecution—Woghin declared in court papers: The company denies "any wrongdoing whatsoever," rejecting any "fault or liability or wrongdoing."

A year later Woghin was back in court, this time utterly contrite as he stood before a judge in U.S. District Court in Brooklyn to plead guilty to two charges related to fraud and obstruction. Contrary to his earlier defiance, Woghin confessed that he had taken part in the accounting fraud, had covered it up to elude government investigators and had ordered employees to do likewise. He could get five years in prison.

"Your honor, I am ashamed to be standing here today," he told the judge on Sept. 22, 2004. By then the full extent of the fraud at Computer Associates was clear. CA admitted that, desperate to avoid falling short of Wall Street estimates, execs had prematurely booked $2.2 billion in sales in fiscal 2000 and 2001. The feds say the fraud was $3.3 billion and involved more than 360 contracts. The practice was so institutionalized that insiders called it "the 35-day-month."

Fifteen CA people were fired or forced to resign; five have pleaded guilty to charges including fraud, conspiracy and obstruction of justice. The ousted chairman and chief executive, Sanjay Kumar, awaits trial. Why, then, was CA brass allowed to stick around for months after the scandal broke, running up

Wyly was dismayed that despite this rampant larceny, no big investors had stepped forward to help him challenge Wang and the CA board, but he decided to stand up, to do something, even if most of CA's shareholders just sat on their hands. For this fight, Wyly formed Ranger Governance in 2001, which quickly sent a letter to CA stockholders: "Once an investor puzzles through their pro forma pro rata [a newly invented accounting phrase created by CA and their new CPAs, which in plain English meant, "Forget what we called revenue and profit in the past—we are going to show it to you again in the future] reporting, we believe it's clear that performance can honestly be described as anemic."

Wyly reached out to all stockholders, but knew there was one pivotal CA shareholder, Walter Haefner—if he could not get Haefner to join him, there would be no hope of winning the proxy fight. His relationship with Haefner, a 90-year-old Swiss billionaire and Thoroughbred owner, went back decades, and, in another ironic twist, Haefner's huge holdings in CA were a direct result of the business he had done with Sam Wyly. As was mentioned earlier in chapter five, Wyly had bought Haefner's European computer services enterprise in 1968 in exchange for debt and equity in University Computing, and Haefner then began to invest in Wyly's Datran. (Of the $100 million lost when Datran was shut down, $40 million was Haefner's.) In the post-Datran recapitalization, Haefner got a very big chunk of University Computing; when CA bought UCC in 1987, his stock was converted to 20 percent of CA's stock, substantially more than what the founding Wang brothers had. At its peak in January of 2000—the pinnacle of the bull market in tech and telecom stocks—his 123 million CA shares were worth more than $9 billion. But 18 months later, the value of his stock was cut in half, so Wyly thought he might be open to a change in leadership.

Wyly repeatedly made it clear that he did not want to run CA, he just wanted to see regime change happen in a way that new people at the top were honest and competent. And he wasn't willing to settle for a few cosmetic changes and half-hearted promises to do better. He wanted to clean house. As he explained to one reporter: "I'm a digital guy. It's either a one or a zero."

Even with all the ammunition he had accumulated against CA, Wyly's proxy fight was a long shot. He knew that most shareholders in any big company are "passive investors"—pension funds and mutual funds—and that 20 percent of all shares typically don't vote. The "control bloc" at CA—meaning the insiders, plus Haefner—held slightly more than 28 percent of the stock, so the odds of "winning" the election were minuscule. He took the fight public anyway.

A short time later, Haefner declined to cast his votes against the incumbents. In a letter to Wyly, Haefner explained that Wang and CA had done too much for him over the years.

When he read that, Wyly knew there was no way he was going to win control of the company, but he knew that a proxy fight would shine sunlight on the corruption, and that sooner or later, change would come. So he fought on—he bought full-page ads in *The New York Times* and *The Wall Street Journal* that said, "Throw these Long Island bums out." He and Perkins did a road show for investors, and their message finally began to gain traction. A few weeks before the August 29 vote, CalPERS, the massive public employees' pension fund in California, which held 5 percent of CA's stock, shocked the sleepy world of institutional owners—and CA's board—when it abruptly switched its vote and said Wyly's charges had substance and that his slate of candidates for the board would be a good thing. A short time later, Proxy Monitor, the voting advisory service, followed suit, as did Institutional Shareholder, the other consultant who advised owners on how to vote.

CA's board was stunned, and scrambling to win the PR battle. It countered with a frantic campaign that lasted up to election day, including a full-page ad in *The Wall Street Journal*: "Don't let these Texas bums take over."

On election day, which Wyly called "Liberation Day" for Computer Associates' shareholders, his Ranger Governance slate got 25 percent of the vote. *The battle is lost*, thought Wyly, *but not the war.* He knew his fight had changed much, and that there was now blood in the water.

Seven months later, in March of 2002, in spite of the many promises by Wang and Kumar of better performance, CA's share price declined further, on its way to a July 2 low of $7.61. That meant $100 of CA stock in January 2000 was worth about 10 bucks just 19 months later.

Wang and Kumar, feeling the pressure, threw a fig leaf on a bonfire: they announced they would appoint two independent board members, form a

Why are these men smiling?

Charles B. Wang
Computer Associates Chairman

Sanjay Kumar
Computer Associates President and CEO

Russell M. Artzt
Computer Associates Executive Vice President

Is it because they're the only ones who made money on Computer Associates' stock over the past five years?

- The Computer Associates Board of Directors granted Messrs. Wang, Kumar and Artzt <u>more than $1 billion</u> in Company stock in 1998.

- Two months after this grant became effective, the stock plummeted.

- In fact, CA stock has returned a <u>negative</u> 11% to shareholders over the past 5 years, versus a software industry average of <u>positive</u> 171%.

- What's more, CA management has damaged its credibility by using accounting gimmicks to mask poor performance.

It is time for new leadership at Computer Associates.

There is a better way, and a better team poised to lead the company into a brighter tomorrow.

Ranger Governance, led by software pioneer Sam Wyly, is proposing new management under a truly independent Board of Directors.

Ranger Governance has a plan to unlock the value and potential of Computer Associates.

The new Board will strategically realign the company into four decentralized business units, and create a culture of innovation, accountability, extraordinary customer service, and real growth.

Integrity. Innovation. Increased Value for CA Shareholders.

Now <u>that</u> would be something to smile about.

committee to improve employee relations issues and end the company's suspect method of reporting results. All of these changes had been part of the Ranger Governance agenda, and Wyly welcomed them, but he knew they were not enough to change the basic culture of the company.

But change was coming. Investigators were finally starting to look more closely at the CA cesspool. In late 2001, federal prosecutors in Brooklyn launched an investigation into whether CA had used accounting tricks to inflate its earnings to trigger that $1.1 billion bonus Wang, Kumar and CA cofounder Russell Artzt had pocketed. Shareholders were suddenly restive in the wake of the massive Enron scandal, which broke in October of 2001, wondering if they could trust corporate fiduciaries. The decline of CA's stock far outpaced every comparative index, so Wyly concluded the company was far more vulnerable now than it had been during his first proxy fight. In 2002, he was ready to launch another proxy fight, and pulled together the Ranger Governance group for a meeting.

This time, he spoke to his team about people. He told them he was still bothered by CA's treatment of former Sterling employees, such as Ray Hannon, the press- and investment-relations man who had worked for him at both University Computing and Sterling Software, and was being denied his monthly pension check by CA; and was frustrated that nobody at company headquarters in Long Island would answer his letters or phone calls. Abusing former employees was inbred in Charles Wang's company culture; it was anathema to Sam Wyly's corporate ethos.

The Rangers debated the pros and cons of another proxy battle, and like the great collegiate debater he had been, Wyly listened attentively to the concerns of his people and answered each query. They all knew little had changed since they'd lost that vote—everyone in the room could do the math, and it was obvious they couldn't win this proxy fight, either. But this decision wasn't being put to a vote.

Wyly leaned forward in his chair, calmly folded his hands on the table and said, "We're doing this for Ray."

On February 20, 2002, it was revealed that the FBI had joined the probe by federal prosecutors in Brooklyn into CA's accounting practices. The next day Computer Associates had the worst-performing stock in the S&P 500, as its shares slid $4.40 to $20.91.

After being sent to jail, Kumar charged that Wang was intimately involved in the wrongdoing at CA. Prosecutors were unable to support those accusations against Wang, who never used e-mail or voice mail.

On June 28, Ranger Governance announced another proxy fight, and this time put forth a slate of five candidates. The battle of newspaper ads raged for four intense weeks and then, in late July—a month before the vote—CEO Sanjay Kumar asked to meet with Wyly. The two men got together, talked for a while and Wyly walked out of the meeting with some promises and some cash. Kumar solemnly swore that serious change was on the way; that Wang would be gone in a few months; and that more "independent directors" would come aboard. He also agreed to pay Wyly $10 million to drop his proxy fight. About three months later, on November 18, 2002, CA chairman Charles Wang resigned, and Kumar took over.

Kumar loudly proclaimed that CA was a good, honest company, and that he would set things right. Instead, he got quickly swept overboard as prosecutors, regulators and angry shareholders finally took hold of CA and gave it a good shaking. In August 2003, CA agreed to settle some lawsuits filed by shareholders who had accused the company of accounting misdeeds by issuing shares that totaled almost $150 million. Six months later, senior vice president Lloyd Silverstein pleaded guilty to criminal charges for lying to prosecutors and lawyers about whether the company had booked phony revenue, and charged that other CA executives had urged him to tell those lies. Four months after that, the feds filed charges of accounting fraud against chief financial officer Ira Zar, vice president David Rivard and senior vice president David Kaplan for holding open CA's books for extra days at the end of each quarter in order to book additional revenue. All pleaded guilty. So did general counsel Steven Woghin, who had instructed a CA accountant "to respond to questions from [an auditor] with half-truths and vague answers."

"Sam has turned out to be more right than he knew," William Brewer III, Wyly's lawyer, told *The Deal* in 2005.

At long last, CA's board finally showed some spine—they fired most of the top brass, and gave a sharp shove to Kumar, who stepped down in June 2004. A few months after his departure, CA paid more hush money to surly shareholders—this time $225 million —as part of an agreement it signed with federal officials that gave CA immunity from prosecution as long as it stopped the criminal behavior there and cooperated with the prosecutors chasing CA's former top execs. Gary Lutin, manager of an investor-sponsored, online public stockholder forum, ripped both shareholder settlements. He told *The Deal*: "The directors essentially used shareholder funds to buy themselves a 'get out of jail free' card."

In April 2005, a new CA board established a Special Litigation Committee (SLC) to investigate allegations made against 22 current and former employees. A year later, Kumar pleaded guilty to lying to federal investigators and directing employees to lie about the fraudulent accounting. He was sentenced to 12 years in prison.

Wyly was pleased to see many of these crooks marched off to jail, but was aggravated about the $400 million paid as compensation to shareholders. He and his investor group claimed to have lost more than $100 million in the scandal, and he was pissed that CA's board didn't go to bat for shareholders by attempting to recoup settlement, legal costs and ill-gotten gains from the lawbreakers, but instead signed an agreement to let the feds handle the problem.

His lawyer Brewer told *The Deal* that the $400 million in compensation worked out to only three cents on every dollar that shareholders lost in the CA scandal. "That ought to be given back by [cofounder Charles] Wang and Kumar and people who benefited to the tune of all that money," Brewer declared.

In an amazing twist to this sordid tale of corporate thievery, Charles Wang never spent a day in jail and was never even formally charged with a crime. He got away with blaming his protégé, Kumar, for the all the rot at CA. It was hard to believe that this chronic micromanager—who had boasted that the dragon had only one head—

could have been unaware of such pervasive, systemic malfeasance for so many years. But proving otherwise was seemingly impossible because Wang never used e-mail or voice mail, so there was not a good evidence trail, and CA's labyrinthine accounting "system" seems to have been designed to obscure the facts from Day One.

In April 2007, however, CA's Special Litigations Committee revealed it had "uncovered credible and corroborated evidence [that] Wang both directed and participated in the 35-day month practice." It even said he had negotiated some of the back-dated deals himself. In August 2008, Kumar filed an affidavit in U.S. District Court (from prison) that substantiated the SLC's charges. He said Wang not only knew about those 35-day months, but exploited them, and had been doing so before Kumar joined CA in 1987. He said the practice was "firmly entrenched" at the company when he arrived and that Wang had "personally directed this practice in [Kumar's] presence." He also said that three former board members—former Senator Al D'Amato, ex–board chairman Lewis Ranieri, and Russell Artzt—all knew about the practice.

All four men denied the allegations. No one stepped forward to support Kumar's accusations, and none have been indicted. Wang is still happily and comfortably retired.

Meanwhile, all the top management and the board of directors at Computer Associates have been replaced, and every month, Ray Hannon gets his pension check from CA.

Endnotes

1 CNET Business News, July 5, 2000; New York Stock Exchange.
2 CA paid almost $4 billion for Sterling Software in 2000, and $780 million for University Computing in 1987.
3 Source: Morgan Stanley Dean Witter.

Wyly: "It costs consumers about a cup of Starbucks coffee a month extra to buy cleaner energy."

THE DIRTY POLITICS OF CLEAN ENERGY

"There are no passengers on Spaceship Earth. We are all crew."
—Marshall McLuhan

In 1997, when Sam Wyly decided to create a clean-electricity company, it was more about legacy than business, and he was determined to answer an important question: "How can the world be powered without being poisoned?"

He wanted to create a profitable, sustainable business in the loss-ridden clean-energy industry, and build it into the most successful enterprise of its kind in America. And he wanted to overturn the laws and regulations that protected the utility monopolies and open the way for competition that would bring about real innovations in renewable energy.

By this point in his career, Wyly had already been in the energy game for some time, and he'd given much thought to environmental issues. Back in 1973, his Earth Resources Company faced a serious and expensive decision. Lead, which had first been added to gasoline back in 1927 to take the "knock" out of your car's engine, was shown to be toxic to humans, so the Environmental Protection Agency initiated a "phase down" program—large refineries were ordered to make the expensive conversion comply quickly, but smaller, independent refineries, such as Wyly's Delta Refining Company, were given until 1982 to do so.

Since most American cars and trucks used leaded gas, Wyly knew he could sell leaded fuel for another decade before doing the conversion—drivers weren't going to trade in 50 million cars overnight. Deferring the huge conversion costs was the "smart" play for independent refiners.

But Wyly and his brother, Charles, and their CEO, Dan Krausse—decided to make the conversion as quickly as they could, and told their engineers to find a way to both eliminate the lead and keep their products profitable. The Wylys made their case to their public: "We believe that modernizing our Memphis refinery sooner will pay better dividends over the long haul." In 1978, ERC completed a major expansion of Delta Refining that not only produced lead-free gas, but dramatically increased the quantity of products it produced. Far from harming profits and shareholder value, the early investment in expansion and cleaner fuel added great value. In 1979, the Ayatollah Khomeini overthrew the Shah of Iran and the price of oil tripled. Simultaneously, profit margins from the pump all the way back to the refinery and the barges that hauled crude oil up the Mississippi River expanded just as production was increasing.

In 1980, two years before the mandated conversion for smaller refineries, Wyly sold the already converted ERC for a $57 a share, some $40 over the share price a year earlier, and 570 percent of the IPO price 10 years earlier, and this was accomplished in a decade in which the average stock was down.

Another key moment in the greening of Sam Wyly came a decade later when Christiana Wyly—at 11, the youngest of his four daughters—asked her father: "What are you going to do about all these toxins being dumped into the air?"

"What am *I* going to do about it?" he responded, somewhat defensively. But her question got him thinking. He could donate money to environmental causes, but there were lots of other good eleemosynary investments too, including his backing of the *Jim Lehrer NewsHour* and *Sesame Street* on Dallas's Channel 13. He wanted to join the battle, not just as an activist, but in the world he knew best, as an entrepreneur. He knew real solutions would only come from innovative businesses, just as they always had.

By 1997, Wyly had six children and nine grandchildren (now 11, plus two great-grandchildren—McAmis and Savannah). He was doing all the good-citizen things: he recycled at home and at work; he insulated his home in Aspen with denim blue jeans; when Toyota introduced the Prius hybrid that year he, his son Evan and his daughter Laurie Wyly Matthews were among the first customers. But he longed to do something substantial—he wanted to create a clean electricity company, which he would call Green Mountain. (He got the name from his study of the American Revolution and the story of Ethan Allen and his cussedly independent Green Mountain boys of Vermont.) He hoped Green Mountain would be a good long-term investment both financially and ethically. It would be an investment in the Earth, in the future. The trends that would eventually make 2010 the hottest year since 1880 were already well in place all over the world.

Wyly's idea was to ride the swelling wave of deregulation in the utility markets (each state or town had to choose between continuing its electric utility monopoly and allowing competition) to build a national electric company based on clean energy. He believed that those newly deregulated markets would open up opportunities like those that had emerged in telephone and data services after the breakup of the AT&T monopoly. In Wyly's vision, Green Mountain would become the MCI or Sprint or AOL or Sterling Commerce or Google of electric power—and avoid the economic fate of Datran, which had pioneered trails for all of the above.

In three deregulated states—California, Pennsylvania and Massachusetts— new power providers could sell electricity to consumers in competition with local utilities. They could use the local utility's transmission lines—just as phone competitors could use AT&T's local lines—and could buy power from sources all over the power grid.

There were and are three grids in the USA: the East Grid, the West Grid and the Texas Grid. Green Mountain would offer renewable wind or solar energy or other electricity generated in a way that was a lot cleaner than the old coal plants, which were then producing 50 percent of America's power. Most new competitors would say, "We sell it cheaper!" But Green Mountain could say, "We sell it cleaner!"

Wyly envisioned the growth of a green entrepreneurial class—professional business innovators who could thrive in a competitive energy market, contribute en masse to a cleaner environment and earn the profit they must earn to pay the cost of capital. He knew that if entrepreneurial, intellectual, organizational and creative intensity could be applied to the deterioration of air quality, the results would surpass anything the federal government would do any time soon.

The biggest obstacle was the entrenched monopolies. Unlike AT&T's nationwide monopoly on telephone calls and computer data transmission, each electric utility was a statewide or local city monopoly. This meant he'd have to break them up one at a time, state by state. But that didn't worry him much. The utilities seemed vulnerable in a world growing more aware of the Earth's frailty day by day and already seeing the economic benefits of the bust-up of former monopolies, from trucking to telephones to airlines. And Wyly liked what the numbers told him. Green Mountain's research showed that 20 percent of U.S. consumers would pay a small premium for an environmentally friendly electricity product. The company decided to focus initially on residential electricity. With 100 million households in the United States spending $100 billion annually, the potential seemed vast, and most new competitors would go after the corporate customer first.

Another obstacle, one Wyly hadn't anticipated, would be the Greener Than Thou crowd. Green Mountain was "not green enough," some would say. "Too capitalistic," others would whine. They would also question Wyly's political history. "A lot of them didn't believe you could vote for both George Bushes and lots of Republicans and also be a tree-hugger," he recalls.

Green Mountain opened for business in August of 1997 in California, the first state to deregulate its electricity. When his long-time friend and colleague Richard Hanlon, who was on the board of America Online, told him about some of the remarketing AOL was doing with companies, Wyly saw an opportunity for mass exposure. Green Mountain negotiated a marketing coalition with America Online, and the deal seemed to be locked down. Then Hanlon had a visitor.

Eric Keller, the senior manager of AOL's Business Affairs unit, stuck his head in Hanlon's door one afternoon. "I just want you to know," Hanlon remembers him saying. "Even though we are just about to sign a deal with Green Mountain, we are going to have to tell them no. Enron has made us an offer we can't refuse."

Houston-based Enron Corporation, which wanted to land a chunk of California's energy business, had offered AOL $5 million if it would do no deals with Green Mountain.

After the AOL deal blew up, Wyly began to look at an IPO for Green Mountain to raise much-needed capital. Hanlon suggested Wyly talk to a banker he knew at Prudential. Wyly did, and liked what he heard. "The banker began putting stars in everyone's eyes by saying, 'This is a $500 million deal!'" Hanlon recalls.

Not long after, Hanlon's phone rang. It was Wyly. "Richard, we are going to do the biggest IPO in history!" he told him. "Prudential has committed to underwrite and they have sales agents in almost every town in America. They bought the Bache Brokerage and they are determined to take a big bite out of Goldman Sachs's and Morgan Stanley's and Merrill Lynch's underwriting business."

In March 1999, Green Mountain changed its name to Greenmountain.com to exploit the market's love for all things dot-com and filed with the Securities and Exchange Commission for a proposed stock offering. There had been hundreds of successful dot-com IPOs in the previous five years, but most had raised less than $100 million. Greenmountain.com's plan was to sell $500 million in stock.

Small sensitive planet
seeks caring individuals

Imagine a company where Internet commerce, basic consumer needs and the environment all intersect. A place that easily empowers ordinary people to make a real difference—one click at a time.

greenmountain.com

Choose wisely. It's a small planet.

PROSPECTUS

25,000,000 Shares

greenmountain.com

Choose wisely. It's a small planet.

Common Stock

GreenMountain.com Company is offering shares of its common stock in an initial public offering. Prior to this offering, there has been no public market for GreenMountain.com's common stock.

We anticipate that the public offering price will be between $11.00 and $13.00 per share. The shares of GreenMountain.com will be included for quotation in the Nasdaq National Market under the symbol "GMTN."

	Per Share	Total
Public offering price	$	$
Underwriting discounts and commissions	$	$
Proceeds, before expenses, to GreenMountain.com	$	$

See "Risk Factors" on pages 9 to 17 for factors that you should consider before investing in the shares of GreenMountain.com.

Neither the Securities and Exchange Commission nor any state securities commission has approved or disapproved of these securities or passed upon the accuracy or adequacy of this prospectus. Any representation to the contrary is a criminal offense.

The underwriters may purchase up to 3,750,000 additional shares from GreenMountain.com at the public offering price, less underwriting discounts and commissions, to cover over-allotments. Delivery of the shares will be on   , 1999.

Prudential Securities   **BancBoston Robertson Stephens**

Deutsche Banc Alex. Brown
Volpe Brown Whelan & Company
FAC/Equities
First Union Capital Markets Corp.
The Robinson-Humphrey Company
E•OFFERING

            , 1999

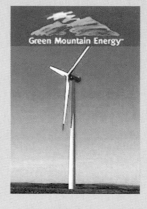

Green Mountain Energy

Above, left: Green Mountain president Paul Thomas urges Texans to use solar panels.

Above: Attempting to salvage Green Mountain, Wyly tried to piggyback on the dot-com bubble by turning it into an e-company—urging consumers to "Choose wisely" by signing up on the Web.

Left: In this 1999 tombstone, Prudential Securities, BancBoston Robertson Stephens and other underwriters set out to raise $500 million in a Greenmountain.com IPO.

Prudential anticipated a total market value of $3 billion, which would have been a sporty debut for a company that had just 72,000 customers in two states and had reported a loss of $46 million in 1998 on revenue of $1.5 million. (But it would have been peanuts compared to most of the 340 IPOs that year, such as Webvan at $144.6 million or Time Warner's record-setting payment of $150 billion—in AOL currency, of course—for America Online, which Time Warner would sell 10 years later for $2 billion.)

Everything looked good for the IPO, but the timing was off by a matter of months, because the dot-com boom suddenly went bust and punched the air out of Wyly's IPO. ("I saved my letter from Prudential saying they were going to raise us five hundred million bucks," Wyly says. "It's up there on the wall along with my Confederate war bonds and defaulted bonds issued by Czarist Russia.") The company reclaimed the Green Mountain Energy name, and Wyly began seeking capital from private investors. The company pushed ahead, opening for business in Pennsylvania, and then began promoting wind and solar projects there and in California.

Hanlon, who had joined the Green Mountain board early on, worried about the millions of dollars being pumped into the business every month, as did Dallas Mavericks owner and fellow board member Mark Cuban. "Mark and I would look at each other and roll our eyes because Sam's general managers had grandiose plans beyond any means of financing them," Hanlon recalls.

In 2000, Wyly found the deep pockets he needed—$50 million investments each from BP, the oil giant, and Nuon, the Dutch electric utility. Formerly called British Petroleum (originally Anglo-Persian Oil), BP was one of the "Seven Sisters of World Oil," but it had developed wind and solar projects, made its gas stations sun-powered and withdrawn from the Global Climate Coalition—50 corporations and trade associations that still claimed global warming was an unproven premise. By 2008, BP had $361 billion in gross revenue (third largest in the world), and was still making massive investments in renewable energy projects.

The deal also brought to Green Mountain a BP executive named Paul Thomas, who had been in charge of its North American oil and gas trading. Thomas brought a scientist's intelligence, an activist's passion and a Wyly-esque ability to dream big. As president and CEO of Green Mountain, he quickly expanded its energy alternatives to wind, solar, water, geothermal, landfill gas and biomass, or whatever electricity was cleaner and reasonably competitive on cost. Natural gas is twice as clean as coal—it emits half the CO2 and a lot less mercury, sulfur dioxide and nitrogen dioxide, all poisonous gases—and the U.S. has big supplies of natural gas. It costs consumers, Wyly is fond of saying, "about a cup of Starbucks coffee a month extra to buy cleaner energy."

Sam Wyly had a great instinct for picking people to work with, and he also had a good eye when it came to picking a priest.

Sally Bingham had been active in environmental causes for years before she became an Episcopal priest and took her cause to the pulpit. In the '90s she founded the Regeneration Project after borrowing $1,000 from each of 12 friends—"My disciples," she jokingly calls them—and fashioned a new way to fight global warming with some collective clout. She organized churches, synagogues, Buddhist temples and mosques to buy green power generated by wind and solar energy providers, and to reduce the energy consumed in their facilities. She believed that as stewards of God's creation—the Earth—churches and congregants had a religious and moral obligation to protect the environment.

While she was working toward a divinity degree at the University of San Francisco in the mid-'90s, the Jesuit school mandated that she study the world's religions. In her readings, she was struck by how few preachers ever spoke of nature in sermons, and went to her parish priest. "Why don't I ever hear about ecological issues from the pulpit?" she asked.

"Well, we are saving souls," he told her. "We leave that up to the secular environmental community."

"Well, that is really odd," she said. "Because if God created all this and we love God, why don't we protect it?"

Bingham decided to do just that. Ordained an Episcopalian minister in 1997 after a grueling nine-year process, she was told she could not mention the word "ecology" until she had first learned all of the skills of the priesthood. If that weren't enough, she was completely bald as she took her vows because she was fighting off cancer, a battle she won. Finally she was allowed to do the work she felt she had been called to do all along, which was to help save creation.

She continued enlisting congregations around the country to support green companies her group had approved. One of them was Green Mountain Energy—

though it was young, she was impressed both by its mission and its missionaries. "Of all the companies that we interviewed with," said Bingham, "Green Mountain was far and away above the others in terms of values, in terms of the kinds of people that worked for the company. They were a company that we were comfortable taking in partnership to these congregations."

Wyly and Green Mountain were happy to support Bingham's project and to have her endorsement, especially as her campaign to amass green

The irrepressible Reverend Canon Sally G. Bingham might be the world's greenest theologian, and has spent decades "tending to God's creation."

congregations around the country began to take off (her Regeneration Project now had more than 4,000 congregations in 23 states). But in March of 2000, Sam and his son Andrew, a "just the facts, ma'am" political conservative, ignited a controversy that whipped Bingham's environmental followers into a frenzy.

It began when they spent $2.5 million to create and run television and print ads supporting their old family friend, Texas Governor George W. Bush, over Arizona Senator John McCain during the Republican presidential primary in New Hampshire. The ads—sponsored by a group created by Wyly called Republicans for Clean Air—stressed Bush's few environmentally friendly achievements in Texas and contrasted those with McCain's vote in the Senate against funding renewable energy. The problem was that most professional environmentalists considered Bush, the son of oil money and big business, an enemy who coddled the Earth's despoilers.

The ads came at a crucial time, during the New York, California and Ohio primaries, and Bingham's phone started ringing off the hook. "You sold us a bill of goods!" one caller said indignantly. "Green Mountain Energy's founders are *Bush* people!"

"What are you talking about?" Bingham asked.

"Look at *The New York Times*! Look at CNN! Look at Fox!"

There she found a full-page ad endorsing Bush, paid for by the Wylys. Bingham, who had never met Sam Wyly, sensed she was in trouble. "The California church people who had believed in me and thought that we were environmentally conscious and that we had integrity were furious," she recalls. "They said, 'Anybody who supports Bush is not somebody who understands the environment. I am getting out of Green Mountain.'"

Bingham was also the chair of the Episcopal diocese of California's Commission for the Environment, and suddenly the people on the committee who had met the Green Mountain staff, who had all become customers of the company, were leaving Green Mountain, too, and they were blaming Bingham for leading them astray.

She defended Wyly, telling people that his political friends had nothing to do with what Green Mountain provided. She said, "Look, you don't go to every company that you own shares in or every car you buy and find out what is the political preference of the people who sit on the board of directors. This is stupid. Stop blaming Sam. Sure, he likes George Bush. So what?"

The greener-than-thou crowd was suspicious of Wyly's commitment to renewable energy because of his long friendship with the Bush family.

But her flock was adamant—if Wyly supported Bush, he must, by default, not be an honest green guy. The Wylys had supported Bush family campaigns going back to George H.W. Bush's runs in Texas for Congress in 1966 and president in 1980, and then for vice president in 1980, as well as George W. for congress in West Texas in the '70s and for governor in the '80s. Wyly always had maintained his independence and his distance from them, staying away from specific policy issues. The only exception to that was when, during the Texas legislative session before the 2000 election, Wyly had helped environmentalists like Tom "Smitty" Smith's Public Citizen, then in league with energy entrepreneurs who wanted the right to compete with the utility monopolies, win passage of a bill which mandated that old coal-burning power plants reduce their air pollution. Then-Governor Bush had wanted the compliance to be voluntary (which the greenies considered a joke), but Wyly helped Dallas Democrat Steve Wolens persuade him to go along with the House bill. In Texas, Wyly was known as an Adam Smith free-trade businessman, a Republican and an environmentalist. But outside Texas, many environmentalists never got past the first two before they wrote him off.

Bingham decided to find out for herself what Sam Wyly was about. On March 15, 2000, one frenetic week into the controversy, she wrote him a letter that explained she was a priest in the Episcopal diocese of California, and had been promoting Green Mountain Energy for the last two and a half years. "I cannot," she wrote, "continue to promote Green Mountain Energy until you, Sam, can look me in the eye and tell me that you care more about renewable energy than you do about getting George Bush elected president." At best, she expected a mildly contrite letter in response.

Forty-eight hours after mailing that letter, her phone rang. It was 8:15 a.m. "Sally Bingham, please," the voice on the phone said.

"This is Sally."

"Hold a minute, please. I have Sam Wyly on the phone."

Bingham's face reddened. "I sat down as if the president of the United States was on the phone," she recalls, "and thought, *Now, what should I do?*"

Wyly told Bingham he wanted to look her in the eye. "I am going to be in Seattle speaking to the Climate Institute over this coming weekend. Can you fly up there? I'll have my plane pick you up."

"I'm sorry, Mr. Wyly," Bingham said. "I can't get on your airplane. It will only give fuel to these people who think that I'm a big promoter of Green Mountain or I'm getting some kickback from it." She declined an airline ticket for the same reason, then suggested he come to San Francisco.

"I'll be there in two weeks," Wyly said.

Bingham was flabbergasted. "He doesn't know me," she thought. "Sam Wyly calls me—me, an Episcopal priest. Not only does he agree to come to San Francisco, he agrees to stay at my house." She began to sense that Wyly had a serious case to make in his defense, and that he valued her and her work.

She decided that if Wyly had a message for her, some of her doubtful colleagues might want to hear it as well. And if they liked what they heard, they could help her divine the truth about him. She called her associates at Environmental Defense Fund in Washington to see if there was any interest in lending her some serious expertise. "Sam Wyly is coming to my house," she told them. "I need an expert to be here to figure out whether he is for real or not."

Bingham was surprised to learn that most of them knew all about Wyly—his businesses, his wealth and his politics—and were willing to make the trip. She called Hal Harvey, president of the Energy Foundation in San Francisco; Bill Reilly, who ran the EPA for President George H.W. Bush from 1989 to 1992; and Ralph Cavanna, who was the senior attorney, codirector and energy guru for the National Resources Defense Council. She ended up with a menacing gauntlet through which Wyly would have to run if he wanted her support.

The collective expertise Bingham had assembled would be an acid test: If Wyly was just another greedy capitalist investor looking to make a buck and not really concerned about the environment—as some believed—he would not have a prayer of surviving this meeting.

Sam and his wife, Cheryl, arrived at about nine on a Saturday morning, and came with no lawyers or wingmen. Bingham had divided the day into two sessions: the first, a morning meeting with the environmental skeptics; the second, in the evening, a gathering of Republican-leaning environmental activists. The Wylys disappeared into her guest room for about an hour, and the early group began to gather at 10 a.m.

Finally the Wylys came down and Cheryl, smiling, left to do some San Francisco sightseeing and shopping. She did not seem worried about her husband's welfare, and Bingham soon learned why. Ready for the bloodletting to begin, she instead watched Wyly's unpretentious charm, disarming candor and amazing depth of knowledge blunt it from the outset. "He sat down, and everybody started to have a conversation with him," remembers Bingham. "And it was easy. We went around the room. But he was relaxed, he was warm, and he didn't seem intimidated. And I had a powerful group of people around who had understood the renewable energy business for a long time. Sam was informative, he was open in his conversation with these folks, and soon they were all with him."

They talked about public policy in Texas, and got into both Bushes' spotty environmental record, including a discussion of how George W. had, in their view, stomped some eco-legislation in Texas when he was governor. "Sam was able to explain both sides," Bingham recalls. "There were places where he had to agree that Bush hadn't done the right thing on this particular renewable energy issue. But he was amazingly knowledgeable."

Wyly was grilled for two hours, during which he drove home his contempt for the overreliance on Arab oil, the slow-to-move nature of the electricity monopolies, his interest in a competitive energy market and his belief that there was "enough energy from the sun and wind and other sources of energy to power the world for years to come, and we ought to use it." He explained the roots in both Rachel Carson's and Adam Smith's philosophies of Green Mountain's motto: "Choose wisely; it's a small planet."

The evening dinner with a very different group produced the same result. It became clear that the several sides of Sam Wyly—the businessman, the entrepreneur, the investor, the political donor and the pursuer of clean air—could coexist to the benefit of all of them. The merger of clean energy and capitalism, a union many environmentalists instinctively found repugnant, was not merely possible, but vital.

"He is an entrepreneur," says Bingham. "There are obviously ways to make money with cleaner energy. When you do that, everybody wins." She disagrees, however, with Wyly's characterization that cleaner power through Green Mountain costs just "an extra cup of Starbucks coffee a month."

"It's not a cup of coffee," she says. "It's a latte."

Like her associates, Bingham was a little shell-shocked by the way Wyly obliterated their cherished stereotype of wealthy Republicans. "I am not an early riser, but I got up at six a.m. and took a long walk with [him and Cheryl] down at Christie Field," Bingham says. "In just a very short period of time, I grew very fond of them. I was just in admiration of the fact that he is a Republican, he is exceedingly wealthy and he could take any road he wants to in terms of what he wants to do with his money. The fact that he has chosen to help this country get off its dependency on foreign oil is commendable."

Some months later, Bingham flew to Aspen, where the Wylys spend several months each year, and on whose pristine trails they have walked countless miles. It is a place so beautiful that it would be hard to live there and *not* be an environmentalist.

Said Bingham, "This is the way the Holy Spirit works."

When Green Mountain began marketing electricity in California, there were three central issues to contend with: stability, value and perception. The stability question played on consumer fears, and it was a gorilla. Did consumers prefer to keep their government-controlled rates or would they risk competition and its downside—market vagaries such as potentially volatile (hopefully lower, but possibly higher) rates, plus a lot of business failures? Competitive markets are messy.

And what value did customers place on "going green"? The case Green Mountain had to make was that signing on with them meant an increase in cleaner power purchased *somewhere* on the grid, and that demand would allow more windmills and other cleaner production. It answered the question a lot of caring people asked themselves: "What can I do personally?" Wyly was offering customers a way to be "a good citizen of the planet."

The third issue—perception—was about educating consumers. Many people buy the oil-and-coal-company story that there is no man-made pollution problem, and that global warming, if it is really going on at all, is part of a natural cycle. So why spend even a nickel more on electricity? Wyly's answer was that the low cost of "dirty electricity" was an illusion, a big lie that we tell ourselves. Like smoking cigarettes, where the real costs include personal and public healthcare costs, coal-generated power has what economists call "externalities," costs that really aren't paid by a single consumer in a monthly electric bill. The real bill must include the cost for all the damage to people on the planet caused by pollution, and the butcher's bill grows by the day. Wyly found that once people saw the real costs for dirty electricity, the epiphany often converted them. But winning this battle of ideas and evidence felt like fighting a world war door by door.

Early on, California looked like the perfect place for Green Mountain—its citizens seemed "green" (they were already protecting their Redwood forests), and the state had deregulated its electrical utilities in 1996, hoping to contain rising electric power costs. Given the state's huge population and vibrant green movement, he saw it as fertile ground, but he didn't know California was headed for an epic electricity disaster.

During the '90s, while the state's population was growing by more than four million, its economy had unparalleled new business growth and energy demand was spiraling, not a single power plant was built. California's energy supply was choking on red tape, as were a lot of other businesses.

"It was an extremely arduous process to go through regulatory requirements to put new facilities on line," said Gillan Taddune, chief environmental officer for Green Mountain. The 1996 so-called deregulation bill—a model of bad law—allowed out-of-state supply but also established, and then *froze*, extremely low prices for electricity. The lawmakers did not understand markets. The California Power Exchange index Green Mountain used to price power became meaningless once trading on the exchange ceased. Wholesale prices were frozen at high levels while the market waited for state officials to set a course for state power purchases, and utilities tried to stop paying credits owed to customers who had chosen alternative providers. Federal Energy Regulatory Commission Chairman James Hoecker summed the situation up succinctly in December of 2000: "This version of competition was a disaster."

On February 1, 2001, California Governor Gray Davis ended retail choice for electricity consumers, but the death notice was buried in a bill that authorized the state to buy power on long-term contracts. Four days later, Green Mountain pulled out of California, and turned its 52,000 customers back to the local monopolies.

Green Mountain focused now on Texas, the largest electricity market in the United States. It was also one of the nation's top polluters—one giant power plant, owned by Dallas-based TXU Energy (and ironically named "Big Brown"), was

putting 389,000 tons of contaminants
into the air each year. The state was
badly in need of cleaner sources of
energy, so Texas State Representative
Steve Wolens and Senator Dave Shipley
went to California, studied their program and said, "If this is deregulation,
Texas wants no part of it." Where California got it wrong, Wyly concluded,
Texas would get it right.

Because Green Mountain Energy created a lot
of new customers for "clean air through clean
energy," Texas had a larger installed wind tur-
bine capacity than the next three states
combined in 2010.

Before joining Green Mountain,
Taddune helped shape Texas's very different version of deregulation. In 1997,
she was chief economist for the Public
Utilities Commission in Austin when
the issue was being hammered out
with the electricity companies' would-
be competitors and the state lawmakers. Unlike California's law, the legislation
that deregulated Texas electricity—which went into effect on January 1,
2002—contained a mandate to build an additional 2,000 megawatts of renewable
energy by 2010. (This lofty goal was exceeded as thousands of windmills were
built at the southern end of the Rocky Mountains in West Texas, a place T. Boone
Pickens later dubbed "the Saudi Arabia of wind.")

When the new law was passed, Taddune got the nod to lead the project for the
Texas regulators. She helped develop the first successful renewable energy credit-
trading program, which stimulated competition and had an incentive to drive
down costs. It is now being used as a model in other states and countries.

She first became aware of Green Mountain because it was educating regulators about the benefits of giving consumers a choice in how their electricity was
made. "I liked the fact that Green Mountain gave customers a choice other than an
incumbent monopoly, and provided an environmentally beneficial option," she
says. "With the new, competitive markets, companies like Green Mountain were
out there saying—on the TV news—'Did you know that making electricity is the

largest source of industrial air pollution in the United States, and now you can do something about it?'"

Today, Texas is still the largest electricity market in the United States, 11th largest in the world, and has already built more windmills than California plus the next six biggest windmill-building states. The Texas version of a competitive electricity market *works*. A stream of competitors, green and otherwise, entered the market. Many went bust, but almost 20 continue to compete. Wyly's business model at Green Mountain has succeeded fabulously, encouraging new sources of power to tap. T. Boone Pickens and others have plans to build hundreds of windmills in West Texas and on up the U.S. wind corridor to North Dakota and Canada.

In 2000, Wyly made a TV commercial in which he declared, "California got it wrong. Texas got it right!" And over the next 10 years, as California was losing 100,000 jobs a year and Texas was gaining 100,000 jobs a year, *The Economist* judged Texas the best state in America to start a company, and California the worst.

When Green Mountain went into Connecticut in 2001, it built the largest solar electric power source in the state. But two years later, it had to quit. The state government's policies made it clear that Connecticut intended to protect its electricity monopolies.

Meanwhile, yet another disaster was brewing for the company. NOPEC, a council of governments representing more than 100 communities in Ohio had, back in 2000, selected Green Mountain as its electricity supplier for hundreds of thousands of customers. But by 2003, the welcome mat had been jerked out from under the company's feet. New regulatory obstacles that stifled the company's profits were introduced, and Green Mountain was also hit with newly invented power transmission charges that threatened to bankrupt it in that state.

To make matters worse, Pennsylvania's deregulated market began failing for mostly the same reasons. In 2005, Green Mountain retreated from Ohio and Pennsylvania and reluctantly pulled the plug on service for 480,000 customers.

Wyly now sensed that the nationwide movement toward electricity deregulation that had fueled Green Mountain's rise had ebbed and no one could predict when it would return. Was now the time to cut his losses and put his money and energy elsewhere?

Nope. Instead, Green Mountain began a cooperative retailing program. "Now, in states that continue to be regulated, we are working with incumbent utilities and partnering with them to bring a green product to market," said Paul Thomas. "Through that partnership we can have a material impact on the number of people buying a green product, drive up consumption of green power and help create new projects behind it—totally consistent with our mission."

Green Mountain now works with Portland General Electric in Oregon, the local utility, and with Florida Power and Light. And every year, as if waiting out a bad storm, Green Mountain renews its license to sell electricity in California, Ohio, Pennsylvania and Connecticut.

Green Mountain was the largest company of its kind in the U.S. Its metrics tell the story of its success: by 2008, its customers (in Florida, New Jersey, New York, Oregon and Texas) had received more than seven billion kilowatt hours of cleaner electricity, offset more than 4.1 billion tons of carbon dioxide emissions, and avoided as much CO_2 pollution as the equivalent of planting 300 million trees.

In cooperation with BP and Nuon, Green Mountain spurred the development of 35 new wind and solar energy facilities, built the first solar-powered Ronald McDonald House and designed an award-winning green headquarters in Austin, Texas. It was only the second Texas building to receive the U.S. Green Building Council's Leadership in Energy and Environmental Design (LEED) certification.

The company's "carbon offset" program has spread around the globe. One offset represents the reduction of one metric ton of carbon dioxide, or its equivalent, in other greenhouse gases. Once a carbon footprint is established, an entity can purchase carbon offsets, the revenue from which goes toward clean energy development and "neutralizing" the customer's footprint. The goal is to become at least "carbon neutral." Large companies purchase carbon offsets in order to comply with caps on the total amount of carbon dioxide they are allowed to emit. Individuals or smaller companies purchase carbon offsets to mitigate their own greenhouse gas emissions from transportation and electricity use. For example, an individual might purchase carbon offsets to compensate for the greenhouse gas emissions caused by personal air travel.

By the end of 2007, the company had hit $300 million in revenue and rebuilt its customer base to 1.5 million. In 2009, Green Mountain ranked highest in the

J.D. Power and Associates *2009 Texas Business Retail Electric Provider Satisfaction Study.* That same year the company hit $400 million in revenue. By 2010, Green Mountain's revenue had topped $500 million.

In September of 2010, Green Mountain was sold to NRG Energy, the Princeton, New Jersey, energy giant, for $350 million (after $200 million had been returned to Wyly's investors). Once again, the deal fell in line with one of his principal entrepreneurial goals: Leave a company in the hands of people who can grow it. "They will make Green Mountain a nationwide brand," Wyly said. "It really is a case where one plus one equals more than two.

   "This is a great day for Green Mountain. It's a great day for NRG. It's a great day for Texas and for America. We set out to change the planet, and that's happening."

Imagine a time when "Charge 'er up" replaces "Fill 'er up." The time is now and NRG is at the center of it. From delivering clean energy solutions to new charging stations that power electric cars, NRG is moving clean energy forward—for every generation. Now that's something to shout about. To find out more visit **nrgenergy.com**

Moving clean energy forward.

In 2010, energy giant NRG bought Green Mountain, and continued its good work for a cleaner planet.

Andrew and Sam hit the books at Sam's home in Dallas.

WE NEED A CAT

Most of this book has been devoted to entrepreneurship on a grand scale—*very* big business—but it ends with the smallest business Sam Wyly owns: Explore Booksellers, in Aspen, Colorado.

It sits in a 4,922-square-foot Victorian house built during the town's 1890s silver mining boom, about the time William Jennings Bryan was making his "Cross of Gold" speech and Colorado's silver miners were cheering for him rather than his opponent, who was defending the gold standard for the U.S. dollar. The bookstore's first floor is a warren of shelves and leather chairs with an eclectic array of titles; there are more books upstairs along with the Pyramid Bistro restaurant. Wyly's daughter, Kelly O'Donovan's Elliott Yeary art gallery is three blocks away and Sam and Cheryl have a home named Asylum about six blocks away, built of huge white pine timbers, clapboard painted green, and anchored on a huge rock. "As recommended in the Bible," Wyly says with a smile, "where it speaks about building on solid foundations, not on shifting sand."

In August of 2006, the 30-year-old bookstore was put up for sale by the heirs of its founder, Katherine Thalberg. This distressed the local intellectuals and guardians of the town's unique culture, who considered Explore a local literary landmark. (Aspen is an extremely literate community—more than 60 percent of residents over 25 have bachelor's degrees or higher.) Wyly thought it was an important part of the local culture as well, and hated the idea of the bookstore falling victim to real estate developers who would turn it into condos for rich people who only came to town a few weeks a year. And so he offered to buy it.

But when Thalberg's three daughters announced they were going to sell him the bookstore, they faced surprising questions from shocked locals and both daily newspapers. "Was Sam Wyly really the right sort to own the only bookstore in this unique resort town? Wasn't he a bottom-line guy, a buddy of Nixon, Ford, Reagan and the Bushes? Was Explore headed for a Rush Limbaugh Symposium and an Ann Coulter Reading Room? Was the vegetarian bistro going to start serving cheeseburgers?"

Cheryl and Sam bought the store in January 2007, and it was not long before those doubters came around, and even came around to personally thank the

Left: Cheryl and Sam with their dog Julie at Explore Booksellers in Aspen, a recent investment of love by both of them.

Above: Kashmir was brought in to oversee the reading habits of the mice.

couple for saving this important piece of Aspen history and continuing its contribution to its unique culture.

Unlike with his other businesses, Wyly does not plan to build this into a global enterprise, and he vows there will never be an IPO for Explore. The first time he and Cheryl met with a room full of employees, the two of them answered everyone's questions, and then Sam asked, "What do you need?"

The response: "We need a cat."

So, another new addition to the enterprise is Kashmir, a big, gray, female cat from the newly expanded Cheryl and Sam Wyly Animal Shelter in Aspen. There is also a new carpet in the bookstore, plus fresh wallpaper in the veggie-centric, nutrition-focused bistro and new energy-efficient lighting. Cheryl is the new, one-woman board of directors and meets with employees over avocado omelets, braised tofu or artichoke strudel.

Some people, those who don't know Sam Wyly, say it is his hobby company, his Aspen plaything. They suggest that Explore Booksellers is, for him, a trivial pursuit.

But they are wrong. Sam Wyly loves books, loves to read and knows that everything he has accomplished and all that he has been blessed with came to him because he read . . . and then read some more.

INDEX

ACKNOWLEDGMENTS:

My father, Charles, publisher of the *Delhi Dispatch,* and my mother, Flora, the first entrepreneur I knew, gave me boundless love, an appreciation for the written word and the confidence to attempt the impossible. I was educated and encouraged by the writings and teachings of Mary Baker Eddy and taught personal lessons in courage, trust and teamwork by the coaching of Raymond Richards. These people formed my character, and without their influences, the business successes that are the subject of this book would not have been possible.

My wife, Cheryl, and my six children continue to give me strength, inspiration and joy, and have supported me spiritually throughout the process of completing this project.

To my brother, Charles, and all the other leaders and employees of the companies we created, I give my deepest thanks. The stories of success (and failure!) in this book are your stories.

I also thank Duncan Bock and Shoshana Thaler at Melcher Media and Susan Tiholiz and Karen Wade in my office for their unrivaled creativity and tireless effort in producing this terrific book.

Melcher Media would like to thank Chika Azuma, Kay Banning, David E. Brown, Anne Calder, Holly Dolce, Danielle Dowling, Shannon Fanuko, Barbara Gogan, Austin O'Malley, Lauren Nathan, Katherine Raymond, Karen Sanders, John Schneider, Julia Sourikoff and Megan Worman.

PHOTO CREDITS: